VOLUME 33 • NO 3 • JULY 2004

GW00725468

Horseman of the Acropolis, London: will he get home to Athens in time? (p187)

WEBSITE NEWS UPDATED WEEKLY
WWW.INDEXONCENSORSHIP.ORG • CONTACT@INDEXONCENSORSHIP.ORG
TEL: 020 7278 2313 • FAX: 020 7278 1878

BUILDING JERUSALEM

URSULA OWEN

Walls are built to keep some other world at bay, yet they shut in as much as they shut out. In a world where the inclination to solve problems by separating and containing remains as powerful as ever, *Index* looks at the political and social motives for building walls, and at the lives disrupted by these man-made borders.

In Berlin, there are only fragments left to remind us of the most famous wall of our time, but following its path in what was East Berlin still gives the strong sense of a divided city. The sad barrier of derelict buildings that passes through Nicosia, dividing Cypriots from one another, seems to symbolise the normalisation of partition in the minds of the Greek-Cypriot community (p25). The result of the several walls built between Mexico and California is not increased security but the death of thousands of immigrants (p48). And despite the six-year-long peace process in Northern Ireland, Belfast walls still carry dramatic pictures and slogans of the war that is so hard to end (p53).

The newest and most contentious wall is in the West Bank, where Israel is building what it calls a security fence (p66). Most of the Israeli population regard it as part of the solution to the challenge of suicide bombers. For the Palestinians it is illegal, taking as it does more Palestinian land, separating residential sections of Palestinian towns from their fields, and creating ghettos such as Qalqilya, with a single gate for entry or exit and watchtowers every 50 metres where Israeli soldiers can shoot invaders. It didn't stop militants from cutting through metal grating and firing at cars travelling on the trans-Israel highway in June 2003.

In Jerusalem, apart from making daily life a misery, a good deal of the wall separates Palestinians from Palestinians rather than from Israelis, so it has no apparent rationale as far as keeping suicide bombers out is concerned. As currently planned, the wall will eventually put 50 per cent of the West Bank in Israeli hands, dividing it into two distinct cantons and making a two-state solution unsustainable. Ironically, most Israelis, while supporting the wall, do not want a single-state solution.

Meanwhile, there are other kinds of confinement. The Roma in Central Europe are seen by some as a threat to the new European identity – with its emphasis on 'high wealth, growth and well-being' (p58). *Index* looks at the cultures of the new countries of accession (p128), and of those, like Bulgaria, still waiting in the wings (p211) .

And in the run-up to the Olympics in Athens, we take a controversial look at who really has a right to the stolen and appropriated artefacts in the world's great museums (p187). ❏

IN THIS ISSUE

<< More sinned against . . .

than sinning. Israel's newly released
whistle-blower talks to *Index* **page 29**

Writing on the walls >>

Walls have a bad name: they disfigure
the planet and divide its people. Felipé
Fernandez-Armesto looks at a long history
page 38

<< May the force be with you

Umberto Eco tells Europe:
'Unite or die' **page 130**

Loot! >>

Sending Lord Elgin's Marbles
back to Greece **page 187**

CONTENTS

2   **URSULA OWEN**   Editorial

NEWS & MEDIA

6   **In the news**

8   **MEHRAK GOLESTAN**   Dirty Kuffar
Islamist rappers meet cyber-censorship

11   **ALEXANDER REYNOLDS Terror in Thailand**
Bangkok tries to get to grips with an Islamic insurgency

14   **ANIA DABROWSKA Freedom is a big word**
A celebration in pictures of South Africa's 10th anniversary

18   **MARCEL BERLINS Libel tourism**
Welcome to London, libel capital of the world!

21   **MICHAEL GRIFFIN True today, false tomorrow**
A writer finds a libel writ on the breakfast table – and his book gets pulped

25   **TABITHA MORGAN Aphrodite's other island**
Cyprus stays divided as Greeks vote their Turkish neighbours out of the EU

OPINION

29   **JAMES THACKARA A man more sinned against than sinning . . .**
The release of Mordechai Vanunu provokes a discussion of our nuclear future

36   WRITING ON THE WALLS

38   **FELIPÉ FERNANDEZ-ARMESTO This story doth a wall present**
The very long history of walls & Omid Salehi's photos of same in Tehran

46   **KAMILA SHAMSIE High on walls**
A lesson in irony from Pakistan

48   **RUBÉN MARTÍNEZ Fortress America**
How the Great Wall of America brings death in its wake

53   **GLENN PATTERSON A strange kind of peace**
Belfast wins a 'Keep Britain Tidy Award' – with photos by Namiko Kitaura

58   **IRENA MARYNIAK Think Roma, say Jew**
The ghettoes remain and discrimination becomes 'official' in Europe

64   **MARTIN ROWSON Stripsearch**

66   **STEPHANIE LE BARS & MARION VAN RENTERGHEN Walking the wall**
Israelis say it's a security fence, Palestinians call it the wall of apartheid

78   **WENDY PULLAN A one-sided wall**
An old solution for a very modern problem

83   **RAJA SHEHADEH A drive on a forbidden road**
The trials and tribulations of getting home after a night out

88 EYAD EL SARRAJ Crossings
Playing the waiting game in Gaza

91 AVRAHAM YEHOSHUA Why the Zionists were right
Lament for the death of optimism

96 FLASHPOINT A matter of conscience

98 INDEX INDEX

128 MEET THE NEIGHBOURS

130 UMBERTO ECO May the force be with you
A strong case for a united Europe

135 MARTIN PLUHACEK-REINER Czech Republic: Always the bridesmaid
The eventful history of Brno

140 JAAN KAPLINSKI Estonia: A home named Tammiku
A tale of deportations and conquest on the road to today

148 LÁSZLÓ KRASZNAHORKAI Hungary: City of phantom gentlemen
The ghosts that walk the streets of Gyula

156 NORA IKSTENA Latvia: Looking for the Livs
On the track of a vanishing people

161 MARIUS IVASKEVICIUS Lithuania: The howling wolf
Matchmakers and malls in Vilnius

168 ANDRZEJ STASIUK Poland: Vanishing point
The multiple exits and entrances of a Polish escapologist

172 VALERIU NICOLAE Roma: Exclusion within
'It has to be better; we've known the worst'

175 DUSAN DUSEK Slovakia: Home of the heavenly hairdresser
The Pope, the hairdresser and a good bowl of soup

180 KATARINA MARINCIC Slovenia: Window on Ljubljana
Lives that hide behind windows

183 MICHAEL FOLEY Bulgaria: Waiting in the wings
And next time it's the Balkans . . .

187 CULTURE

187 EDWARD LUCIE-SMITH Loot!
Who owns the Arch of Titus?

201 BABEL WENDY PEARLMAN Palestine: Voices under occupation

211 DIARY LEDIO CAKAJ & MARIA BURNETT-GAUDIANI August in Albania

218 LETTER ESTHER MOIR Zimbabwe: Absolute scarcity of everything

IN THE NEWS

CHOCOLATE COCK-UP A coalition of black groups has protested against food manufacturer Masterfoods, claiming its use of the counting rhyme 'Eeny, meeny, miney, mo' in an ice-cream advertising campaign is racially offensive – even if the offending line is not cited. The poster ad shows five spoons of varying sizes next to a tub of Galaxy chocolate ice cream, with a strap of the rhyme's opening line that invites consumers to pick one of them. The rhyme, of course, continues 'catch a nigger by his toe' and, like 'ring-a-ring o' roses', is deemed to be a contemporary playground response to real historical events, in this case the trade in African slaves. 'They are using a nursery rhyme that many people know as being profoundly racist and brutal,' said Simon Woolley, coordinator of Operation Black Vote. 'The amazing thing is what this says about the advertising industry. It shows how few minorities there are in senior roles in these companies.'

VERBAL BENCHMARKS Unworldly judges in England and Wales have been told to watch their tongues after Lord Chief Justice Lord Woolf unveiled a guidebook in May dealing with the treatment of race, religion, disability, gender and sexuality issues in court. Some of the advice offered in the *Equal Treatment Benchbook* is fairly standard, including the use of 'they', instead of 'he' or 'she', and the substitution of 'postal worker' for 'postman'. Other suggestions are more intriguing. Use of the expression 'visible minorities' is not recommended because it implies the existence of 'invisible minorities' and particular care should be taken with 'asylum', since it has accumulated a pejorative sense through association with people with no genuine claim. Some idiomatic phrases, the book helpfully points out, including 'sleeping policeman', may actually be confusing to people from different cultural backgrounds.

GREAT HEADLIGHTS! If hot-blooded males in Iran seem to spend an inordinate amount of time talking about cars, it's more than likely they're weighing up girls, according to the *Persian Dictionary of Argot*, an academic study of Farsi slang that has turned into a surprising bestseller. Less surprising, perhaps, is the fact that the languages of lust and mechanics should start to merge when public contact between the sexes is banned and young people have to cruise around in single-sex cars to flirt with each another. So Tehran youth use a car code to avoid prying ears. A 'zero kilometre' is a virgin, an 'overturned car' is a non-virgin, while a girl who is pregnant has certainly 'been in an accident'. 'Hubcaps', 'headlights' and 'axles' refer to . . . well, you work it out. Car models also make it into street language and a peasant bride is referred to as an Iranian-made 'Peugeot 405' – not the flashiest vehicle to drive. No one is sure how the dictionary got past the censors but, despite being in its sixth edition, it's almost impossible to find in the bookshops.

THIEF IN WOLF'S CLOTHING A satire about the adventures of a fake Iranian cleric, which won the best-film trophy at Tehran's international film festival in February, is not making the country's religious authorities laugh out loud. *Marmoulak* (*The Lizard*) recounts the adventures of Reza Marmoulak, or Reza the Lizard, a petty thief who escapes from prison disguised as a mullah only to discover and exploit the extraordinary powers his stolen robes bestow on him in a conservative and respectful society. Though clearly a critique of the over-mighty clergy, the film scraped past the censors with only minor cuts and was an immediate success in Tehran. Outside the capital, *Marmoulak* has been less lucky. It was banned in Mashad, Orumiyeh, Rasht and the holy city of Qom, while copies have been stolen from screening rooms elsewhere. But Vice-President Mohammed Ali Abytahi praised the film on his weblog, adding wryly that he hoped that his approval – as a religious leader – would not harm the film's box-office takings.

SATIRE SHORTAGE The president of an African country, feeling out of touch with what his people are thinking, sends out an official on a mission to find out what they say among themselves. On his return, the official reports that people are complaining bitterly about shortages of food and fuel. The scenario of *Super Patriots and Morons*, a satirical play produced by Daves Guzha, could be set anywhere in Africa but, after 20 performances in Harare, Zimbabwe's capital, it was eventually banned in May. The censorship board has not given any reason for the ban. Guzha denies *Super Patriots* is about Zimbabwe, though the fuel queues featured in the play are widespread under President Robert Mugabe's rule (see 'Letter from Zimbabwe', p218). ❏

Compiled by **MG**

DIRTY KUFFAR

MEHRAK GOLESTAN

ISLAMIST RAPPERS TAKE ON THE ABUSE
OF IRAQI PRISONERS IN THEIR OWN STYLE

The words 'Dirty Kuffar murder innocent Iraqi civilian' appear against a black backdrop. We then see CNN footage of US marines laughing and cheering as they gun down an unarmed Iraqi man, afterwards bragging: 'Hell, yeah, it was awesome. Let's do it again.' The screen then fills with menacing images of Islamic militants wearing balaclavas and waving guns in front of banners. Then the baseline kicks in and the militants begin their rap.

This is 'Dirty Kuffar', the latest rap music video on the Internet inciting us to 'Jihad against the Western Crusaders'. 'Kuffar' – 'unbelievers' in Arabic – chillingly informs us:

> There's a new name for disbelievers
> Now we have to call them Dirty Kuffar
> If they don't respect the Almighty one
> Then we throw them in the fire where they'll burn, burn, burn.

The images of the rappers are superimposed over scenes of Al-Qaida training camps and factions such as the Hezbollah, intercut with news footage of US troops and vehicles being blown up and attacked. We are also shown the 'Dirty Kuffar' in question: these include George W Bush, Tony Blair (who is branded 'Bush's lapdog'), Colin Powell, Ariel Sharon (whose face is digitally morphed into a pig bearing the Star of David on his forehead), Saddam, the British National Party and the French National Front. US troops land on Iraqi soil while slogans such as 'Send them home in body bags' flash on the screen. The video ends with the 9/11 plane crashing into the Twin Towers against a soundtrack of laughter and a list of countries that have been 'victims of US violence since 1945'. The latter totals 56.

'Dirty Kuffar' is the debut release from Sheikh Terra and the Soul Salah Crew, a group of British-Asian Muslim rappers about whom very little is known. It is only their accents and the specific genre – an amalgamation of US-style hip hop and Jamaican-style dancehall – that reveal their origins to be British. For obvious reasons, they keep their true identity a closely

Sheikh Terra of the
Soul Salah Crew.
Credit: Reuters

guarded secret: at no point in the video do they expose their faces. No contact numbers, no email and no website where the video can be downloaded; only the record label Digihad. News of the video's existence has passed purely by word of mouth.

All very mysterious!

Originally, links to the video were posted on some fundamentalist Islamic sites. After a few days, the sites were shut down: attempts to log on resulted in 'page not found' rubrics.

However, a number of US teenagers had already managed to download copies of the video and had posted it on their weblogs; but again, a few days later, many of the sites were nowhere to be found. The author of one weblog even reported receiving emails from official bodies instructing him to remove the offending material.

It is unclear how access to these sites is being prevented, but it seems that 'perpetrators' are being targeted individually rather than by entire Internet Service Providers or networks. Sites that provide links to the video tend to be left alone; it is only sites that actually 'host' the video that appear to be a problem. Is all of this evidence of cyber-censorship by the powers that be? Maybe.

Sheikh Terra and the Soul Salah Crew would certainly not be the first rappers to promote political ideology or to use religious ideas. Current US rap group Wu-Tang Clan are well known for their affiliations to Louis

Farrakhan's Nation of Islam and there are a number of Christian rap outfits such as Pryme Minister or Royal Priesthood.

The trend is not particularly new. During the late 1980s and 1990s, the New York activist rap group Public Enemy released a string of blistering attacks on corporate America – AmeriKKKa as they called it – in the form of songs such as 'Don't Believe the Hype', 'Impeach the President', '911 is a Joke' and 'Fight the Power' which contained controversial lyrics such as:

> Elvis was a hero to most
> But he never meant shit to me
> 'Cos he was a Racist simple and plain
> Motherfuck him and John Wayne

Fans of hip hop pride themselves on the fact that it is a universal genre that has many influences and is manifested in the diverse categories that exist within rap music – gangster rap, political rap, commercial rap, rock rap, etc. For every walk of life there is an internal rap genre; there even exists a group of 'gay rappers' in a culture that is largely homophobic. The beauty of rap music lies in the fact that it is constantly expanding as rappers rap about anything and everything within their experience and internalise outside influences.

The difference with Sheikh Terra and Co is that they are not 'rappers' who use religion and politics to make their rap music 'cool'. On the contrary, they are using rap music to make their politics and religion 'cool'! hip hop is being hip hopped as the 'insiders' – Islamic fanatics – take over the 'outside influence' of hip hop.

By current rap standards, Sheikh Terra and Co are not amazing; in fact, they are not even very good, just barely average. But the quality of the rapping is not an issue; it is the message they are conveying. One sometimes wonders if the Soul Salah Crew are actually aware of the full implications of releasing 'Dirty Kuffar', especially at a time when allegations of abuse of Iraqi prisoners by US and British troops are sure to add to the already substantial anti-West sentiment that exists in the rest of the world and is increasingly evident in the ethnic minorities living in Europe. 'Dirty Kuffar' is aimed at Muslim youths who reside in the West and walk the difficult line between the two worlds: a sensationalist piece of propaganda designed to further confuse the confused. ❏

Mehrak Golestan *is a musician and writer*

TERROR IN THAILAND
ALEXANDER REYNOLDS

THERE IS A GUERRILLA WAR BREWING
IN THAILAND BETWEEN THE COUNTRY'S
SECURITY FORCES AND MACHETE-
WIELDING MUSLIMS ON MOTORBIKES

It all began with a raid on an army depot in January and culminated in April in a bloody stand-off at a historic mosque. Over 166 people have died since the beginning of the year and the latest exchange could be the overture to a long-term low-intensity conflict.

Behind the smiles and *wais* of popular tourist destinations, few know of the 5 per cent Muslim minority concentrated in the southern provinces of Yala, Pattani and Natrathiwat close to the Malaysian border. The region is dominated by Muslims who speak their own dialect and feel alienated and disenfranchised as a result of heavy-handed treatment by Bangkok bureaucrats.

Bangkok thought it had contained Muslim separatism in the south by the late 1980s, but it has resurfaced with a vengeance. The region is poverty-stricken and there are high levels of unemployment. These provinces have been trouble spots for many generations. In the past, Muslim groups such as the Pattani United Liberation Front, the Barisan Revolusi Nasional and the Gerakan Mujahadeen Islam Pattani have called for the provinces to be incorporated into Malaysia. They complain of heavy-handed treatment from the police and armed forces but stress that most Muslims want only respect for their culture and peace in the region.

Into this political crisis comes the dynamic figure of Prime Minister Thaksin Shinawatra. His standard procedure is to approach the chaos of politics with businesslike solutions. After dealing with Sars and the recent outbreak of H5N1 avian/chicken flu, Thaksin is confident he can quell the daily violence in the south and has personally taken charge of ending the unrest. Despite several visits to the region, he has yet to find a consensus.

More important, no one knows – or agrees on – who is behind the wave of terror: local Muslim separatists, drug-crazed youths or Jemaah Islamiah, the South-East Asian wing of Al-Qaida.

The flashpoint for these new troubles was a surprise raid on an army base in Narathiwat in early January in which the attackers murdered four soldiers and looted the armoury: 375 M16-A1 assault rifles, three rocket-propelled grenade launchers, two M-60 machine guns and 2,000 rounds of ammunition have yet to be recovered despite a lengthy investigation and an extensive search of the provinces. One theory has it that they were smuggled out of the country and ended up in the hands of Indonesian rebels in Aceh. To the embarrassment of the prime minister, Najmuddin Umar, MP for Narathiwat and a member of the New Aspiration Party which is part of Thaksin's ruling coalition, was arrested for suspected links to separatist groups and for plotting the January raid.

Soon after the Narathiwat raid, martial law was imposed throughout the region. To date, heavy-handed policing has failed to stop a wave of spontaneous attacks on government officials, teachers, police, soldiers, railway workers and even Buddhist monks. Many schools have been set alight; teachers are to be armed. Since the death of a railway worker, soldiers from the Royal Thai Army now guard trains throughout the region. The south has also been subject to a bombing campaign. At first the bombs were crude incendiary devices attached to parked motorcycles; then came an explosion at a Pattani nightspot close to the border and a recent theft of ammonium nitrate, a fertiliser used in bomb-making. There were fears that a large device would be detonated during the recent Songkran – New Year festival – but the security forces maintained a high presence and the event passed without incident.

Then came coordinated attacks during late April, when insurgents attacked 15 security posts in Pattani and Songkhla. The Pattani ambush started with the fatal knifing of three policemen at 4am and ended with a 2pm siege at Krue Se Mosque, a symbol of Pattani's Islamic heritage. After an exchange of fire with the insurgents, soldiers bombarded the mosque with rocket-propelled grenades and tear gas, killing 32 people. Three soldiers died in the firefight and seven were hurt. According to a local resident, 54-year-old Duangjai Waesani: 'It was nothing short of a war zone.' The attacks in Songkhla were more extensive: police stations, checkpoints and military camps were attacked in the Bannang Sata district and the Krong Pinang sub-district; many of the insurgents died in the exchange with security forces.

The prime minister dismissed these attackers as drug-crazed youths and claimed the insurgency had nothing to do with Islam. 'We will root out the cause of the violence, which is not at all related to separatism or religious conflict,' he said after one of the bloodiest episodes. Others in his cabinet disagree.

For some time, Jemaah Islamiah have been suspected of funding and training separatists in bases across the Malaysian border. Some of the suspects in the recent stand-off at Krue Se Mosque were found to be wearing JI symbols on their clothing. Thai forces have been monitoring movement across the border with Malaysia and have maintained a strong visible presence in an attempt to win the hearts and minds of the local population.

Riduan Issamudin (aka Hambali), deputy to JI's alleged leader, Abu Bakar Ba'asyir, was arrested last year in Ayuthaya, Thailand, in a joint Thai/US Intelligence Service operation. A plot to bomb embassies in Thailand was later busted by police in Singapore. Though the JI link is still tenuous, the style of April's attacks bears its hallmarks: coordinated, surprise attacks on soft targets. A highly placed source in the Fourth Army believes that JI and a Malaysia-based cell of the Kampulan Mujahideen Malaysia (KMM) are involved in the Thai insurgency problem, and that JI and KMM mobilised and financed the unrest to the tune of Baht 300 million (US$7.3 million). In the last five months, nine suspects with JI links have been arrested in Thailand. Seven out of the 32 slain in the mosque shoot-out are not Thai and are thought to be Indonesian. Lt-Gen Pisarn Wattanawong-keeree is '100 per cent sure' that they are foreign insurgents and is requesting DNA tests to identify insurgent corpses. All the dead have been identified save these seven. There are those who think the problems in the south plus the presence of Thai soldiers in Iraq make the kingdom a target.

An independent commission is to be set up to analyse the problems of the south and to investigate whether the Royal Thai Army overreacted at the Krue Se Mosque. Meanwhile, Muslim groups want to see the revival of Deputy Prime Minister Chaturon Chaisaeng's peace proposal. This calls for the lifting of martial law in the region, an amnesty for suspect insurgents, more Islamic schools, increased recruitment quotas for the police force and civil service and Baht 12 billion (US$294 million) in development money. Many think this proposal, if implemented, could prevent an escalation in unrest in the long term. In the present global climate of fear generated by 'Islamic terrorism', the problems of south Thailand can no longer be ignored. ❏

Alexander Reynolds is a freelance journalist working out of Bangkok

FREEDOM IS A BIG WORD

ANIA DABROWSKA

A CELEBRATION IN PICTURES OF
SOUTH AFRICA'S 10TH ANNIVERSARY

Khayelitsha township, Cape Town.
Above: young mother and baby in their new home in South Africa's biggest township
(population 1 million plus). Right, top: the way it used to be . . . Right: the new housing
that is beginning to transform the township. While the old makeshift shanties still dominate,
government funding has subsidised local housing cooperatives to build better homes with
electricity and piped clean water; local trade and enterprises and the signs of relative
wealth are all increasing. Credit: all photographs Ania Dabrowska

Opposite: ex-journalist dismissed for extreme right-wing views. The graffiti reads: 'Here lives a stupid old Boer. By chance a King. "Thou shalt not follow the majority in that which is wrong" – Torah'

Left: Khayelitsha church Black Jesus campaigns against Aids

Below: Camps Bay, Cape Town: a million miles away, the once 'whites only' cocktail bar now caters to wealthy locals and tourists

LIBEL TOURISM

MARCEL BERLINS

WELCOME TO LONDON,
LIBEL CAPITAL OF THE WORLD

It's become a tiresome cliché: 'London is the libel capital of the world.' And, as a result, it's become the most popular focus of 'libel tourism' (the words are usually used pejoratively). But what do these terms actually mean? And should we be worried, on freedom-of-expression grounds?

This is the perceived danger. The libel laws of England, compared with those of just about every other country in the world, are particularly friendly to claimants. The procedures are relatively simple and the rules of evidence favour the alleged victim of the libel. In particular, it is for the writer or publisher to prove that what was written was true – not for the claimant to prove that the allegations were false. Moreover, English juries tend to be more sympathetic to apparently distressed individuals than to the rich newspaper or publishing groups responsible for defaming them; the levels of compensation awarded, though nowhere near as high as they used to be, are worth fighting for.

In addition, over the past few years, another element has entered the English legal arena: 'no win, no fee' litigation, by which losing claimants do not have to pay anything to their lawyers. If they win, the lawyers are entitled to charge far more than their usual fees – up to double. Until no win, no fee, libel claimants had to find their own money (a lot of it) to finance a court case. State-funded legal aid was not available so, in effect, anyone not well off was excluded from the libel courts.

There's another aspect to London's status as libel capital. A claim may be brought in the High Court only if there is an English connection – the book or magazine must be sold here and the claimant must have a reputation to lose in England. In practice, however, the connection doesn't have to be substantial. Many successful claims have been brought against books or newspapers read by very few people in England.

Libel tourism is an inevitable result of a laid-back and sympathetic libel regime. Why struggle to bring a case in a country that makes it difficult to do so – the US, for example – when other countries are so welcoming?

There is nothing new in seeking to exploit the easiest path to compensation. In 1987, Martin Packard, a former naval commander, sued in the High Court over false allegations in the Greek newspaper *Eleftherotypia* that he had betrayed the resistance movement against the military junta that had ruled Greece, and was implicated in the murder of an English journalist. A bad libel, certainly, but the circulation of the newspaper in England was a mere 40 copies; nevertheless, the jury awarded a record £450,000.

In the early 1990s, a hostile biography of the oil tycoon Armand Hammer went on sale in the United States without any legal consequences. The moment the book was published in England, however, even though it had modest sales, Hammer pounced and sued, citing 147 instances of libel. It was expected to be Britain's biggest and most costly libel trial. Then Hammer died, and his lawsuit with him.

The most recent batch of libel tourism has been spearheaded by Saudi interests. Earlier this year, Sheikh bin Mahfouz won substantial damages against a small publishing house, Pluto Press, over a false claim in *Reaping the Whirlwind* by Michael Griffin that he was related by marriage to Osama bin Laden and supported terrorism.

In December last year, Mohammed Jameel successfully sued the *Wall Street Journal* European edition, which has only a small circulation in England, over untrue allegations that his bank accounts had been monitored by anti-terrorism enforcement agencies.

Saudis are not the only libel tourists to have spotted London's great charm for seekers of libel damages. The Russian businessman Boris Berezovsky successfully sued the New York-based magazine *Forbes* in London, where it sold relatively few copies, and not in the US, where the vast majority of its readers live. When, in 2002, the *New Yorker's* investigative journalist Seymour Hersch wrote a series of articles highly critical of Richard Perle, one of George W Bush's most influential advisers, Perle publicly announced his intention to sue – in London, but not in the magazine's home city.

But what's more troubling than cases actually brought against writers is the chilling effect of libel tourism: the outbreak of cold feet among publishers of vaguely controversial writings. Craig Unger's bestseller, *House of Bush, House of Saud: The Secret Relationship between the World's Two Most Powerful Families*, was not much liked by the Saudi royal family. They couldn't do much about it in the US but the possibility that someone mentioned in the book might bring libel proceedings in an English court was enough to make the publisher Random House stop Secker & Warburg, its UK subsidiary, from publishing it there. It's not that they doubted its accuracy; they dreaded the costs of fighting the case in court. No doubt they also took into account the fact that the Sheikh bin Mahfouz who featured prominently in the Unger book was the same person who'd just won damages against Pluto Press. The deputy chairman of Random House wrote apologetically in the *Bookseller*, the publishers' journal: 'UK libel laws and legal processes are stifling legitimate and responsible freedom of speech.'

Random House was also the publisher of the equally acclaimed *While America Slept: The Failure to Prevent 9/11* by the equally respected investigative journalist Gerald Posner. It revealed that an Al-Qaida operative had told his captors in Pakistan that some high-ranking Saudis had known about the 9/11 plot but didn't tell the Americans. That book, too, Random House has decided, will now not be published in England. Posner was philosophical: 'If Random House spends US$500,000–$600,000 in a UK court defending my book, it will certainly get a nice pat on the back. But that's additional money the publisher has to spend for the right to buy and publish a book. Unless the book does extremely well, the publisher can possibly be out hundreds of thousands of dollars defending the rights of an author in court.'

Is this the beginning of a sinister trend? Two books not published do not yet amount to a mass assault against freedom of expression. But financial factors are increasingly dominating decisions on whether or not to publish a book or run an article. If publishers, proprietors and editors believe that they're vulnerable to libel claims that will cost huge sums to defend – whether or not the claimant is a libel tourist – they will be scared to publish. The only way to redress a balance that so favours claimants is to change the laws of defamation in England and Wales. That reform should start with reversing the burden of proof. If you claim to be physically injured and bring a legal action, you have to prove your injuries. If you claim you've been libelled, the law should make you prove that what's been written about you is false. That change alone would dramatically reduce libel tourism – and the threat to freedom of expression. ❏

Marcel Berlins *is visiting professor in media law at Queen Mary College, University of London, and lecturer in media law at City University in London. He is legal columnist on the* Guardian *and was the presenter of BBC Radio 4's* Law in Action *programme*

TRUE TODAY, FALSE TOMORROW

MICHAEL GRIFFIN

WHAT HAPPENS WHEN A SUPPOSEDLY
IMPECCABLE SOURCE DENIES THE TRUTH
OF HIS STATEMENTS, AND THE EQUALLY
RELIABLE NEWSPAPER THAT REPORTED
THEM PRINTS AN ABJECT APOLOGY?

I had been called to a breakfast meeting near Villiers Street in London with a libel lawyer and my publisher, and was quietly confident by the time the secretary brought coffee and sandwiches to the room. We had received a letter from the legal advisers of Sheikh Khalid bin Mahfouz about defamatory statements contained in my book, *Reaping the Whirlwind*, published in June 2003.

Reaping was the fruit of seven years' work based on a close reading of day-by-day reports on the Taliban and Al-Qaida from Afghanistan, Pakistan, Saudi Arabia, the United States and elsewhere. Through the accretion of detail about key personalities, their movements, sponsors and allies, and the geopolitical ferment that surrounded Afghanistan at a time when Central Asia and the Caspian were both in geopolitical flux, I felt I had developed close to Ouija-board sensitivity to the least fluctuation in the regional ionosphere.

I had not foreseen Al-Qaida's attacks on the World Trade Centre and the Pentagon – who had? – but I was well placed to interpret what happened next, and to trawl through countless news reports for the gist of a political thriller that began not on 12 September but a generation earlier.

Besides, I consoled myself, I had my footnotes. Every fact and nuance in the book, every policy elaboration, was anchored to what I considered a reputable information provider, whether print, media website or specialised newsletter, or to that authoritative fount of knowledge, 'intelligence sources', usually cited as the basis of articles in the equally trustworthy *New York Times* or *Washington Post*. I had sifted and connected these dots, hints and gleams of information, and assumed that the image that emerged was as close a reflection as possible of a world of opacity in which there were vested interests in separating cause from effect, and blurring the difference between friend and foe.

The libel lawyer quickly punctured my self-assurance. Courts in the UK presume that a newspaper article is false, not true, and that it is the writer's duty to pursue to its origins the veracity of every assertion he or she makes in the course of a book (there were more than 1,300 citations in *Reaping*). Did I know the name or motivation of the Associated Press journalist in the Cairo news bureau who reported a linchpin of the 9/11 narrative in July 1999 when Osama bin Laden mysteriously surfaced after disappearing from the Afghan radar for six months? It was this report, and a couple of echoes elsewhere in the media of the time, that set running one of the hares that partly underpinned the suit against *Reaping*, and persuaded Random House not to publish investigative journalist Craig Unger's *House of Bush, House of Saud* in the UK for fear of litigation.

Had I not understood, the solicitor asked me suavely, that journalists routinely make false allegations to elicit a denial, indeed any response at all from the subject of their enquiries? Well, no, I had not realised that 'quality' journalism had the same moral avoirdupois in the eyes of a British libel judge as muckraking.

Added to the legally indefensible character of news reporting is the un-reliability of 'intelligence sources', a matter that has become only too trans-parent since the 'dodgy dossier' affair in the UK and an invasion of Iraq launched on the pretext that Saddam Hussein possessed weapons of mass destruction (WMD).

My false allegation that there was a family relationship between the bin Laden and bin Mahfouz families stemmed, in fact, from a claim to the Senate Judiciary Committee in September 1998 by former CIA head James Woolsey, one month after President Bill Clinton approved the missile attack that destroyed Al Shifa pharmaceutical plant in Khartoum in reprisal for Al-Qaida's suicide bomb attacks against its embassies in Nairobi and Dar es Salaam. Woolsey retracted the allegation in December 2003 – over five years later – in a video-link cross-examination by James Price QC in the High Court of Justice during a libel case brought by Mohamed Abdul Latif Jameel against the *Wall Street Journal*. The by then out of office director conceded that his error was 'lost in the confusion of the past'.

For him, perhaps. Unrevised 'facts' that are allowed to linger in the public domain for half a decade tend to achieve a certain permanence in the landscape of received information. The revised edition of *Reaping the Whirl-wind* had been in the bookshops for three months by the time Woolsey was finally called on to correct his error, an act that reinforced the notion of retroactive defamation: that an allegation that was 'true' in one period of time, according to a credible intelligence source, is no longer true at a later period; and that anyone who repeats this allegation in the first period of time can be successfully prosecuted in the second, after the source has publicly withdrawn his assertion.

In the Jameel case, the *Wall Street Journal* tried to use the defence of 'qualified privilege' – that information from reputable sources was in the public interest – but failed to convince Mr Justice Eady, who 'found that the journalism failed to meet the high standards required to establish a duty to publish', according to Martin Soames, writing in the *Guardian*. 'This is a recurrent and deeply worrying aspect of terrorism-related journalism,' Soames continued, 'in which strong evidence is hard to find.'

The pitfalls facing writers on contemporary affairs – I hesitate to say 'investigative journalism' – will only be multiplied following the *New York Times*'s admission in late May that much of its reporting on Iraq and WMD was tainted by the same intelligence sources that led to the pulping of my book. In a rare display of mortified candour, the *NYT* cited 28 articles on Iraq published between October 2001 and February 2003 that were flawed by an overdependence on claims by 'Iraqi informants, defectors and exiles bent on regime change', accounts that were 'eagerly confirmed' by US intelligence officials convinced of the need to invade Iraq. 'Articles based on dire claims about Iraq tended to get prominent display,' ran the apology on 26 May, 'while follow-up articles that called the original ones into question were sometimes buried. In some cases there was no follow-up at all.'

The flagging of these articles followed quickly on the demotion of Ahmad Chalabi from the Pentagon's favourite Iraqi to an alleged stooge of Iranian intelligence, which had supposedly tricked the US into invading Iraq. An important and fabulous story, but how can one go about establishing the truth of the allegations against Chalabi with both media and intelligence sources so compromised, and for so long?

Perhaps the only way of recounting these stories that lie temptingly on the borderline between fact and 'factoid' without incurring legal action is through film. Michael Moore's documentary *Fahrenheit 911* covers some of the same ground as the books by myself, Unger and Gerald Posner (*While America Slept: The Failure to Prevent 9/11*), another author whose book will not be published in the UK, though in a more polemical fashion and with less of the dangerous detail. Though the big-screen documentary is a genre of fairly recent origin, it has, to my knowledge, only been contacted by lawyers once. Last October, James Nichols, brother of the Oklahoma City bombing conspirator Terry Nichols, lodged a lawsuit against Moore on charges of libel, defamation of character, invasion of privacy and emotional distress during the filming of his Oscar-winning *Bowling for Columbine*.

In the film, Moore asks Nichols for an interview and steers the conversation round to gun ownership. Nichols tells Moore he has a gun under his pillow and Moore gets him to show it to him. Nichols's lawyers are asking for US$36 million in damages for 'tricking' their defendant into an interview.

With *Fahrenheit 911* now set for release in 700 cinemas, a lot of people in the George Bush camp will be rooting for Nichols. ❏

Michael Griffin is a freelance writer and broadcaster specialising in Afghanistan and Al-Qaida

APHRODITE'S OTHER ISLAND

TABITHA MORGAN

GREEK-CYPRIOT POLITICIANS AND
CLERICS BOOT OUT REUNIFICATION
AND CYPRUS'S SAD LITTLE WALL HAS
TO ENDURE FOR SOME YEARS YET

Walk through the narrow twisting streets of old Nicosia and you could be forgiven for thinking the barriers that divide the city are really rather attractive. Salmon-pink geraniums sprout from piles of old sandbags, purple convolvulus twines around the bases of cement-filled oil drums. One enterprising restaurateur has improvised an open-air dining area in the middle of what was once a busy thoroughfare but now ends abruptly with a wall.

And although the militarised no man's land that divides the city still contains large quantities of unexploded ordnance, Cypriots are actually at far greater risk from the chunks of masonry that occasionally fall from the derelict buildings on the edges of the buffer zone.

This, in a way, is the problem. A combination of neglect and casual normalisation have served to solidify the barriers that mark the city's physical division. In a similar way, familiarity of a kind has reinforced the island's partition in the minds of the island's Greek-Cypriot community.

Reunification was intended to change all this: on 24 April, in simultaneous referenda on each side of the island, Greek- and Turkish-Cypriots would vote in favour of entering the European Union as one nation, demonstrating as they did so the principles of pluralism and reconciliation that underpin the European ideal. Greek- and Turkish-Cypriots would be joined together in a loose federal state with each constituent state retaining autonomy over its own affairs, but with a single international identity. Forty years of inter-communal friction would be brought to an end with the stroke of a pen.

The UN proposal that was to bring about this transformation – known in Cyprus as the Annan plan after UN Secretary-General Kofi Annan – was not an easy read. The result of years of negotiations, it ran to some 9,000 pages of complex legal jargon. Little surprise then that few Cypriots managed to read it all, but looked to their politicians and the media for clarification and guidance.

The weeks leading up to the referendum became particularly charged in the south of the island where both political and religious leaders urged the Greek-Cypriot population overwhelmingly to vote against reunification. In an emotional television address, lasting nearly an hour, President Tassos Papadopoulos condemned the Annan plan, arguing that regardless of the concessions made to Greek-Cypriots, he did not believe Turkey would ever adhere to the terms of the new constitution. His message was clear: don't trust Turks.

The president's anti-unification stance was echoed by the powerful Greek Orthodox Church. One leading bishop threatened that those who voted in favour of reunification would 'lose their place in the kingdom of heaven'.

Former Greek-Cypriot government spokesman Michaelis Papapetrou, a supporter of reunification, believes that the president failed in his duty to explain the basic outlines of the plan to the electorate. 'The president himself tried to misinform people,' says Papapetrou. 'He deliberately gave them a very distorted picture.'

The president's rejectionist arguments acquired a particular resonance because they tapped into a widespread fear of both Turks and Turkey that has been tacitly encouraged in the decades following the island's de facto division after the Turkish invasion in 1974. Time and again, Greek-Cypriots voting against the plan explained that they did not want to live alongside Turks.

There are around 90,000 mainland Turks in northern Cyprus. Most came after partition when the Turkish government offered land and incentives to settlers, part of an attempt to alter the demographics of the country. Their arrival was met with understandable dismay by Greek-Cypriots who had been forced from their homes in the north in 1974.

Many of the settlers – mostly impoverished Anatolian villagers – have been on the island for 30 years now; their children and grandchildren were born here. And throughout that time they have been systematically demonised and vilified by the Greek-Cypriot media and by politicians who claimed that if only Turkish 'settlers' were expelled from Cyprus, reunification could be achieved painlessly. To suggest otherwise became unpatriotic.

Their rhetoric was directed primarily at the 200,000 Greek-Cypriot refugees from the north who now form a powerful political lobby group. Their right to return has become an emotive political doctrine that few politicians have had the courage to question publicly. Under the terms of

Limassol, Greek-Cyprus 2004: anti-reunification graffiti.
Credit: Ania Dabrowska

the UN plan more than half of the refugees would have been allowed to return to their former properties; the rest would have received generous financial compensation. This pragmatic solution was wholly unacceptable to those such as Ioannis Sherkersavvas from the coastal town of Kyrenia in northern Cyprus. He acknowledges that Greek-Cypriot politicians might have misled him in the past but maintains he has an inalienable right to farm his family's land. 'The land is a continuous thing,' he says. 'It fed my grandfather and my great-grandfather and it should be returned to us so we can feed our children and their children's children.'

Sherkersavvas's children and grandchildren are likely to share his views. Greek-Cypriot schoolchildren are taught in great detail about the atrocities committed by the invading Turkish army in 1974 but learn little about the Greek-sponsored military coup that prompted Turkey's intervention. Most are equally ignorant of the decade of discrimination and violence that preceded it, when the island's Turkish-Cypriot minority lived in fear, eventually leaving their homes and livelihoods to seek safety in urban ghettos.

By ignoring entire chapters of the island's history, the education system encourages children to believe that Greek-Cypriots were unique in their suffering. There is little in the school curriculum that encourages youngsters to come to terms with the past, while the system of rote learning in state schools discourages them from thinking for themselves or questioning the received version of events.

Turkish-Cypriot peace activist Sevgul Uludag believes this approach to teaching has created a deeply conservative society and stifled public debate. She argues that without freedom of expression 'people . . . stop thinking; they don't take the risk of thinking in a different way'. Perhaps it's not surprising, then, to find that Greek-Cypriots identify primarily with the Greek 'motherland' rather than seeing themselves as Cypriots first and Greeks second.

Yiannis Papadakis, an anthropologist at the University of Cyprus, believes both communities suffer from what he terms 'ethnic autism'. In the same way that those with autism have difficulty listening to or communicating with the outside world, Papadakis says Cypriots have become 'so enclosed in their own feelings of self-victimisation they have become oblivious to the pain and suffering of others'. While both communities suffered civilian casualties, many of whose remains have never been found, Papadakis claims that if someone from either side uses the word 'missing', 'they are only talking about their own missing, they would not even consider that the word might apply to the other community'.

Taking all this into account, it is probably inevitable that the majority of Greek-Cypriots are fearful of living alongside Turks and oblivious to the suffering of Turkish-Cypriots. But until something can be done to build trust between the communities, the climate of racism and xenophobia that prevails in the southern part of the island calls into question Greek-Cypriot claims to be citizens of Europe. ❑

Tabitha Morgan *is based in Nicosia and covers Cyprus for the BBC*

MORE SINNED AGAINST THAN SINNING
JAMES THACKARA

Eighteen years ago, Mordechai Vanunu, an Israeli scientist working at Dimona
nuclear facility, revealed that Israel had an atomic bomb project, a secret that had
clouded US–Israeli relations since the days of Kennedy and Ben Gurion, and might
have involved collusion between the countries. Vanunu was kidnapped in Italy,
returned to Israel and sentenced to 18 years' imprisonment, nearly 12 of which
he spent in solitary confinement. In April this year, James Thackara went to Israel
for Index on Censorship *to greet Vanunu on his release from Ashkelon Prison.*
Ursula Owen interviewed Thackara on his return.

First of all, I was astonished that though the international press was outside
the gates at Ashkelon to cover the release of Vanunu, not one interview, as
far I could see, devoted itself to any heightened or visionary debate about
the morality and the existence of nuclear weapons in Israel or anywhere
else.

Israelis call their position on nuclear weapons their 'nuclear ambiguity'.
That ambiguity has legal significance, reflecting in turn a moral riddle. A
few years ago, the UN General Assembly brought a case at the International
Court of Justice in The Hague, on the legality or otherwise of nuclear
weapons. The Algerian president of the court passed on it, saying, in effect:
'Nuclear weapons are legal in times of peace, illegal in times of war.' In
some way, this reflected the concept of ambiguity. But in the case of Israel,
it also reflects the nature of the Holocaust State: the Jewish people's plight in
the twentieth century and the nature of the Jewish state in relation to all
other states. It is a unique state aware of its uniqueness; the rest of the world
is also aware of its uniqueness; and it deals with things in a unique way.

We have Israel saying it doesn't have nuclear weapons, and they could
have anything from 150 to 400 warheads, some of them thermonuclear; it
also has three German submarines able to carry cruise missiles. It's a major
world nuclear power. We invaded Iraq for weapons that do not seem to
exist (though they might have been close to existence at one time). The
Israelis have avoided the kinds of inspections required by the Atomic
Energy Agency by staging *vernissage* inspections by the US. I think it has put
both countries in quite an awkward position.

When Truman became president in 1945, at the time of Potsdam, he didn't even know there was a BOMB so, when he was told, he thought it was just a slightly larger bomb. He wasn't particularly distressed to go along with the army's powerful ambition to drop the bomb. The business of secrecy is very dangerous in nuclear weapons.

It's important to remember that nuclear technology has got way ahead of morality. However, simply to deny a secret project belongs to the primitive stage of nuclear weapons, the 1940s and 1950s. We are moving out of that stage; and my comment at the moment I met Mordechai Vanunu was that his release meant the necessary end of it.

Nuclear weapons are very much a project of twentieth-century ideologies: ironically, the people building nuclear weapons often felt they could bring peace to the world. In the early stages, when the US and the USSR had primordial power over this project, it produced a kind of 'conversation' between Russians and Americans, a peaceful conversation based on the assumption that since they both had nuclear weapons and could incinerate each other and everybody else, they weren't going to do things in the usual way but would use little countries around the world to fight proxy wars for them. And that's how they did it, all conducted with the pawns and not the major pieces.

Now, more and more countries have nuclear weapons. And lo and behold, this is very uncomfortable for those countries that thought they had this power, because they thought they were rather responsible; now other people with religions that don't agree with them, with racial prejudices that aren't in accord with them, don't actually accept everything the primordial group tells them. So there is now a kind of nuclear community, in which there is a discourse that goes on within the nuclear establishment, which is a kind of alternative government.

For Israel, the exclusiveness of what happened to the Jews in the Holocaust is enshrined in their state. This exclusiveness, they believe, allows them to do things that other states do not do. It is at the root of why they have not joined the Atomic Energy Agency and do not reveal their nuclear capability. They have great confidence in their superior moral nature, and feel justified by the imperative of survival. Israel feels it is surrounded by anti-Semitic, aggressive people. For Ariel Sharon, this involves occupational thuggery that has put Israel in the position of a neo-colonial country.

Jerusalem 21 April 2004: Mordechai Vanunu at St George's Cathedral.
Credit: Rex Features / Amar Amar

Vanunu's abduction in 1986 came at a time of flux for Israel: it was redefining itself, having a form of identity crisis. It had occupied territories after the 1967 war and it gradually became clear that the territories were not going to be returned. This produced a moral dilemma for Israel as well as security issues on the ground. The fact that Israel had a nuclear project was not at the forefront of most Israeli anxieties, problems and guilt. It was developing its nuclear project and what was apparently a reactor project was moving into a weapons project.

Vanunu initially took security oaths based on a research project; he was not concerned about that. Gradually, however, he became aware that he was being involved with major proliferation. He found himself inside a totalitarian, repressive, secrecy-ridden state of denial and repression, an anti-human organisation – the world's nuclear community. He decided to take responsibility for what he was doing. This was particularly poignant for him because he wasn't a high-level scientist and he is often insulted by those who claim he is not important enough to be taken seriously. He decided he didn't want to be involved in this lie any longer and was gradually persuaded that it was important for him to say something.

While we waited for Vanunu to come out of prison I was interviewed by what I believe is the second largest paper in Israel, *Ma'ariv*. The journalist became more and more interested, more and more sober. At the end he turned to me and said: 'I want to speak to you personally. The Israel that Vanunu is coming out into is not the Israel he went in from. I believe that Vanunu will be accepted and admired by my generation of Israelis.' He made a personal apology to me about what happened to Vanunu. The interview did not get into the paper and, a few days later, they conducted a poll asking Israelis what they thought should happen to Vanunu. One of the options offered was 'kill him'. Paranoia has produced the most appalling kind of conservatism. And this plays into the nuclear state aspect of Israel, because nucleonics is always totalitarian, undemocratic and conservative. But the poll in *Ha'aretz* showed something like 50 per cent wanted him released, 30 per cent thought he should be kept under house arrest and silenced, and maybe 20 per cent that he should go on being punished for ever. In a north London liberal synagogue, I heard a man who claimed to have been at the Dimona project say: 'Vanunu betrayed Judaism, he converted to Christianity, he was a low-level technician. He betrayed his family, they denounced him. He betrayed the Jewish state. He is no better than Adolf Eichmann. He should be executed.'

We are not going to have disarmament in our lifetime, or the lifetime of our children, but in 100 years civilisation will evolve away from nuclear weapons. Meanwhile, the presence of nuclear weapons in Israel is Israel's greatest impetus to joining the community of all the races and religions of the world as an equal – if it admits they are there. I can't say that to build instruments that are portable gas chambers and weapons of extinction is a sign that the human species is a sane species on this planet. However, given the primitive state that humanity is in and has been in for a long time, I would say that to have nuclear weapons is to assume an enormous, aggravated responsibility. A few years ago, the Marshall McLuhan Institute in Canada said that nuclear weapons were the great teacher, and there should be a nuke in every marketplace. I would say there is a moral content in nuclear weapons, because it involves a conjunction of moral authority and powers of mass ecological destruction. When God wanted to punish people in the Old Testament, He infested the world with floods, plagues and violence. Nuclear weapons are a plague and a flood – it is in fact the Old Testament God enshrined in science.

In the post–Darwinian age, a large number of people say God doesn't exist, or God is dead. Even if they claim to believe in God, people feel that they should be doing something to improve the planet. If you take on nuclear weapons, in a sense you are saying, well, God might have had virtue on His side but we have gone beyond God now; man is responsible for everything. Every last ant on this planet is in the realm of human responsibility. And this weapon is saying to us, don't let other people solve your problems, don't argue with your neighbour because you are not going to get anywhere with him, because antithesis is going to produce Armageddon. For God's sake, get on with the business of solving the problems of the world. And here I would admonish the Israeli state: nuclear knowledge has a sacred aspect to it. It is something that belongs to everybody and when Klaus Fuchs gave away the secret of the implosion principle to the Soviets, he did it because he felt tortured that nuclear knowledge, which is larger than any nation or religion, was not being shared – in this case with our *ally*, Russia.

An Israeli negotiator said – and Afif Safieh, a Christian representative of the PLO, made similar comments – that in every negotiation with the PLO the fact that Israel has a bomb project is an appallingly disheartening aspect of the discussion, because it is saying Israel is absolute. And this creates a nuclear arms race in the Middle East: the Iranians, the Iraqis, the Syrians –

everybody – would like to have nukes so they can sit at the negotiating table with the Israelis.

Nuclear weapons are dangerous things to have on your territory because they not only give you a kind of sovereignty and immense moral prestige if they are not abused, they also put you in a position of having to defend the terrain that the nuclear project is on because it is too dangerous to have it fall into anybody else's hands – Osama bin Laden's, for instance.

I think the release of Vanunu will force Israel to come clean. It's important that Vanunu walks as a free man on the planet, is not assassinated, is not harassed, not muzzled. After being locked away for 18 years, how could he have secrets dangerous to Israeli security? After 18 years' quarantine, a head of Dimona would not be likely to have up-to-date dangerous secrets – especially as Vanunu put everything he knew in the public domain in 1986. Vanunu wants to leave Israel, he's said that in letters, he has been totally open about it. He wants to go to Congress – to do what? It seems that so great is the angst underlying US–Israeli relations that the same people who use US tractors to trash the homes of unarmed old women can't find the courage to give this man the passport he is guaranteed by Israeli law.

At the moment he's living in an Anglican cathedral in Jerusalem, quite close to the old city, to the Damascus gate. When I visited him, there were heavily armed police at both ends of the road, presumably to protect him. It would be a major international incident for Israel if anything were to happen to him; they don't want him dead. There were conspicuous Shin Beit [Israeli secret service agents] outside masquerading as reporters. To get in, I just had to hand a slip of paper to an attendant of the church saying 'James, *Index on Censorship*'. He came back five minutes later, the gates were cleared, I was let in and we walked straight across the cloister into the colonnade. He looked over his shoulder and then said, 'Now go left.' We hurried down the colonnade into an austere cloister with a long monk's table. And there, after 18 years, was Mordechai Vanunu sitting at the end of the table, with one brother Asher on the other side and Meir, his other brother, at the end. He rose to meet me – he'd been told by his brother who I was – and we spoke for maybe half an hour. It was one of the most beautiful things I've ever experienced. Because this man was totally calm, totally gentle, totally unhostile, apparently not angry, completely sane, witty and funny, and *innocent*. I put the question: how did he stay sane? And he said that they would question him regularly, he was under continual questioning because they wanted to understand why he felt the way he did. As I understood it, his reply was that he was able to preserve his sanity by something I took to be akin to personal ideological discourse. He would spend his whole time thinking about what they had said, what the implications were, and replying to them. This mixture of Socratic discipline, heavy exercise, these confrontations with his persecutors, but also his interlocutors and his contact with humanity, was what preserved his rational powers and kept him calm; probably even, I would imagine, supplied him with a certain sense of humour in a situation that was far from funny.

I would emphasise, and I don't think Vanunu would argue with me, that this man should not be seen as first and foremost a human rights victim. It is a human rights case, but he had access to certain newspapers, he was able to read, he asked his friends to send him videos and films. This was not a man who was nailed to a cross and hung in public view; this is a person who was kept out of sight to guard a secret. I think it's important to see that this man is a censorship hero of a very particular kind.

This man was crucified in a very modern way. He was quietly separated from humanity and made a prisoner of the nuclear state, which would not allow him to debate what every human being on the planet should be debating. This is a particular kind of modern psychopathology; it is insane; it reflects the psychotic state the human species is in. ❏

James Thackara *has had a long involvement in nuclear issues and the Vanunu case, and is the author of* America's Children *(Chatto & Windus, 1984), a novel dealing with the Manhattan Project and the fate of Robert Oppenheimer*

Tehran: The face of things to come; walls go secular in 21st-century Iran.
Credit: Omid Salehi / 135 Photos, Tehran

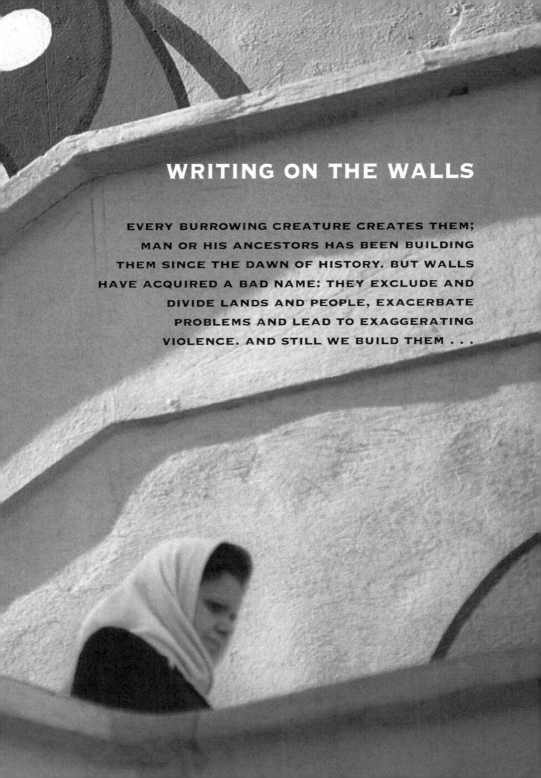

WRITING ON THE WALLS

EVERY BURROWING CREATURE CREATES THEM;
MAN OR HIS ANCESTORS HAS BEEN BUILDING
THEM SINCE THE DAWN OF HISTORY. BUT WALLS
HAVE ACQUIRED A BAD NAME: THEY EXCLUDE AND
DIVIDE LANDS AND PEOPLE, EXACERBATE
PROBLEMS AND LEAD TO EXAGGERATING
VIOLENCE. AND STILL WE BUILD THEM . . .

THIS STORY DOTH A WALL PRESENT
FELIPÉ FERNANDEZ-ARMESTO

West Tehran: fantasy towers prefigure those now rising all over Tehran.
Credit: all photographs Omid Salehi / 135 Photos, Tehran

Walls have a bad name. We associate them with exclusion, with the radical modification of landscape, with human arrogance that wants to shut out nature, or with human greed that evades sharing. They disfigure the planet and divide its people. Yet every tunnelling, burrowing creature, in a sense, creates them. It is as much in our nature to surround ourselves with them as it is in birds' to enclose their nests, or insects' to spin cocoons, or beavers' to wall-in the flow of rivers.

Of course, it depends what you mean by walls. Was the first hunter to draw *frondure* around him to create a covert making a wall? If so, the first wall a hominine made was a stratagem and a subterfuge, designed to confer an advantage in violence. The first walls we now know about from direct evidence were discontinuous – posts or stones or large bones, shifted and righted, to define the drive lanes that led Pliocene megafauna to their deaths. In the days when people had lots of big mammoths and aurochs to hunt, this was the hunters' favourite method: drive them over an abyss, where hecatombs piled up, and where the bones often remain to this day, or into a mire or lake, where the creatures lost manoeuvrability and could be relatively easily dispatched by spearmen. Like the fencing of corrals, which were probably invented soon afterwards, the walls of drive lanes were designed to keep creatures in, not to keep humans out. Exclusion was a later refinement.

Even the most rudimentary dwellings have walls of a sort. Most 'cave men' did not live in caves but scraped together shelters nearby. Stone Age caves were usually reserved for ritual activities, burials and art. The earliest surviving ruins of the walls they built are about 20,000 years old. People who lived on the Eurasian steppe propped mammoth bones and stretched hides over them to construct their houses. Structures of this sort conferred scant security from predators or assailants, but they did shut out the wind.

However, these apparently innocent enclosures provided more than shelter. They prefigure a use to which walls have always been put: they are displays of power. The mammoth bones surely signified more than useful building materials for the people who piled them up. They were trophies of amazingly successful hunting, of acts of violence executed on creatures immensely more powerful than men. They were means of appropriating magic, and symbols of the defiance of nature. Ever since the era of the mammoth–hunters, we have used walls to convey messages: the means and materials of which they are constructed say how rich or powerful we are. To make the message clearer, we decorate them with reliefs, adorn them

with sculpture, hang them with flat art, or smear them with graffiti. Or, if we want to be really intimidating, we leave them blank and deliberately ugly. A bleak, faceless wall, or one relieved only by random scorch-marks or streaks of blood, is as eloquent as the carved façade of a temple or cathedral.

When did walls become defensive weapons in human warfare? Pre-humans who knew about shelters and hides almost certainly practised warfare. Jane Goodall's discovery of warfare among chimpanzees makes that overwhelmingly likely. Hominines were pretty good at throwing – so they probably fought with missiles. This means they had a use for walls in warfare for aeons before any evidence shows up in the archaeological record. The earliest direct evidence of large-scale inter-communal violence – which takes the form of concentrations of large numbers of dead bearing wound-marks of kinds likely to have been inflicted in battle – dates from about 13,000 years ago. The fighters of that era could have built formidable forti-fications around their villages had they so wished. The people of the culture archaeologists call Natufian, from about 12,000 BC, constructed permanent dwellings by digging into the earth and supporting hide or rush roofs on drystone walls. Defences could have been constructed on similar lines, but, as far as we know at present, no one bothered.

Jericho was the first settlement known to have been enclosed, or largely enclosed, by a wall of dressed stone. Kathleen Kenyon discovered it in 1956. The first wall of Jericho was built over 10,000 years ago: it was over three and a half metres high, with a huge tower that contained 1,000 tons of stone. Because Joshua 'fit de battle' here and made the walls of Jericho tumble down, it is hard to resist the assumption that the earliest wall was a defensive measure. Such an assumption would almost certainly be misleading. Other towns of the period, or a little later, which are almost as big as Jericho, had no defences. Jericho's wall must either have had some special symbolic significance or ritual purpose peculiar to its location; or, more probably, it served to deflect the floods and mud shifts that tumbled and slid from the hills around the Jordan valley.

Men are just one kind of menace. In the growing cities of the next few millennia, the use of walls as a means of defence against armies was therefore probably a development of their role in fending off natural adversaries. They were not a universal device among what we loosely call early 'civilisations'. The Egyptians did not favour them, whereas the Sumerians did. The Myce-

Tehran: body-beautiful advertising gym

neans did, while Cretans did not. So specific cultural considerations must have affected the decision. Like other features of early civilisation, large-scale wall-building was a form of conspicuous consumption, which mopped up seasonally idle labour, immortalised rulers and conferred prestige. In some of the wonder-lists of the ancient Greek tourist trade, Babylon was noted not only for its 'hanging garden' but also its walls, reputedly broad enough for four chariots to ride abreast behind the topmost parapets. For such walls served, in a sense, to keep people in as much as to keep them out: they were for demarcation as well as defence, defining the city and fomenting civic spirit.

The huge projects of frontier fortification indulged in by despotic master builders of antiquity – symbolised for us by the Great Wall of China – were not entirely useless as defensive measures. Just by virtue of their scale, they were designed for a psychologically intimidating effect on the barbarians who beheld them. The Great Wall appears so often on Chinese maps of what we think of as the late medieval and early modern periods that it must have had a big part to play in Chinese perceptions of the nature of the state. The sheer façades were genuine obstacles to invaders who relied on horses. But, because of the obvious problems of manning, neither the Great Wall, nor any of the lesser fortifications that echoed it, ever achieved a particularly creditable record in defeating determined invaders. For much of Chinese history, the frontier was south of the wall.

It is commonly supposed that the development of powerful artillery and sophisticated siege techniques eventually made defensive walls redundant. The opposite is true. The most redoubtable city walls ever were built in the eighteenth century, precisely in response to such developments. The large-scale destructions of city walls in Europe in the late eighteenth and early nineteenth centuries were the result of urban growth and enlightened distaste for monuments thought to represent a benighted, medieval past. Walls remained as powerful as ever, because what made them powerful – what makes them powerful – is their symbolic meaning.

They have returned in the twentieth and twenty-first centuries, because the latest technology favours them. Long-range surveillance techniques mean that walls can function with limited manpower to keep neighbouring communities apart and – for the first time in history – to stifle the enterprise of individual migrants. But the control of humans' freedom of movement is

Tehran: mourning the martyrs of the Iran–Iraq war 1980–88

*Left: Felestine (Palestine Ave), Tehran: commemorating the Palestinian intifada
Above: West Tehran: wounded war veteran of the Iran–Iraq war*

still only part of the wall-builders' rationale. The Berlin Wall served, it is true, to stop refugees getting out, and Israel's 'security wall' may have been conceived to stop terrorists getting in. But what the walls say is more important than what they do. 'We want to impose a culture different from yours,' said the Berlin Wall to West Berliners. 'We will define the boundaries around here,' says the Israeli wall to Palestinians. Walls may have ears: they surely have mouths. ❑

Felipé Fernández-Armesto is the author of Civilisations *(Macmillan UK, 2001). He is professor of global environmental history at Queen Mary College, University of London*

HIGH ON WALLS

KAMILA SHAMSIE

'Why do you have walls around your house?' I was at university in the US when a friend asked me this question.

'High crime rate in Karachi,' I replied, thinking, *Isn't it obvious? Why else?*

It was months, maybe years, later that it finally occurred to me that if there's a high crime rate in a densely populated city, walls don't make sense. After all, walls are what prevent your neighbours from seeing into your house and reporting 'suspicious activity'. Walls don't protect, they isolate. What's more, they're not terribly effective at keeping people out. When you go to see who rang your gate-bell and find a man pointing a gun at you and demanding to be let in, all the walls in the world won't help you. (Why should criminals bother with breaking and entering when they can find effective methods of merely entering?) Besides, most gates are easy enough to climb up and jump over, even if the walls aren't. So, really, all that walls do is render ineffective the 'neighbourhood watch', making it necessary to find other ways of keeping your house under constant surveillance.

And thus walls lead to armed security guards whose sole purpose it is to ensure that no one unwanted gets past the walls (or through the gate) – the side benefit of having these guards is that you are assured of the presence of loaded semi-automatic weapons in your vicinity at all times. A secure thought, if ever. But then again, security guards can be paid off by criminals.

So it's best, actually, to hire a private security company to set up an elaborate alarm system triggered by motion sensors. You may find your pet dog activates the sensors several times a day, in which case you may need to get rid of the dog, particularly if he is in the habit of licking strangers' faces rather than ripping out their throats. The private security company will compensate for the loss of your pet by installing a 'panic button' in your house that will make you feel as though you're living in a high-tech Hollywood movie. If you press the panic button, someone from the security company will call you within three minutes and ask for the code. If you fail to answer correctly, they'll dispatch a van full of armed men to your house to deal with the armed men who have broken in.

Feeling safe yet? The only problem with the panic button, and the whole alarm system, is that it's connected to the phone line. So if someone cuts your phone lines before breaking in, the system is disabled. Of course, a yellow light will start blinking in the video room of the security company's office to let them know your phone lines are cut – but, since the video room isn't monitored 24 hours a day, it's purely a matter of luck whether or not anyone will see the blinking yellow light.

Why do it? Why go through the rigmarole of the walls, the guards, the alarms, the barbed wire on the walls and the spikes protruding from the top of the gates? In part, of course, because you simply hope breaking into someone else's house will be less trouble for lazy criminals than breaking into your mini-fortress. And, yes, the guards, the wire, the alarms, even the pet dog with an air of ferocity about him aren't entirely without effect in dissuading intruders.

But there's a deeper pathology at work behind the high walls of Karachi's houses (you can judge the affluence of a neighbourhood by the height of its walls). Talk to people who've had their houses broken into, and you'll soon detect, in all of them, an anger quite different from that of people who've been held up at gunpoint in their car, or on the street. That such a thing should happen in one's house! There is a rage in there that does much to explain walls.

But let's backtrack and recap: walls that keep your neighbours from noticing if anything is amiss in your house; security guards who bring guns into your neighbourhood instead of keeping them out; security companies who spend millions on elaborate technology but can't hire someone to watch a video screen; not to mention the barbed wire that doesn't last very long in Karachi's sea air and will soon rust away and disintegrate. Every precaution is a lesson in irony. But push past the irony and what you come to is this truth that lies at the very root of the rage I mentioned earlier: you cannot keep yourself safe. In trying to do so you only draw attention to yourself, make those who wonder such things wonder what exactly it is you're guarding so ardently. How valuable is the prize for finding a way through your levels of safety?

You cannot be safe, but you want to believe you can. You're desperate to believe you can. How do you create for yourself that façade of safety? Here's the first step: you build a higher wall. ❑

Kamila Shamsie's *most recent novel is* Kartography *(Bloomsbury, 2002)*

FORTRESS AMERICA

RUBÉN MARTÍNEZ

IT WON'T STOP THEM COMING AND
MIGRANT DEATHS WILL INCREASE,
BUT THE US IS BUILDING ITS OWN
GREAT WALL OF EXCLUSION

Last summer I stood on the banks of the Rio Grande in Big National Park, Texas, and for a few moments I had trouble reconciling the fact that for some 1,000 miles the river – known to Mexicans as the Rio Bravo, the raging river – forms what is perhaps the most contested border in the world today.

It was August, and it was hot, yet there were no hordes of migrants gathered on the Mexican side readying to ford the slow, knee-deep waters (at many other points along the river, the waters can be deep and the current can be powerful enough to drag you under). Neither was there a phalanx of US Border Patrol agents waiting on this side. There was no evidence of the battery of surveillance equipment omnipresent at popular illegal crossings near San Diego, Tucson or El Paso – video cameras and seismic sensors, helicopters and unmanned 'drone' aircraft (the same kind currently being used in Iraq and Afghanistan).

Indeed, there wasn't a fence, not even an obelisk announcing my side as American or the other Mexican. There was only the gentle rush of the river, the summer sun sparkling on the wavelets, and all around me – in the canyon cut by millions of river-years, in the stratified heights of the Sierra del Carmen, in the very sand I stood upon – the geological evidence that the land was here long before we or the border were, and would be here long after this very human frontier is lost to time.

In the midst of my reverie, two teenagers and an adult man appeared on the opposite bank. They called out a greeting to which I responded. The boys jumped into the river and came across to my side, clambering up on to the rocks above the waterline. They had now officially and illegally entered the United States of America. I took a quick look behind me; still no Border Patrol in sight.

The crew introduced themselves as denizens of Boquillas del Carmen, a modest town on the Mexican side, within plain view of the American shore. The older of the boys fished a plastic ziplock baggie out of his pocket. Inside was a stamped letter bearing an American address – a relative living on this side. He asked me the favour of dropping it off at the post office a mile down the road. If he attempted to do so himself, he explained, he might indeed be apprehended as an 'illegal alien'.

Now the younger of the boys piped up and said that tomorrow was his birthday and would I do him the favour of buying some chocolate frosting at the general store (next to the post office)? I told him I would, and I did, though later I wondered how many 'birthdays' he'd had recently.

The father of the boys never completely crossed the river, preferring to sit on a rock about 25 feet from shore. He told me that things hadn't always been this way. Gringos and Mexicans had moved back and forth at will, he said, dating back to 1848, when the Treaty of Guadalupe Hidalgo designated the river the boundary between the United States and Mexico. In the wake of 9/11, the Border Patrol had suddenly clamped down on this little 'informal' crossing. Presumably, Al-Qaida was about to smuggle dirty bombs across the Rio Grande.

Dragging this region into the post-9/11 national security state devastated the livelihoods of residents in Boquillas. For decades, the town had subsisted largely on the trickle of American tourists ferried over on canoes and hosted at a couple of modest bars. Likewise, Mexicans had shopped and worked across the river in the US.

Before departing, the boys asked if I wanted to cross over to their side for a visit. I looked at the river, at the village rising from the sand on the opposite bank and at my new friends. And I realised that for the first time in my life, I was seeing the line between the US and Mexico the way Mexicans generally see it. If I crossed the river, I'd become an illegal American in Mexico. And if I returned to the US at the same spot, I'd be an illegal American in America.

It is one of the great regrets of my life that I didn't cross. Quixotic or not, I should have jumped across that river – because in the end, that's what it is, a river, and rivers are meant to be crossed like mountains are to be climbed.

Afterwards, I began to think that this is precisely the real problem at the US–Mexico line today: that we, Americans, don't cross over and see the border as the citizens of the developing world see it, those who live in the global realm, a world without borders. Americans do get around, of course – but as tourists, as consumers of the 'other'. From the migrant point of view, borders are permeable rather than solid, moving rather than fixed, politically expedient rather than morally imperative.

In America, we speak of migrants as 'illegals' because they have broken the letter of immigration law. But from the migrant point of view, US immigration policy seems to be breaking the laws of nature – or at least of globalisation. For fiscal year 2004, the federal government has budgeted over US$9 billion for border protection. Credible politicians talk of building a wall along the entire southern frontier, the Great Wall of America.

And yet, to date not a single suspected terrorist has been apprehended trying to make illegal entry on the US–Mexico line. (Most national security experts agree that the much more likely scenario is for terrorists to attempt entry along the largely unguarded Canadian border; as for the 9/11 hijackers, all entered *legally* on tourist or student visas.)

The most concrete result of a decade's worth of restrictive immigration policy is not a more 'secure' nation but the death of thousands of undocumented immigrants. Several walls – none of which runs for more than 20 miles – have been raised at the most heavily trafficked illicit crossings but they haven't stopped or even stemmed the flow. Like water following the path of least resistance, the smugglers push their human cargo around the walls and thus into much more isolated and hazardous desert terrain. Every year since the first wall was built (at San Diego in 1994), the number of migrant deaths at the line has increased.

EVERY YEAR SINCE THE FIRST WALL WAS BUILT, THE NUMBER OF MIGRANT DEATHS AT THE LINE HAS INCREASED

This year, by all accounts, will see a massive increase in migrant crossings, apprehensions and deaths. At the beginning of the year, President George W Bush proposed a 'guest worker' programme. The proposal was lambasted by advocates of immigrants' rights as institutionalised exploitation (there would be no guarantee of citizenship after a worker's 'contract' expired, no mechanism for family reunification, and the reform would only target immigrants in the lowest wage brackets), but for many other observers – in particular the migrants themselves – Bush had taken a step, however tentative, in the right direction; and many who'd been waiting for just such a signal decided it was the right time to cross over.

Unfortunately for the migrants, the Bush plan is more of a symbolic election-year stunt – apparently an appeal to those Latino citizens in the US (many of whom once crossed illegally themselves) who hold the proverbial

US/Mexican border, Mexico: and the sun came out on the other side.
Credit: Alex Webb / Magnum Photos

'swing vote' power in several key states. It is highly unlikely that there will be a vote on Bush's plan, or on the Democratic Party's more liberal alternatives, this year.

But the toll is already obvious on the border. Some 84 migrants have perished on the Arizona stretch of the border since last October, a rate triple that of the previous 12 months. On average, one migrant a day perishes on the US–Mexico line; in the last decade, well over 3,000 migrants have died attempting entry.

I have written about the border for going on 20 years now, and while I admit I probably indulged rhetorical excess back in the 1980s when I compared the situation here to the old divide between East and West Berlin, today the comparison is rather more precise. With billions of dollars' worth of technology, the presence of some 10,000 Border Patrol agents – in addition to Customs, Drug Enforcement Agency and other federal officers – we are finally achieving in deed what restrictionist politicians have envisioned with their rhetoric: Fortress America.

The problem for the wall-builders is that the migrants continue to cross anyway. The Border Patrol tallied some 1,400 detentions in south-eastern Arizona *on a single day* last month. The general rule of thumb has long been that for each migrant detained, another gets through.

A long hot summer is predicted for the drought-stricken American Southwest. A new record number of deaths will be set. The politicians will try to proclaim success in 'sealing the border'. But the migrants by their very numbers – those who die, those apprehended and turned away, those that make it into the interior – will tell us otherwise. ❑

Rubén Martínez *is the author of* The New Americans *(The New Press, 2004) and* Crossing Over: A Mexican Family on the Migrant Trail *(Pantheon, 2001)*

A STRANGE KIND OF PEACE

GLENN PATTERSON

Sandy Row, South Belfast: you have been warned: this is a protestant stronghold.
Credit: all photographs Namiko Kitaura / Fabrica

In August 1969, eight years almost to the day after the advent of the Berlin Wall, rioting in Belfast led to the hasty erection of a peace-line between the Protestant Shankill and Catholic Falls Road – or rather, for most of its length, between the Shankill and Springfield Roads. Thirty-five years on – 15 years from the fall of the Berlin Wall, 10 years from the IRA ceasefire, six years from the Good Friday Agreement – that 'temporary' peace-line, reinforced and extended to over half a mile, still stands, as do the 16 others created in its image in various contentious parts of the city. The greatest concentration, like the greatest concentration of murders during the conflict, is in north Belfast, including one, erected since the Agreement, through the middle of a public park.

Above: Falls Road Belfast: nationalist poster supporting hunger strikers of 1981
Right: Ainsworth Street: in loyalist protestant territory

Protestants and Catholics may for the most part have stopped killing one another but that is not to say that they are ready to live side by side.

This was never, by any stretch of the imagination, an integrated city but it is a more profoundly divided one now than at any time in its history. Whereas two-thirds of Belfast citizens were estimated to be living in segregated streets in the 1960s, by the 1980s the figure had risen to four-fifths. Evidence suggests that figure has gone on rising. In his book *The Trouble With Guns* (Blackstaff Press) writer and magazine editor Malachi O'Doherty, a Catholic by birth, tells how during the riots of 1969 he was trying to make his way home from the Shankill Road where he was then working as a barman. Finding himself lost he asked for – and was given – directions to the Falls. It is almost impossible to imagine such a scenario today. Nor is it easy to see how the current divisions can be reversed. Where once there

were through-roads now there are cul-de-sacs; housing at many traditional flashpoints has been cleared altogether and retail developments, industrial parks, even motorways built as de facto buffer zones. A wall, in time, can be dismantled, but how in the world do you overcome six lanes of traffic?

With their backs turned to one another these segregated areas are often further divided into paramilitary zones of influence. If flags and painted kerbstones – green, white and orange, or red, white and blue – will tell you whether you are in a Catholic or Protestant part of town, murals are usually the best guide to which organisation holds sway there. A BBC Northern Ireland investigation earlier this month into antagonisms between loyalist paramilitaries was aptly entitled *Feudal Times*. Though east Belfast has been the focus of the most recent feud, the bloodiest and most protracted one remains that which in summer 2000 split the Shankill Road, Korea-like, between an upper (UVF) end and a lower (UDA) one. Scores of families were put out of their homes. According to one contributor to *Feudal Times*, the road is still traumatised by the events.

My mother's family are Shankill people. A few years back my brother and I drove an uncle, home from Australia, around the streets where he had grown up. He was visibly shaken by the depradations.

It is all the more remarkable, then, that the Shankill has just picked up a 'Keep Britain Tidy' award after an initiative that has involved the removal of 27 murals, sectarian graffiti and paint from 7,000 metres of kerbstones. This is not – as one overenthusiastic press agency suggested – 'the last vestiges of the Troubles [being] scrubbed away', but it is a start.

In another recent development, senior figures in Sinn Fein and the Democratic Unionist Party issued what appear to have been synchronised calls for a quiet summer in Belfast. (Summers here have traditionally been hot for all the wrong reasons.) Mobile phones, meanwhile, have been issued to community workers either side of certain of the peace-lines to allow them to communicate and mediate at the first signs of trouble.

And all the time housing is returning to the city centre itself, reversing decades of population decline. In keeping with other cities in Britain and Ireland, much of this housing consists of apartments for young singles – 'yuppie flats' as they are still somewhat anachronistically referred to. So far these developments have been largely free of sectarian tension and iconography, though only last month there were ugly demonstrations outside an apartment block on Sandy Row, a working-class Protestant district behind the city's 'golden mile' of restaurants and bars, after rumours that an Irish

Divismore Drive, Ballymurphy: time for a little nationalist sentiment

flag had been waved from one of the windows. Of even greater concern are the attacks in both Catholic and Protestant parts of the city on members of Belfast's still small ethnic minority communities. In loyalist areas in particular, there has been clear evidence of paramilitary involvement.

It seems that while the peace-lines are undeniably popular with those living within a stone's – or a petrol bomb's – throw of the other side (and who knows, were I living there myself they might be popular with me), they have perpetuated into our heavily processed peace a world view where there are really only two types of people: 'us' and 'not-us'.

There are still many thousands of metres of kerbstones to go. ❏

Glenn Patterson is the author of That Which Was *(Hamish Hamilton, 2004) and* Number 5 *(Penguin, 2004). He teaches an MA course in creative writing at Queen's University, Belfast*

THINK ROMA, SAY JEW – YOU WON'T GET AWAY WITH IT

IRENA MARYNIAK

WHEN THE EUROPEAN PROJECT IS
COMPLETED, EUROPE WILL BE HOME TO
SOMETHING BETWEEN 8 AND 12 MILLION
ROMA. WILL THIS MARK AN END TO
DISCRIMINATION?

On 1 May, European accession day, the head of the EU delegation to Slovakia, Eric van der Linden, suggested in an interview that Roma children should be separated from their families and pressed into boarding schools to help them fit into 'the system of values dominant in our society' and contribute 'productively' to the economy. The European Roma Information Office, which reported the statement, was understandably outraged and called for his resignation. Yet this kind of ill-judged talk is symptomatic of a now widespread perception that the Roma community is an embarrassing threat to the new European idea and the culture of high wealth, growth and well-being.

Central European administrations are strongly in favour of this view of the Roma tradition, and in the run-up to accession it surfaced to colour the wording of documents relating to EU policies of social integration. The Slovak 'Joint Inclusion Memorandum' (JIM), prepared with the European Commission and published in December 2003, is hazy on aspects of health and housing ('cumulative disadvantages experienced by the Roma community') but warns of dangers that the Gypsy 'culture of poverty' will be transferred to future generations. The Czech JIM laments the 'serious problems' of the 'cohabitation of the Romani population with the majority community' and complains of Romani 'socially pathological behaviour'. This is language guaranteed to send ripples of anxiety through Brussels. It enhances the image of a resistant community, a generic threat, a clash of cultures.

There is a sense in which new European identity is being more sharply defined by the rejection of the Romani stereotype than by bookish references to Christendom, the Enlightenment or socialism. Roma represent the anti-values against which Europe is shaping itself: we work, they don't; we

Usti Nad Labem, Czech Republic: a Roma boy peeps through the infamous 'wall'.
Credit: Sean Gallup / Getty Images

are responsible citizens, they aren't; we accept democratic rules of association, they do not, and so on. The Roma have been part of the fabric of European society since the thirteenth century, and with a population of 4.5 million in Europe, they form a larger national entity than many EU states. But with the Union looking for a secure, overarching identity that will affirm its uncertain global role, the Gypsy community is being cornered into ever deeper cultural confinement by words and gestures purporting to offer liberation, education, success and assimilation.

WITH A POPULATION OF **4.5** MILLION IN EUROPE, ROMA FORM A LARGER NATIONAL ENTITY THAN MANY EU STATES

This is particularly true in Central European countries, where economic and cultural self-projection often comes down to a well-coiffed look, Milanese footwear, a religious affiliation or a business card. Any digression from the formula can be seen as an affront and an outright challenge to everything that Europe represents and promises to be. Traditionally, the Continental prescription for dealing with suspected cultural resistance has been control by confinement. Unassimilated communities were concentrated, cordoned off, walled in. The segregated ghetto – Prague's Judenstadt, for instance – was a way of life from the fourteenth to the nineteenth centuries. Today, it is more often recalled as a passage to the Nazi killing camps.

David Ferko is a Romani from Usti nad Labem, an industrial town in northern Bohemia in the Czech Republic. Usti has a baroque church and a medieval castle, and offers tours to Terezin (Theresienstadt), the nearby site of a concentration camp where 33,500 Jews died in densely crowded cells, and 88,000 were shipped out to gas chambers in Auschwitz. Ferko took a Terezin excursion and described his impressions in an account written for the Stories Exchange Project, an online forum to encourage dialogue between Roma and non-Roma. 'There were 60 women in this very, very small room with absolutely nothing,' he writes. 'In Maticni Street it looks much the way it does here. People are also crowded into small rooms: 10–15 people. Of course the situation can't be compared . . . But the sense of both these things seems to me to be the same.'

Maticni Street gained notoriety six years ago, when the authorities in Usti constructed a concrete wall two metres high down its centre to separate Romani apartment blocks from private houses on the other side. The Gypsies were noisy, messy and didn't pay their rent. It was 'no more racist than the wall of a quarantine ward or a prison,' Jozef Pospisil writes in the Czech Internet daily *Britske Listy*. 'The inhabitants behind the wall did not observe the law or the principle of hygiene.' Thankfully, international outrage brought the wall down within six weeks; but Pospisil's remarks generated a flood of supportive emails from Czech readers. Subsequently, the government released a grant of US$88,000 to buy up the non-Romani homes in Maticni Street whose owners had initiated the wall's construction.

Throughout Central and Eastern Europe, Romani communities live in segregated areas, are schooled separately and buried apart. One in six are constantly hungry. Those who have integrated know their vulnerability: losing a job or a home can dispatch you straight back to the ghetto. In

Slovakia, many of the country's 400,000 Gypsies live in shanty towns where people while away the hours standing, squatting, staring, kicking a ball, fetching water from the standpipe. Toxic tips, intermingled waste and drinking water fester forgotten. One settlement, Patoracka outside Rudnany, lies on the grounds of a disused mercury mine. In eastern areas Romanies live in stick-and-mud shacks outside villages. Their settlement in Svinja was devastated by flooding five years ago and children go to school dirty because they have had to wade through mud and sewage to get there. Non-Romani are justifiably appalled, so they have built a fence through the playground to keep the dirty children away from the clean ones.

Attempts by Romani families to move outside segregated areas are often blocked by vigilante action. Baseball bats, iron bars, power saws and axes are popular tools of intimidation, and Roma themselves often feel that trying to move out of designated housing is fruitless. Kosice, Slovakia's second city, has evicted thousands of Roma from the city centre as part of a 'beautification project' launched in 1997 by Mayor Rudolf Schuster (now president of the country). Many were crammed into the Lunik IX estate – now the largest Romani ghetto in Slovakia – without electricity, hot water or rubbish collection. 'Roma destroy beauty,' Kosice's leading political analyst Peter Schutz commented. 'They have a different mentality. It is impossible to integrate them. The only option is to move them forcibly out of town.'

Slovakia has very little data of its own on the Roma minority, but the government says that in 2001 about 38 per cent of Romani children were in remedial schools. In the Czech Republic, official estimates suggest that 75 per cent of Gypsy kids go to schools for the physically and mentally deficient, though there is little evidence that most are either. The authorities quote a language 'handicap', a different 'hierarchy of values', 'different dynamics of personality development', and Roma themselves often prefer to keep their children apart because in segregated environments they are safer. But the quality of alternative education offered makes them unemployable.

Joblessness among Czech Roma approaches 70 per cent; in parts of Slovakia it reaches 90 per cent. Last January, the Slovakian government cut state benefits throughout the country, particularly targeting families with more than four children. Many Romani households were left on the verge of destitution. A month later, there were riots in central and eastern Slovakia, two of the poorest regions in the EU. Roma men looted food from shops and the Slovak armed forces undertook their biggest mobilisation since 1989. According to Claude Cahn of the European Roma Rights

Centre in Budapest, in Trebisov, a town with a Roma population of about 5,000, 240 police – some apparently drunk – raided Romani homes for about 12 hours from the morning of 25 February. Doors were kicked in, people were detained and beaten, truncheons and cattle prods were used on children. Radoslav Puky, a 28-year-old unemployed Roma, was found drowned in a canal with a broken ribcage. Police said it was an accident and within a couple of days the media announced that the government would be committing €1.25 million (US$1.5 million) to a campaign to improve Slovakia's image abroad. During a visit to eastern Slovakia after the riots, Prime Minister Mikulas Dzurinda accused the Roma community of 'speculating on the Welfare system'.

This, of course, is the main allegation: laziness, untrustworthiness, 'leeching', as the *Daily Express* calls it. 'What can be said of the Roma wouldn't be allowed to be said of any other ethnic group,' Jeanette Buirski of European Dialogue commented. We prefer to ignore the fact that Roma were slaves in Europe well into the nineteenth century; that they are victims of public antipathy and racial discrimination in the labour market today; that they are politically ostracised, harassed and bullied by police, judiciary and health officials; that Gypsies are victimised and abused – often very brutally – by neo-Nazi skinheads and other extremists; that there is evidence still of the forcible sterilisation of Roma women.

Just 5 per cent of the Gypsy population of Czechoslovakia survived World War II. Many died in the Lety concentration camp in southern Bohemia. In education and the media, Romani history is overwhelmingly ignored or insulted; the site of the Lety prison camp is now a pig farm. In Slovakia, Roma were mostly spared, but after the war a resettlement programme initiated by the communist regime forcibly moved many Slovak Romas west to the Czech side. When the country split in 1993, Roma who had been born in Slovakia found they had no legal right to Czech citizenship. An estimated 150,000 people were obliged to apply for recognition as citizens. Many of those initially refused had lived on Czech territory for over 20 years.

The stateless belong nowhere, have no voting rights, no security from expulsion, can receive only discretionary benefits, cannot legally work or do business. Their children may be taken away from them. They are bound by their own undefined status, strapped in by public denial. In the late 1990s, many Czech Roma tried to leave, encouraged by officials and television. In

August 1997, TV Nova broadcast a programme about the lives of Roma families in Canada. They appeared to be thriving there, on government support. Within weeks, hundreds of Roma had tried to emigrate; Canada responded by imposing visa restrictions. Two months later, another attempted exodus followed – this time to the UK. The British press called it 'an invasion'. Of 560 asylum requests made by Czech Roma in Britain in 1997–8, only three were granted.

Romani hopes of another kind of life outside Central Europe are dwindling. In recent years Slovak Roma have been expelled from Belgium, and Bosnian Roma returned from Italy. They are trapped by their lack of funds, skills and languages and by a disastrous public relations record. Despite media declarations to the contrary, it seems that for practical purposes most Roma are well entrenched where they are. Loose, sporadic talk of a revival of the nomadic tradition has done little for any prospect of significant mobility for Roma in the new Europe. Instead, there are signs of a political awakening: the example of the US civil rights movement has encouraged litigation, lobbying and protest. A growing population, marginalised and denied opportunity for centuries, is looking for ways to respond. Slovak writer Kristina Magdolenova has called the Romani dilemma 'a time bomb in the middle of Europe'. Historically, Roma have been Europe's least belligerent ethnic group; whether they choose to remain that way depends hugely on the rest of us. ❏

Irena Maryniak

Once upon a Time...

① BEHOLD, GREAT KING! AFTER COUNTLESS CENTURIES OF HERCULEAN ENDEAVOUR, THE **GREAT WALL** IS AT LAST **COMPLETE!**

③ FOR **PROTECTION**, EH? FROM WHOM, PRECISELY?

WHY, YOUR IMMENSE **VILENESS**, FROM THOSE **OUTSIDE!** FROM THOSE **OTHERS** HELLBENT ON THE DEBASEMENT AND **DESTRUCTION** OF YOUR **MAGICAL REALM** BECAUSE OF ITS MATCHLESS & SECURE **WEALTH & HAPPINESS!**

⑤ HANG ON! I THOUGHT...

VERILY, SIRE, THE CONSTRUCTION OF THE WALL WAS **PRESSING HARD**, THE WORK **BACKBREAKING** & OFTTIMES **LETHAL**, THE REPAIRS & MAINTENANCE **NEVER-ENDING**; NATURALLY THEREFORE **NONE** OF YOUR LOYAL SUBJECTS, LIVING THEIR LIVES OF **LUXURY** & **EASE** IN THIS **HAPPY HAPPY LAND** WOULD **DREAM** OF LOWERING THEMSELVES TO ENGAGE IN SUCH **AWFUL TOIL!** SO OF COURSE WE CONSCRIPTED **MILLIONS** OF THE **BARBARIANS** FROM BEYOND AS OUR BEASTS OF **BURDEN!**

©Martin Rowson '04

WALKING THE WALL

STEPHANIE LE BARS &
MARION VAN RENTERGHEN

FOR THE ISRAELIS IT'S A 'SECURITY FENCE';
FOR THE PALESTINIANS THE 'WALL' THAT
TRACES AN ILLEGAL COURSE APPROPRIATES
THEIR LAND AND EXACERBATES THE
TENSIONS BETWEEN THE TWO COMMUNITIES

Old Ahmed, parked on the front line, knows how to make himself comfortable. He's erected a Bedouin-style tent open to the four winds on the hill overlooking his house, his olive groves and his animals; here he sits day-long in his red-checked *keffir*. There is a carpet piled high with cushions where you can sit to take refreshments – the narguile and a dish of hot sand for heating up the coffee are ready for chance passers-by. A TV set sits in a corner as Ahmed tells his beads and reflects.

Ahmed is an Arab-Israeli from the outskirts of Oum Al-Fahm, an Israeli town completely occupied by Arabs who, like him, acquired Israeli citizenship in 1948. There are some 1.3 million Arab-Israelis out of 6.7 million Israelis. From his tent, the hills stretch towards Lebanon; one can see Nazareth and, further down towards the south-east, the Palestinian town of Jenin in the West Bank. The houses of the village of Taybe, also in the West Bank, are opposite nearby. Members of Ahmed's family live there but, like his old friends who have lived there all their lives, they can no longer meet him.

An electric fence, several metres high, now runs along the edge of his fields, separating him from Taybe. It starts several kilometres away on the edge of Salem and descends southwards bordering roads reserved for the use of Israeli army patrols. These are protected by great coils of barbed wire on each side, and a pathway of smoothed sand that will betray the footsteps of any would-be intruder. One day, as Ahmed was contemplating the barbed wire, soldiers accosted him.

'What are you doing so close to the fence?'

'What is your fence doing so close to my house?' he asked in return.

You have to travel from north to south along the West Bank to comprehend the real nature of this 'security fence' – the Palestinians call it 'the

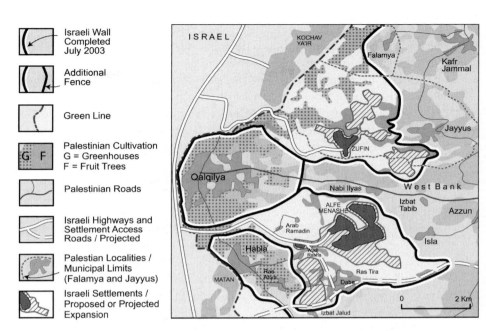

Israeli Wall Completed July 2003

Additional Fence

Green Line

Palestinian Cultivation G = Greenhouses F = Fruit Trees

Palestinian Roads

Israeli Highways and Settlement Access Roads / Projected

Palestian Localities / Municipal Limits (Falamya and Jayyus)

Israeli Settlements / Proposed or Projected Expansion

The intrusion of the wall into the West Bank round Qalqilya, illustrating the isolation of the town from its agricultural land as well as the integration of existing or planned Israeli settlements into the enlarged configuration of Israel. Courtesy Pengon, www.pengon.org

Wall' – unilaterally decided on by Israel and started in July 2002 to protect it from the infiltration of Palestinian suicide bombers. And you have to criss-cross from one side to the other as you go if you are to understand the extent to which this project, which will eventually encircle the whole of the West Bank, crystallises the tensions between the two communities. It's a high-stakes game, a metaphor for the conflict itself.

Fear, terrorist madness and the failure to find any political solution are behind Israel's decision to build the fence. By the end of 2003, only the northern stretch – 140 kilometres from Salem to Elkana – and a few sections near Jerusalem had been completed. But once it is completed, the whole thing will stretch to at least 600 kilometres, isolating the West Bank in the same way that the Gaza Strip has already been so firmly bottled in that no suicide bomber has been able to get out for the past three years.

The idea, proposed initially by the Israeli left and rejected by the right on the grounds that it would define the frontiers of an independent Palestinian state, was finally agreed on by those close to Prime Minister Ariel Sharon. With the exception of some intellectuals and human rights groups, virtually the entire population of Israel, traumatised by 10 years of suicide bombings, have come to accept the idea. According to Agence France Presse, there have been 819 deaths on the Israeli side and 2,608 among Palestinians since the beginning of the second intifada in September 2000.

The Palestinians might have settled for a watertight barrier that guaranteed the borders of their state and freedom within. But this line that zigzags back and forth makes their daily life even more impossible. Above all, far from following the 'green line' – the ceasefire line that marked the borders of the two communities between 1949 and 1967 – the new fence encroaches several kilometres into Palestinian territory with the aim of enclosing, and thus perpetuating, the Israeli settlements. As a result, land confiscations are increasing and the battle over names goes on. It's purely a security fence, insist Israelis, not a border. No, insist the Palestinians in turn, it's an 'apartheid wall'; nothing more than an alibi for further theft of their land, forcing them into exile by strangling them economically.

There are two ways of following the barbed wire. A motorway on the Israeli side runs alongside or keeps it in sight from a distance. On the Palestinian side, it means crossing stretches of rough earth and olive groves, using tortuous roads, often not tarmacked, crossing uncertainly from one village to another, changing cars each side of roadblocks or military checkpoints and long waits at each control point. You can wait for hours with no certainty that the military will, in the end, let you cross. In other words, you cannot skirt the barbed wire on that side, but end with running up against it.

From Salem, some kilometres south of Oum Al-Fahm, the wall does follow the 'green line'. But then it makes a long detour deep into the occupied territories to protect three Jewish settlements, in the process imprisoning 10 Palestinian villages. The villages are in a kind of no man's land: in Israeli territory but without citizenship or rights. Something like 200,000 people – maybe 400,000 by the time the project is completed – are trapped between the wall and the 'green line', which they are forbidden to cross. Sitting at the juxtaposition of these two entangled worlds, adding to the geographical complexity, is kibbutz Metzer, home to around 500 people.

The kibbutz could have been trouble-free, an instance of peaceful cohabitation between the surrounding Palestinians and the Israelis who settled here in 1953 with scrupulous respect for the 'green line', without nibbling away a single iota of land. The founders of the kibbutz, Argentine Marxists with a social conscience sharpened by their experience of Juan Perón's dictatorship, established friendly relations with their Arab neighbours, particularly those in the village of Kaffin.

'It has become the tradition here,' says Don Avital, secretary-general of the kibbutz. 'We worked together, went to each other's weddings and funerals, shared everything: the wells, electricity, roads. We even had a joint football team!' But then came the second intifada and Kaffin became a crossing point for suicide bombers from Jenin. 'Obviously, we had to stop that,' says Avital.

Hence the wall. In the autumn of 2002, the military informed the villagers of Kaffin that 'for security reasons' the fence would cut through their village, dividing it in two. On the one side, the village and its people; on the other, the fields, the wells, the olive groves – everything essential to the lives of the farmers. Not even the presence of a Jewish settlement justified such a division. Taisir Harashi, mayor of Kaffin, appealed to his kibbutzim neighbours for help. There were many meetings. 'In theory,' says Don Avital, 'the Palestinians had one week to appeal against the decision. But it is virtually impossible for them physically to get to the tribunal and make their case.'

Everyone in the kibbutz fought for the fence to follow the 'green line' and not penalise Kaffin. Don Avital and Taisir Harashi held a joint press conference in the open. 'It was the first time a Palestinian mayor nominated by the PLO had ever entertained the idea of a frontier along the "green line",' recalls Avital. Local officials even got Israeli representatives to admit the 'stupidity of the situation'. A meeting was fixed for 11 November 2002. But one day before, a Palestinian from Tulkarem got into the kibbutz and killed five people, including a secretary and a woman and her two children. The fence went ahead; the villagers were cut off from three–quarters of their fields.

Before the terrorist attack, opinion in the kibbutz was split between those who opposed any sort of fence and those who wanted it to follow the 1949 border. After the attack, no one would hear anything against it. 'A wall might, perhaps, calm things down,' stresses Don Avital, 'but we all still think that any fence that does not respect the "green line" is a tragedy. As it is, the fence is inhuman; it puts Israel's security at risk. Our destinies are linked. Each tree that is confiscated is a bomb waiting to go off.'

That's certainly the case in Kaffin, says Harashi. In 1948, he explains,

70 per cent of the village's land was confiscated. Fifty-five years later, the fence robs people of another 70 per cent of what they had left. True, the military announced they would provide a point of access for the farmers; so far, they have heard nothing more of this. And to this day, they say, they have never been allowed to use the only available crossing point, eight kilometres away, which would give them access to their land.

Meanwhile, the villagers wait anxiously for the arrival of October when they would, normally, harvest their olives. Will they be allowed to get to the groves? How will they transport the harvest? Harashi nervously lights yet another cigarette. 'We can no longer go to Israel [where around 80 per cent of the villagers used to work]; technically, we can't even visit our own places in the West Bank. We can't get to the hospitals, students can't get to the university. I want to go to Baka; I can't. If I want to get to Nablus, there are so many checkpoints it would take a whole day. We are not living in our own country, we are in prison.'

West Bank, Jerusalem 2004: last exit to Palestine. Credit: Larry Towell / Magnum Photos

He gestures to the fields on the other side of the fence; his own, theirs too. 'With the olive groves, one could live a thousand years without working. Without them, our survival is threatened. They want us to quit and leave; that's what this wall is all about . . . taking our fertile land, controlling the wells, cutting us off from the world outside. I try to persuade people to hang on; but how are they going to feed themselves?'

The road to Kaffin shows, better than anything else, the madness of the positioning of the fence. You have to go via Nazlat Isa and Baka Al-Sharkiye, two Palestinian villages that have suddenly found themselves isolated, cut off both from Israel and the West Bank – behind not just one, but two fences. One, already in position, cuts them off from Kaffin; bull-dozers are preparing the ground for the other, which will follow the 'green line'. They have already demolished some 200 shops and numerous Pales-tinian homes at Nazlat Isa. 'They were built without permission,' says an Israeli soldier dismissively.

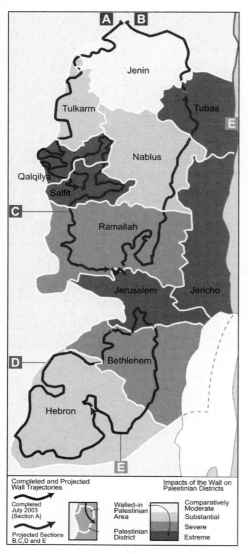

The effect of the wall is rated from 'comparatively moderate' to 'extreme' and is based on a set of criteria that includes territorial cohesion, isolation of Palestinian lands and communities, and communications by road. Courtesy Pengon

Uzi Dayan, a former general and adviser on national security, who was the coordinator for the first phase of the fence, does not agree with the route it is following around Baka Al-Sharkiye. 'I would have preferred it to follow the "green line". This would have minimised friction and cut off as few Palestinians as possible from the West Bank.' But security imperatives decided otherwise. Every time the wall encroaches on the West Bank, the justification is the same: 'for security reasons'. 'We have done our utmost to minimise the inconvenience,' says a soldier, 'minimised the insecurity, the annexations of Palestinian land and the difficulties caused to the civilian population.'

Nazlat Isa is little more than a vast heap of scrap iron. Little remains of the market where many Israelis used to do their shopping, just a few casual stalls. In the midway village of Baka Al-Sharkiye, every productive means of livelihood has been destroyed. Muayad Hussein, mayor of this settlement of some 3,500 people, explains: 100 hectares of land were confiscated and 3,000 olive trees were uprooted, he claims. Traders used to come to sell their produce in the markets of Nazlat and Baka. They no longer come since they can't get there. The mayor himself, a tomato grower, had Israeli customers. 'But now,' he sighs, 'there's not a soul.'

If you want to go back and forth to Baka Al-Sharkiye in the West Bank, you need a permit; even then, you could wait for hours at the Kaffin crossing point. 'Why should I need a permit to visit my own country?' asks the mayor. He goes on: 'They think the people from Baka should be forced to clear out. However, unlike the folk of Kaffin, we have a strong farming tradition. We can survive with our chickens, our sheep, our tomatoes and cucumbers. They will never win.' 'It's a security fence,' not a political strategy, Israeli officers never tire of repeating. 'No way is it a border.'

Heading south, you join the new spic-and-span M6 motorway that runs more or less parallel with the 'green line' and is, naturally, forbidden to Palestinians. This is the way to Bat Hefer, an Israeli residential village, just to the west of the 'green line' opposite the large Palestinian town of Tulkarem. Its 5,000 inhabitants have built their own wall without waiting for the security fence. In 1996, having borne the brunt of Israeli gunfire, they decided to protect themselves behind a two-kilometre-long concrete fence.

David, 31 years old, shows us the bullet holes in the door of his house. 'That happened some months ago,' he says 'proof if any were needed that the wall changes nothing. I was wounded in Gaza in the first intifada. I came here for some peace and quiet. My Palestinian friends at Tulkarem were accused of collaborating with the Israelis and are dead. I don't go there any more.' He heaves a sigh and limps off to his door. Then he turns back: 'Only the army can make any difference,' he says, 'not a wall. Believe me, I know what I'm talking about.'

Where the M6 runs beside Tulkarem and a little further south by Qalqilya, the 'fence' becomes a real wall – sometimes as high as eight metres and flanked by two patrol roads and bristling with watchtowers every 300 metres to protect the motorway.

Right on the border between Israel and the West Bank, Qalqilya and its 40,000 inhabitants have, quite literally, been turned into a prison, shut in by a loop formed by the fence and the wall designed to incorporate two Jewish settlements into Israel. According to the Pengon (Palestinian Environmental NGOs Network), which gathers information on the area, 4,000 of Qalqilya's people have already given up any hope of surviving there and have fled deeper into the territory. The Israeli military justifies its actions here by reminding us that both Tulkarem and Qalqilya are major breeding grounds for suicide bombers. For their part, the Palestinians accuse the Israelis of wanting to 'win a little more land'. The land around Qalqilya, they smirk, shelters the richest stretch of aquifers in the western West Bank. Pengon claims the fence will deprive Qalqilya of 40 per cent of its land and 17 aquifers. 'The Israeli government strategy is clear,' says one of its spokespeople. 'How can you have a viable state that has lost control of its land and its water supplies?'

If you take the road reserved for the use of Israeli settlers, via a checkpoint and up some pretty steep slopes, you can get to the West Bank village of Jayyous in the outskirts of Qalqilya. Here the fence runs six kilometres west of the 'green line'. Villagers can no longer rely on being able to get into town every day. And, like the people of Kaffin, they can no longer get to their own fields: the wall has cut them off from two-thirds of their farmland and from their wells. 'For security reasons,' repeats the soldier in charge of a journalists' tour without going into further details, 'we have to have sufficient depth.' He's referring to the narrowness of Israeli territory around here: 15 kilometres only between Tulkarem and Natanya; 20 or so between Jayyous and Tel Aviv. 'For a terrorist that is nothing.'

He also stresses that there is a gateway open several times daily for the farmers. But what if that gate is closed? No problem, he replies: a number of telephones have been installed for the use of the farmers of Jayyous, Kaffin and elsewhere. If they call, the soldiers are happy to let them through. The villagers greet this information with cynical laughter and wry smiles.

'The regulations for the opening of the gates change daily,' explains Abdellatif Khaled, whose family owns fields on the wrong side of the fence. 'You could go mad. Sometimes entry is forbidden to anyone under 35, at others only those with a donkey can go through. When no particular orders have come down from the military it is open for 15 minutes three times a day. So: get your ass and your sheep used to these timetables! As for the traders who come to buy their stock in Ramallah: do you think they are going to take the risk of waiting six hours for the gate to open? They simply won't come any more. In fact, they've already stopped coming. And without dealers, the farmers have been forced to leave.' While waiting for the wall, 50 or so farmers have erected tents in their fields and live there alongside their vegetables, olive trees and fruit, a few kilometres from home. The rest kick their heels back in Jayyous. They pray – and smoke.

Mayor Fayaz Saleem has stacked up dozens of olive trees and stumps in front of his house. They are his own, some of them up to 600 years old. 'My antiques; my wealth,' as he puts it. Israeli officials admit they have 'uprooted' tens of thousands of trees from Palestinian land in the process of erecting the fence, but claim to have 'replanted' 65,000. 'Where's that then?' asks a member of Pengon. 'If you'd replanted the olive groves of the West Bank we'd have seen them.' Fayaz Saleem looks sadly at his dead trees.

The first phase of the fence from north to south stops short of Elkana, south of Qalqilya, west of Ariel. With its population of 16,000, Ariel is one of Israel's most important settlements. Its position within the heart of the West Bank is a focus for Palestinian hatred and opposition to the wall. The government has made it clear that the fence will take Ariel and its two neighbouring settlements into Israel. This means it will encroach 20 kilometres into the heart of the occupied territories. The Americans, who reckon that the fence generally creates a bit of a 'problem', are opposed to this particular section. The settlers are piling on the pressure, but the project is temporarily frozen and the bulldozers sit idle.

Ron Nachman, mayor of Ariel, is a settler and proud of it. He it was who laid the foundation stone of the colony in 1977. 'Fence? What fence?' he asks ironically. The settlers are unanimous in rejecting any form of protective fortification. Not only does the wall run the risk of becoming a frontier inside 'Greater Israel', it will trap some of them in hostile territory.

However, since there is a fence, Nachman has no intention of being left outside. 'If this is intended to stop terrorist activities, I see no reason why it should not also protect Ariel. We have the same rights as people in Tel Aviv. The government will be held responsible if it decides to abandon 16,000 Israeli citizens to Palestinian murderers. The peaceniks say let it follow the 1967 border. All I know is that there is no "green line" mentioned in the Bible!' Nachman exudes confidence. He reaches into a cupboard and takes out a photograph of himself with Ariel Sharon.

Still not completed but no less explosive is the proposal to take the fence around Jerusalem. It would separate the 250,000 Palestinians of east Jerusalem, who have residency rights, from the West Bank, draw Israeli settlements into the municipality and exclude from the city boundaries many of its natural suburbs. Many tens of kilometres of electric fence, barbed wire and roads reserved for military patrols already separate Jerusalem from West Bank towns such as Ramallah in the north, Bethlehem in the south and Abu Dis to the east. Officially, argues Israel, this is all about protecting 'Greater Jerusalem' – the city within the limits decreed by Israel in 1967 – from terrorists. But for Palestinians, it is no more than a ruse to make any future negotiations on the Holy City impossible.

In Abu Dis, in the middle of a shopping street that only a few months ago linked the suburb to east Jerusalem in a matter of five minutes, thousands of Palestinians, in cars and on foot, now come up against the 'Jerusalem envelope'. In a few minutes, schoolchildren will file through the two two-metre-high concrete blocks there. Down the other end of the street, near the mosque, young men are striding across another barrier, in this case made of stones and barbed wire. An old man tries to do the same. No good. A couple of soldiers emerge from their makeshift barracks and indicate, guns levelled at him, that he should turn and go back.

Leaning up against the concrete, Nihad Abu Ghosh looks over to Jerusalem. 'Every day is an adventure,' he says. 'Last year my children went to school in Jerusalem. Since the wall put an end to any normal sort of life, I've sent them to Amman in Jordan, to my wife's family. Instead of working, I spend most of my time working out how to get round the obstacles that prevent me from getting to Jerusalem.'

Lots of people have taken to 'system D': every morning and every evening they make their way via the privately owned yards and gardens that have remained free of the arbitrary circuit of the wall. To the right, a stone's throw away, Nihad points without a word to the golden walls of the Old Town and the gleaming cupola of the Dome of the Rock. Like most inhabitants of the West Bank, the villagers of Abu Dis have not been able to pray on the mosque esplanade for several months.

The famous Al-Qods University in the Abu Dis district also risks suffering from the proposed division of the territory. According to a recent decision by the Israeli authorities, the wall is due to go across the university's football pitch, annexing in the process almost one-third of the campus. The university's media-friendly president, Sari Nusseibeh, is in favour of dialogue with the Israelis but this particular decision has him up in arms. 'Politically, I think the wall is a disaster for both communities. But from now on, I must do everything in my power to save as much as possible of the university.' The registration office has been moved to the football pitch and permanent demonstrations are organised on the spot in an effort to stop further work on the wall.

South of Jerusalem, Bethlehem has been all but cut off. Already surrounded by checkpoints and earthworks, the town is encircled by 15 kilometres of electric fence, barbed wire and military roads that effectively cut it off from Jerusalem and the north of the West Bank, in particular Ramallah.

In August last year, 250 inhabitants of Nuaman, a hamlet perched on a charming hill between Bethlehem and the fairly new settlement of Har

Homa, were warned that the route of the fence would wipe them off the map. That, 'for security reasons', Israel was proposing to annex their land, their houses and their cemetery and bring it within Jerusalem's city boundary. Their land, yes – but not them: the inhabitants of Nuaman, Bedouins settled there for 150 years, have never had residency rights in Jerusalem.

Henceforth they will be in limbo, like the inhabitants of 15 or so other Palestinian towns and villages that the wall would strand inside Israel. But with this difference: their identity will belong to one side of the wall, what remains of their houses to the other. An Israeli officer has proposed compensation, but they have refused. 'They want our lands to extend the colony of Har Homa,' they confide. 'We'll never part with them. We'll hold fast to our own place. The Israelis dream of having the land without the people who live on it.'

One sees the lorries passing; one sees the long trenches across the hills ready and waiting for the next coils of barbed wire. The work goes on; the first phase of the security fence is near completion. But any decision on the next phase has been postponed. The cost of the present phase has already swallowed up somewhere in the region of US$613 million, and there is a further US$1 billion to be found from somewhere. The US, opposed to a fence that cuts across Palestinian lands and threatens to create new facts on the ground, has threatened to freeze funding by deducting from its annual subsidy the amount Israel invests in settlements. Despite all this, Israel has vowed to speed up the work and have this Pharaonic project finished in six months rather than the projected two years. 'We have to be fast,' says Uzi Dayan. 'The fence is in our common interests since security is one of the conditions of any political settlement.'

For Diana Buttu, legal adviser to Palestinian officials, the reverse is true. 'If security were all the Israelis were concerned about, they would have built their wall on the "green line". Their purpose is something else. But they are working against themselves: if the Palestinians are not to have a viable independent state, they will become citizens of Israel. One person, one vote. That will be the end of the Jewish state and it will all be because of the wall.' ❏

Stephanie Le Bars and *Marion Van Renterghen*, *journalists in Israel, wrote this piece for* Le Monde

Translated by JVH

A ONE-SIDED WALL

WENDY PULLAN

THE ISRAELI WALL, FAR FROM BEING MEDIEVAL,
IS AN ESPECIALLY MODERN RESPONSE, RIFE WITH
THE REMAINS OF COLD WAR OBFUSCATION THAT
VIEWED THE WORLD DIVIDED BY THE IRON
CURTAIN AS AN ESSENTIALLY ONE-SIDED DIVISION

Travelling along the old road from Jerusalem to Jericho one comes to an abrupt stop in the middle of Abu Dis, a village turned semi-suburb at the edge of Palestinian Jerusalem. A massive concrete wall rises eight metres high in the middle of the road, severing it; with no warning, the route is terminated. What was the centre of Abu Dis is now the frontier; shops that had been convenient to passers-by now struggle to stay in business; a petrol station is deserted. And ahead, the wall looms. The Hebrew and English graffiti reveals it as a podium for Israeli viewpoints, pro and con, object of an internal 'conflict tourism'. A colleague tells me that on bringing a (rare) mixed group of Israeli and Palestinian university students to the site, the shamed Israelis cautiously examined it while the Palestinians quickly posed together for photos, defiant, with fingers in 'V' formation. Already this structure has become a perverse sort of monument. And it has been given a history, for chillingly, in large letters, we read: 'From Warsaw ghetto to Abu Dis ghetto'.

This row of prefabricated concrete segments is part of the Israel–Palestine 'security barrier', 'separation fence' or 'apartheid wall'; the nomenclature depends on your perspective. It is part of the lengthy structure that Israel claims will prevent suicide bombers from attacking its people. Whether this will have an effect is debatable but, more immediately, the wall has been used to consolidate Israeli settlements and to chop and fragment Palestinian land, imprisoning communities, separating farmers from fields and groves, cutting off people from their places of work, family from family and friend from friend. The wall is not an international boundary but a division of two peoples which has been imposed by one, the Israelis, on the land of the other, the Palestinians. It joins a select group of similar structures – Berlin, Nicosia, Belfast quickly spring to mind – which in modern

Wall painting at Gilo-Beit Jala: through a glass darkly. Credit: Wendy Pullan

times have acted as radical physical separations in attempts to 'solve' problems unresponsive to other means.

Not all walls still stand, and their circumstances have varied, from general condemnation of the East German policy for containment of its own citizens to some voiced approval from both Protestants and Catholics for the 'peace walls' in Belfast. The main section of the Israeli barrier will stretch somewhere between 300 and 600 kilometres, and eventually wrap around the West Bank, whereas the Irish 'peace walls' block individual streets, the most extensive along Springfield Road being about two miles in length. It would, however, be fair to say that all of these structures represent particular fault lines in human history and have been constructed expressly to separate and divide. In the more extreme cases, they have ruptured and sometimes imprisoned whole areas of habitation. Such walls are but one of the many horrors of war and occupation yet, in their particular tangibility, they can easily act as a focus for much that has gone wrong.

And yet, not all walls impose such draconian conditions, nor are all inherently bad. To some extent, our present understanding is conditioned by the modern study of the nature of borders. At the end of the nineteenth century, the new discipline of political geography began to distinguish between the relatively broad border region or fringe, and the borderline itself which was essentially an abstract line on a map. Such an observation spawned much ensuing interest and research into the culture of border areas; even more significantly, it is also a reflection on the idea that certain lines of division should never be fully realised. In some ways, this recalls practices of many centuries earlier; the Romans, for example, ritually ploughed a furrow, usually circular and known as the *poemerium*, to mark the extent of a new town. Under normal circumstances, the *poemerium* was only loosely echoed in the city walls, which deviated as necessary and were added to and changed over time to represent the practical structures of daily life; the result was an important but distant memory of the *poemerium*.

The point here is that walls both act symbolically and help to structure civic life, and while the two may intermingle, they are not necessarily the same. As much as ancient and medieval walls were necessary for defence, and certainly cities resembled fortresses, the wall had a constitutional role as well. One's right to reside inside offered the freedom, and the responsibility, to participate as a citizen. At the same time, and more often than not, cities extended far beyond their walls, to include a hinterland of agriculture, sea coast, dependent villages, trading networks and sacred sites. Moreover, no city stood alone, and commerce, politics, friendship, cultural exchange and, yes, war depended upon what lay beyond the walls. Gates were major land-marks, points of transition and links between inside and out. City gate cultures arose, and with them protocols of behaviour and interaction, some tacit and some explicit. For better or worse, as much as the wall demarcated and separated, it was also a means of connection and mediation.

Along with its symbolic content, the culture of the 'thick' wall as one that structures differences and transitions, thereby embodying and fostering a certain richness of meaning, has mostly disappeared. The problem arises today when walls are built to embody the abstract line, in effect making concrete what should remain elastic. And yet, can we rid ourselves of walls? Probably not, for even in a globalised and electronically linked world, the removal of all borders and bounds is hardly possible and, in fact, undesirable. Today some Berliners regret the total obliteration of the wall and wish to reinstate some form of demarcation as an acknowledgement that their unified city derives from both East and West. Clearly, the need for remem-brance is a driving force but, in addition, no one wants to live in a feature-less and homogeneous world.

Identity normally requires some form of recognition or attachment to place which in turn depends on structure and differentiation. Beirut, which has had its own terrible divisions, and a 'green line' of death and destruction which has been referred to as a 'stoneless wall', has been facing these issues during its reconstruction. In recognition of the various communal groups that lay claim to the city, Lebanese sociologist Samir Khalaf suggests that there is a need for both intimacy and distance, malleability rather than confinement and exclusion. Permeability is crucial, where boundaries and motion exist in reciprocity. The static wall and the ability to traverse and transcend it are a key combination frequently ignored, and all too often the imposition of separation structures is specifically intended to restrict unreasonably or eliminate passage. The wall is assigned a one-dimensional role and the control of movement becomes an insidious and primary weapon widely used in civilian conflicts. This produces a new type of topography, created by barriers and checkpoints that remake the existing landscape and dominate every aspect of daily life, physical, psychological and symbolic.

It is frequently remarked that the Israeli wall is an astonishingly medieval solution for a modern problem; a heedless rejection of Montesquieu's pronouncement that 'with the invention of gunpowder, the impregnable place ceased to exist'. But, beyond some atavistic hope for protection, the medieval comparison falls short, for this wall supports no mediated transitions that orient society, nor does it offer any means to articulate difference. It is a very thin wall indeed; a laceration that reinforces no more than the boundary. It has spawned only destruction, with the Israeli army demolishing all vegetation, buildings and other forms of human presence along its path in the name of security. Clearly, whatever border region there could have been is being shattered, any hope of permeability that might allow and promote recognition and experience of the other side will soon be blocked. Rather than dredging up some residue of the pre-Enlightenment past, I would posit that this situation is an especially modern response. It is rife with the remains of Cold War obfuscation that viewed the world as divided by the Iron Curtain but relied upon the reality of that division as being essentially one-sided, so that either sector could imagine but never know the other.

This is not to say that both sides of the wall are always equal. The case of the Palestinians is particularly loathsome, for they suffer from Israel's policy of containment and ghettoisation. For them, the visible side of the wall is viewed from a damaged and restricted interior. But for both sides, whether by volition or imposition, the wall is there to suppress all forms of engagement – violent, peaceful or otherwise – so that for many there is a turning away and a removal of the conflict from the immediate consciousness to some darker depths from which it is bound to emerge ever more hideous. Such walls permit the populations behind them to grow horns. They foster a curious disengagement with reality, described in one Belfast study where they 'allow people to see what they want to see on the other side, the image of their enemy'. In effect, the conflict becomes a representation of itself, spiralling into unrecognisable and uncontrollable permutations from its one and only side.

Human curiosity may sometimes provide the impetus to look beyond the wall, but too often, as with the observation platform set up in Ledra Street in Greek Nicosia to peer into the Turkish sector (p25), the result is literally a framed and constructed image; authentic experience of the other side becomes increasingly distant. It is not a surprise that next to that viewing platform, in a store front, a nationalist museum was established. Strangely more provocative is the Turkish side, which remains a quiet backwater unknowing or uncaring of being observed. A small café is wedged in against the wall, and on this backdrop is painted a blank window. It is a tease, an image of an opening that points to the other side but goes nowhere and imparts nothing.

In Israel, the painting of walls is becoming common, a grim new art form perhaps. Along the new roads and motorways built as safe routes for Israelis to reach West Bank settlements, walls are erected at points of possible friction, usually when the road passes a Palestinian village or town. A solid concrete construction on either side of the Jerusalem–Modi'in Road is covered by a mural of a viaduct; through the arches the scene is painted with green meadows and blue sky. Flanked on both sides by this strangely imagined countryside, one speeds along the narrow and restricted road, wondering just who is being imprisoned here. A more distressing example is found on the wall just south of Jerusalem that separates Israeli Gilo from Palestinian Beit Jala. There, residents of Gilo gaze into a panorama that depicts a small village in the landscape, recognisably Arab in its topography and architecture but also reminiscent of something more ancient, almost biblical. The sun shines and the painted landscape is peaceful. But in this village there is no trace of people, it has been cleansed. The one-sided wall has become an image of delusion, beckoning to those who venture near to enter into its deceitful grip. And we can only strain to think what can be the way back from here. ❏

Wendy Pullan *is senior lecturer in architecture at the University of Cambridge and director of the Conflict in Cities research project in Jerusalem*

A DRIVE ON A FORBIDDEN ROAD

RAJA SHEHADEH

Whether or not it was prudent to risk going through back roads at night where several motorists have been shot trying to get back home was questionable. But neither of us was in the mood to be prudent. We just wanted to get home.

My wife and I had driven to Beit Hanina, a Palestinian suburb north of Jerusalem, to pay condolences to a family friend. It is not uncommon after such a sad occasion to want to live it up. So we decided to continue to Jerusalem and have dinner there.

We dined and had a good visit with friends from whom we had been separated by the closure. How quickly one can forget about occupation and all the restrictions it places on our life and movement. But when I looked at my watch and realised it was already 9.30pm, I knew my respite was over. Only half an hour to get to the Kalandia checkpoint. We now rushed as though demons were pursuing us. When we got there we found two other cars ahead of us. One was allowed through – we didn't know why – while the other was forced to turn back. When our turn came we were apprehensive.

We simply said we lived in Ramallah and wanted to get back home.

'I can't let you, it is past 10 o'clock. This checkpoint closes at 10.'

I looked at my car clock. 'But it isn't 10 yet,' I said.

'It is 10.49,' the soldier said.

Now I remembered that Israel had already changed to summer time. The Arafat-run Palestinian Authority had decided to delay turning forward the clock for no apparent reason except perhaps to distinguish Palestine from Israel.

'But you've just let this car through.'

'Yes, because he had a pregnant woman.'

'It's not a big deal to let us pass. We're tired and we just want to get home,' I said.

But the soldier was not budging and we were not in the mood for pleading or giving long stories about sick family members we had to rush home to see. In retrospect this might have been a mistake!

'You could go through Surda,' the soldier said, suggesting that we use back roads.

West Bank, near Jerusalem 2003: Kalandia military checkpoint on the way to Ramallah.
Credit: Larry Towell / Magnum Photos

'But it wouldn't be safe at this hour,' I blurted out.

'For you it would. You're not Israeli,' the soldier said, as though cars in the dark blinked their ethnic origins.

Then I thought of my lawyer's card and presented this to the soldier. He had a round pleasant face and was wearing dark glasses even though it was dark. He examined it then looked at me and said: 'But it wouldn't be fair to let you through just because you're a lawyer and not to allow the others. Now would it?'

I wasn't sure whether I heard him right. 'Did you say "fair"?' I asked.

The soldier's only reply was to motion with his little finger for us to turn the car round and leave.

I stayed put. I couldn't believe my ears. The soldier was annoyed that we were refusing the order his little finger had made. With the full force of his hand he pounded on the bonnet of the car, startling us. We should have screamed, but we didn't. We could have argued more with this soldier and challenged his world view. And yet confronted by a claim of fairness from an Israeli soldier, a member of an army that has been in occupation of our land for over 35 years, who has destroyed our life and brought us to this point of having to beg to be allowed to get back home in the evening after having had dinner in Jerusalem, we were rendered speechless.

Silently, without saying any more, I turned the car round and left.

We first drove down the long stretch of a new settler road towards the juncture known as Eun el Haramieh (the eyes of the bandits), where travellers in Ottoman times used to be waylaid and robbed. It was a straight, long, modern road that bisected our countryside and rearranged it. The road signs indicated Israeli settlements: Shilo, Ofra, Dolev. There was hardly a mention of Arab towns; you couldn't see any. An Israeli driving through would see no sign of Arab presence in this land. It was as though these Israelis had painted a reality for themselves and were living it, shielding all other realities from sight. It was a repeat of what Israel had done to its Arab citizens, confining them to small ghettos and giving most of their land to their Jewish neighbours.

The whole road was lit up. Entirely lit up, as though it was inside an urban centre, to make it safe. I was thinking of the large amount of funds it must have taken to build these roads and light them up like this. There were no other cars on the road. The well-built, lit-up road was entirely desolate. The enterprise was not working: those for whom it was intended were too scared to use it and it remained empty. Most of the time I was not sure where I was, where Ramallah was, where all the landmarks I used to navigate my way back home were. All I could see was a long expanse of a straight, empty road cutting through the darkness.

Then we saw a turning to the west we assumed could be the road that would take us to Ramallah. We took it. Soon enough, we came upon a mound of earth. The road was closed by the army. We could see the village of Silwad which is only a few kilometres north of Ramallah, but could not get to it. This road was not intended for the use of the Palestinian residents of Silwad, nor were we expected to be on it. We backed up and continued on the straight desolate road so well lit by the orange light. Finally, we found what we assumed would be the Atarah intersection and took it. If this was it, we should be just south of Birzeit, whence we could drive up to Ramallah. 'Halamish,' Penny said in triumph, reading the road sign, 'this is our crossroad.' Our new road markers were now Israeli settlements!

The road we were now on was no longer straight and it was not lit. The bushes on the side were ominously high and dark and I was wondering more than ever whether we were being prudent driving at night on this road. What if a group of armed men should emerge from these bushes and shoot us? I can well understand why they would, but what use would this be? There was nothing to distinguish our car at night from the colonisers'. If we got shot, it would simply be our fault for having been so frivolous as to go for dinner in Jerusalem. Then I began to think: the fact that this road was unlit must mean that it was not used by settlers, otherwise it would have the usual precautions they take on the roads used by them. The fact that we were on a non-settler road was a comfort, and I no longer felt as worried. Penny remained silent and later told me that she had remembered that it was here, on this patch of road, that a friend of Amer, a driver we know, was killed. Fortunately, I did not know this worrisome fact.

As we drove uncertainly in the dark, I began to have another worry on my mind. What if we came across an Israeli army jeep? We would be all alone with the murderous soldiers in this desolate dark road. My agitated mind had revived the memory of the death of a relative soon after the occupation. He had been driving alone near Latrun close to the border with Israel. He was stopped by an army jeep and killed; then the soldiers took his black-and-white chequered *kuffieh*, dipped it in petrol from his car, and set his corpse on fire. A few days later, his burned remains were found by a shepherd.

Fortunately, we were spared more meetings with the army. We drove slowly in the dark feeling uncertain whether this was ever going to get us home. Then I saw a yellow taxi van approaching. I blinked my lights and called on him to stop and asked for directions.

'Continue straight until after the bridge and then take a dirt road to your right. This will get you to Birzeit,' the driver said and sped away. I followed his directions and eventually found myself driving in Birzeit where the unseen and unwanted live. Despite the lateness of the hour, the town's market was still open and young college couples were strolling in the tree-lined streets. Through back roads I had come upon people in invisible communities who are shielded from the view of the colonisers who assume they do not exist. From Birzeit I drove without incident to Ramallah.

It is true this was a scary drive. It was also dangerous. We were lucky nothing happened. But I am glad to have had the experience. To see the country with its new night-time arrangements; to hear this soldier speaking about fairness indicating how shut off from reality he was; to see writ on the land the untenable position of the insolent, determined settlers who are not in tune with the times, making believe for themselves that the country, to which they have given Jewish names, was theirs only because they were not allowing other than their kind to use the roads or exhibit any signs of presence. All this was most edifying. It made me realise that Israel's settlement programme was a passing phenomenon and was not going to survive. It's anachronistic. The Ottoman Empire, after a 400-year presence here, also had to leave. But before they did, they destroyed our landscape by felling all the trees for fuel during World War I. How much damage will these settlers have done before they leave?

At the condolence, I had spoken to a friend who does business with industrialists in Hebron, a city of over 100,000 inhabitants. He told me the hard-working people there were still able to go on with their lives. He said some had built new factories and were trading with China. In trade fairs, the name of Hebron was posted as though it were another country. And nearby was Kiryat Arba, a Jewish settlement of several thousand fanatics who prayed all day and lived on the support of the crazy Americans and fundamentalist evangelical Christians who support Jewish settlement in Palestine to hasten Armageddon and the Second Coming.

Time is on the Palestinian side, I thought, after I finished this harrowing drive. The Israelis have been inflexible, the spoilt children of the world who are allowed to get away with murder because of the sympathy felt towards them because of the Holocaust. But this emotional dispensation will not continue for ever.

When I got home and thought about the experience, I remembered an entry I read in the diaries of Khalil Sakakini, who worked as an educational inspector during the British Mandate over Palestine. In it he describes a trip he took in the mid 1940s from the north to the south of the country. 'We drove the whole day,' he writes, 'and all I saw were Arab towns and villages. I did not see a single Jewish settlement. What then is the big fuss being made about Jewish colonisation?'

Meanwhile, to his surprise, the unseen people were organising, training and arming themselves; and when the time came, they emerged from their 'invisible' locations, and fought and won a war that ended up forcing out those who had only seen their own kind and failed to see the enemy in their midst. Sakakini, too, was forced out of his new home in Jerusalem, never to return. Sixty years later, whose eyes am I to trust? ❏

Raja Shehadeh is a Palestinian lawyer and writer who lives in Ramallah. His first book, Strangers in the House: Coming of Age in Occupied Palestine *(Profile Books, 2003), was followed by* When the Bulbul Stopped Singing: A diary of Ramalleh under siege *(Profile Books, 2003)*

CROSSINGS

EYAD EL SARRAJ

Rami Heilbronne called yesterday. He is so happy for Mordechai Vanunu, whose release from an Israeli prison has given the international community of peace and human rights a moral victory (p29). Rami is a fighter and a staunch campaigner for justice. He is like a brother to me. He is dismayed that he is unable to enter Gaza and I am mad that we are not allowed to see each other. His only crime is that he is an Israeli; mine that I am Palestinian and live in Gaza.

Living in Gaza is exciting, painful, involving, frustrating, rewarding and joyful. Israeli occupation has turned Gaza into a prison, but Gaza is home. Visitors are welcome to explore our side of the fence. Driving through crowds of people and cars on holed roads is a journey of discovery: of poverty and chaos. Grim faces meet you along broken pavements, some with defiant looks, others with broken humility. Women, modestly dressed, are almost invisible. Many cover their heads, some are veiled. To the foreign eye they may all look the same. Are they oppressed or are they empowered by a defiant identity?

Playful children stop to give you a piercing look, some curious, some angry. Smiles are rare. If you step out of your car to have a closer look, you may wonder why a child looks eight when he is 12 years old. You may ask them what makes them see Arafat as a father and if is it because he is as helpless as their own.

Coming from Israel you will not escape the temptation to compare. You wonder how, in a tiny piece of Earth, there can be two different worlds. Going further and deeper into Gaza you may feel the despair of life in refugee camps, in squalor and in pain. If you dare to visit Rafah you will see shocking scenes of devastation: homes demolished, fields razed, life destroyed. It is overwhelming. You may feel humble as you discover that beneath the ashes there is a glowing spark of dignity. These people have a determined faith in divine justice. They believe God is greater than Sharon and even Bush. You may feel anger at politicians who have allowed 60 years of human tragedy. As if to make the point even more sharply, Israeli settlements stand on the beaches of Gaza looking like something out of the French Riviera. Palestinians, of course, are not permitted to live there or

Rafah, Gaza 2004:
in the wake of Israeli tanks.
Credit: Brendan Corr / Panos

even enter, except as cheap labour. Seven thousand Israeli settlers control more than one-third of the land and water. The rest is left for 1.5 million Palestinians.

You rapidly realise that anger is dominant in this land and might wonder if this is the root cause of the suicide bombing and the inhumanity of the Israeli occupation. You might become defiant; you might leave with a heavy heart. Many have travelled this road before you; some would not do it again. Others who dared to try were prevented by Israel.

Gaza has been under siege for 15 years. No one can enter or leave without Israeli approval in advance. The siege is occasionally relaxed, then once again tightened with renewed force. Today it is severe. Only diplomats and journalists can obtain the necessary prior approval. Others can spend so long waiting they are persuaded to turn back. John Van Eenwyke, a priest and practising psychologist from Olympia in the USA, and his Jewish wife were stranded for a whole day at the border crossing at Eretz. They were told that they should have applied at least seven days before and then waited for an answer before they could enter Gaza. They weren't allowed to pass. John is an old friend and teaches our students.

Another friend, Ted Rynearson, an expert on dealing with violent death, also an American, was turned away. But John, Ted and Rami are still lucky: like other Americans, Canadians and Europeans they can go back to hotels or flats in Tel Aviv or fly back home. Not so Palestinians, who belong to this different world. They may not try to cross the border unless they are cheap labour, or belong to that category of Palestinian officials who carry disgraceful VIP cards. Those Palestinians who are allowed to cross not only have to wait many hours at the gate, they have only a precise number of hours before they must be back in the cage.

It is not only people who wait long hours and days at the gate; food and merchandise suffer the same fate.

Going to Rafah is an adventure in itself. You might wait for hours at a checkpoint in the middle of Gaza before you are allowed to pass. Israeli settlers are a priority. If any of the Israelis who live in the settlements decide to cross into Israel, the main road is closed for the thousands of us. It could be hours. There are times when Israelis close the crossing for no apparent reason, merely as a punishment. This morning, I was in a long queue of cars on my way to begin a journey to Spain, through Rafah and via Cairo. The long line of cars was growing when gradually we realised that the road to Rafah was blocked by Israeli tanks. No movement is allowed even between villages or towns of the Gaza Strip. Life in the prison came to a standstill. Fumes of anger were coming out of the cars. Passengers and drivers were frenzied. Brawls broke out here and there. It seems that I will not get to see my Spanish friends this time.

Crossing the border to Egypt is another adventure; its name is waiting, but it is rewarding. Israel has recently banned Palestinians between 16 and 35 from crossing to Egypt. After crossing to the Sinai, a wave of joy and relaxation takes over. The open space of the desert fills my soul with beauty, it is almost romantic.

Coming back home from Egypt through Rafah can be more than just waiting. It can be brutal. Palestinians in their hundreds are sleeping on the floor at the Egyptian border, stranded for days before the lucky ones can carve their way forward to be squeezed into a bus that will take 150 passengers with their luggage in the 50 seats for a journey of 40 metres that takes over two hours.

Remember: it can be winter time, it can be cold and there is no heating. Remember: there are children. You may begin to see the irony. Jews today are controlling the borders and manning the barbed electric-wire fences of huge prisons. Are they punishing the Nazis? You may wonder how the victim has won the war and then lost himself. You may ask why Palestinian children think that the best thing in life is to become a martyr, to die. You may wonder why Israeli bulldozers crushed the peace activist Rachael Corrie and killed the British journalist Tom Hurndall. You may ask why Arafat is imprisoned and Sharon of Sabra and Shatila is free. You may question why there is so much hatred and if walls and ghettos are the answer. You may wonder what it would take to make the crossing to peace. ❏

Eyad El Sarraj *is a practising psychiatrist and director of the Gaza Community Mental Health Programme http://www.gcmhp.net*

WHY THE ZIONISTS WERE RIGHT

AVRAHAM B YEHOSHUA

'I TRY TO UNDERSTAND NOT SO MUCH
ANTI-SEMITISM AS THE MECHANISMS
THAT LEAD TO ANTI-SEMITISM'

Two years ago, Avraham Yehoshua and his wife Rivka, a psychoanalyst, lost a close friend, Dafna, in an attack on the Hebrew University of Jerusalem. Yehoshua dedicated his most recent novel to her. The Yehoshuas lost two other friends, both in the attack on Maxime's restaurant in Haifa. Meanwhile, as he gazes at Mount Carmel from the window of his Haifa flat, Yehoshua tries desperately to prove his rational optimism is intact.

For over three years, we've been living in a surreal world afflicted by terrorism. What effect does this have on our collective conscious?

We feel we are victims. And in the strict sense of the word so we are. But we can also see what is happening on the other side and we tell ourselves we are not victims pure and simple; we are also murderers. On the one hand, we feel we are to blame for not being able to protect the most innocent among us – our children. On the other, we are aware of our culpability vis-à-vis the Palestinians. We are in total disarray. We don't understand anything any more. Hence our depression. We clean the streets after each attack, mop up the blood and remove the burned-out carcasses of the buses. And within the hour, television informs us life has returned to normal. Only there are victims in Abou Kabir [Tel Aviv's medico-legal institute]. It's curious: of all the Arab names that were once in use in this country, why choose to keep this particular one?

Right at the beginning of the [second] intifada [October 2002], you said we should abandon any idea of peace now, in favour of a border and a fence.

I never believed in this present fence, only one built along the 'green line'. Several of us realised that the left's concept of land for peace was not working and we were forced to draw our own conclusions. The time had come for radical surgery. I don't agree with Yossi Beilin [the founder of the Israeli 'Geneva Initiative'] and his group that total peace is possible. We have to acknowledge that we can no longer ignore the irrational side of the

Palestinians' behaviour. It is impossible today to impose clear-cut, mathematical solutions. I went to Geneva to support the negotiations because I think it's a good idea to set your sights on a horizon and say how you're going to get there. But the text that was hammered out there has become inapplicable, as much from the Palestinian point of view as the Israeli. We no longer have the time or the confidence; nor do we have partners. Today, the demand for a comprehensive peace is costing our blood. We have to stop the haemorrhage, cauterise the wound and move to an immediate, unilateral withdrawal.

Do you think Sharon could be our de Gaulle?

No, but he has the blood of the workers' movement in him. [Sharon originally came out of the workers' world.] What characterises him is his attachment to the soil; it makes him a farmer of a kind. This is why the father of the settlements is today without doubt the only one who can rid us of this scourge. True, he will give us a border rather than peace. Nation for nation, sovereignty for sovereignty. That's why I also support the formation of a government of national unity with the left to end the 'Six Day' war [1967] conducted by another government of national unity. Those who warn us we risk a new war with the Palestinians want to scare us. If there were a new war, it would not be a war of occupation but a normal, legitimate war. Once we have withdrawn, I want to hear no more of the Palestinians. If we have to make war on them, we shall deploy all our force and crush them. But we should not commit any more war crimes.

Why did you choose to leave Jerusalem for Haifa?

I'm an old Jerusalemite. My father's family arrived in Palestine from Salonica around 1830. My mother's came from Morocco about a century later. I'm a pre-Zionist, a *yalid*, a native speaker. My first 12 novels were about the country; more precisely, about Jerusalem and its Sephardi community, the Jerusalem of my father. Today, the emotional charge of Jerusalem is a metaphysical threat. I can understand why the founding fathers had an unhealthy fear of this city.

Have you never given way to a panic about identity, the fear that 'Israeliness' will disappear?

I've known such moments. When I see that 1 million Israelis are trying to get Polish passports, there's good reason to panic. I'm terrified of all these people, driven here by the Holocaust, becoming Europeans again and leaving me alone here with the old Jerusalem of the *yishouv* [the pre-Zionist Jewish community in Palestine]. Having said that, I still believe in the strength of the Israeli identity. When I see how, after a fashion, we have successfully absorbed over 1 million Russians, I tell myself we must be able, in the end, to create a border and a stable reality with one language, one state and a standard, rooted identity.

Your model sounds republican and Jacobin.

Indeed: republican France is my ideal. That's why I don't accept the criticisms that were directed at us in the 1950s [about the assimilation of immigrants from the Middle East]. We had to create a melting pot and to subject these immigrants to a rational process of modernisation. If the process was unfortunately brutal, it was, nevertheless, essential. When you have a melting pot, it allows dialogue between the centre and the periphery. It's no accident that whenever ideas of multiculturalism and pluralism dominated the Israeli debate, social inequalities were widened. When you leave people to inhabit their own world, the strong remain strong and the weak stay weak.

Despite that, you seem to fear the Jews.

I'm afraid of the poorly defined nature of Jewish identity; of its capacity to infiltrate the lives of others, to live without borders, without limits and without responsibility; to maintain a kind of unfocused existence. I try to understand not so much anti-Semitism as the mechanisms that lead to anti-Semitism. We should draw the lessons of the Holocaust and understand that the problematic nature of our identity is what leads individuals and groups, themselves in an identity crisis, to project such terrible things on to us. The combination of our religion and our nationalism disturbs our neighbours and drives them crazy.

You are personally preoccupied by the contradiction between identities that are too strong and pose a threat, and by the need to forge sufficiently strong links between these identities.

That's probably so. I genuinely believe that the present explosion of anti-Semitism is because Israel, in the process of blurring its legitimate borders, is enraging the Jews, the anti-Semites, the Muslims and the Christians.

So there's a link between your support for the wall of separation and your search for a clear identity.

Left and right both believe it's possible to live everywhere: to live without borders. It's typical of Jewishness. The Jews today don't want borders, but the Zionist knew only too well that they were a necessity. In this sense, [Shimon] Peres and [Moshe] Dayan [the ministers responsible for the settlements in 1967] betrayed Zionism by leaving us without borders.

The troubled Jewish identity feeds the troubled Arab identity and vice versa?

There's no doubt about it. We've plugged our blood system into that of the Palestinians and both our nations are mutually contaminated. Our tendency to confuse lines and identities has resulted in the eruption of an irrational and suicidal tendency among Palestinians. Yasser Arafat is its embodiment. His deep-seated need for anarchy makes him the worst thing that could ever have happened to the Palestinians. We must disengage. It's the key to our mental health and to theirs. This is not a simple mater of government: it is essential that we disengage from other peoples; we have worked ourselves to death for two and a half millennia trying to live among them. We must break with our *dybbuk* [demon, that which possesses us].

I want to end by saying something about the Palestinians. We have to understand that they have gone through a unique experience. Suddenly, a nation, formerly seen simply as a religious community, confronts them with the following: 'Your country is actually our country.' Imagine. It's a traumatic experience; and that is what has driven them mad. We left them 22 per cent of Palestine and now we've taken what's left. By increasing the settlements, what we're saying to them is: 'You will be for ever without citizenship in your own country. You will never have what even a starving man in Calcutta has a right to: an identity card.' We have wounded them grievously and we should be fully aware of this. ❏

Avraham Yehoshua was interviewed for the Israeli newspaper Ha'aretz *by Ari Shavit. This interview was reproduced in* Courrier International

Translated by JVH

No 20
Summer
2004

Mahmoud Shukair
Mohammed Al-Harthi
Rubia'a al-Ossaimi
Ahmed el-Madini
Ibrahim Saadi
Ali Bader
Aziz Azhrai
Samuel Shimon

Abdu Khal
Ali Zalah
Turki al-Hamad
Laila al-Juhni
Youssef al-Mohaimeed
Ghazi Algosaibi
Zainab Hifni
Abdullah al-Taezi

BANIPAL
Magazine of Modern Arab Literature

Feature on
The Novel in Saudi Arabia

Interview with
Iraqi poet Saadi Youssef

Your window on Arab literature today
www.banipal.co.uk
P O Box 22300 LONDON W13 8ZO   editor@banipal.co.uk

A MATTER OF CONSCIENCE

On 21 May 2004, a US military court sentenced Staff Sergeant Camilo Mejia Castillo of the Florida National Guard to the maximum penalty of one year's imprisonment for desertion. He had refused to return to his unit in Iraq, citing moral reasons, the legality of the war and the conduct of US troops towards Iraqi civilians and prisoners.

Amnesty International has adopted him as a prisoner of conscience, imprisoned for his conscientious objection to the war in Iraq despite his having taken reasonable steps to try to secure his discharge from the army.

The sentence was imposed despite a pending decision by the army on his application for conscientious objector status. During the trial his lawyers were not permitted to present arguments relating to his conscientious objection, including describing the abuse he witnessed.

He is currently detained in a military prison at Fort Sill, Oklahoma. The sentence is under appeal, but the appeal process is expected to be lengthy.

Staff Sergeant Camilo Mejia Castillo was deployed to Iraq in April 2003. He began to develop doubts about the morality and legality of the war. In October 2003 he returned home for two weeks' leave. He failed to return to duty in Iraq and filed for discharge as a conscientious objector on 16 March 2004, stating that he believed the war and occupation of Iraq to be 'illegal and immoral'.

'This soldier went AWOL because this soldier does not think that this is a good war,' Mejia told CBS TV later. 'When you look at the war, and you look at the reasons that took us to war, and you don't find that any of the things that we were told that we're going to war for turned out to be true, when you don't find there are weapons of mass destruction and when you don't find that there was a link between Saddam Hussein and Al-Qaida . . . and you see that you're not helping the people, and the people don't want you there . . . to me, there's no military contract and no military duty that's going to justify being a part of that war.'

In his subsequent conscientious objector application, Mejia described the conditions of detention and treatment of Iraqi prisoners, including instances where soldiers were directed to 'break the detainees' resolve', including banging on metal walls with sledgehammers to enforce sleep deprivation and loading pistols near the ears of prisoners. He also described witnessing the killing of civilians, including children.

Mejia has described the evolution of his beliefs, what he witnessed and did in Iraq, all of which compelled him to take a stand on the basis of conscience. His objections to such abuse were made before the publication of photographs of US agents physically and mentally torturing and abusing Iraqi detainees in Abu Ghraib prison in Iraq, but his trial came at a time of heightened media attention on this issue.

A member of his defence team, former Attorney General Ramsey Clark, spoke of the 'incredible irony that we're prosecuting soldiers in Iraq for violations of international law and we're prosecuting a soldier here because he refused to do the same things'.

CBS TV's *90 Minutes* programme interviewed Mejia, a Nicaraguan citizen with legal residency in the US. 'I would say this war is not about America,' Mejia told CBS TV's Dan Rather. 'This war is not about safety. This war is not about freedom. This war should not be paid with the blood of American soldiers. . . . And if I do end up paying with jail, then at least I'll know that it was for the right decision.'

Rather also spoke to Captain Tad Warfel, Mejia's commanding officer. Warfel and 27 of his 127 men were wounded, some seriously, losing limbs and spending months in the hospital; no one in the company died. Two went absent without leave; the other eventually returned and was disciplined.

Mejia told CBS that he has never regretted his decision to go AWOL, especially, he says, when he starts thinking about the 12 or 13 Iraqis he and his men killed in Ramadi. All of them, he says, were civilians simply caught in crossfire, except for one 10-year-old boy with an AK-47 and one adult with a grenade.

'His duty's not to question myself or anybody higher than me,' Warfel told Rather. 'His duty is to carry out the orders that I give him or his platoon leader gives him. We're not paid in the military to form personal opinions or to doubt what our leaders say.'

Amnesty International calls for Mejia's immediate and unconditional release. He is the first US soldier known to be tried for 'desertion' after service in combat in the current Iraq conflict.

Prior to his conviction, Camilo Mejia said, 'I have no regrets, not one . . . I will take it because I go there with my honour, knowing I have done the right thing.' ❏

From Amnesty International and CBS TV reports

A censorship chronicle incorporating information from Agence France-Press (AFP), Allafrica. com, Alliance of Independent Journalists (AJI), Amnesty International (AI), Arab Press Freedom Watch (APFW), Article 19 (A19), Association of Independent Electronic Media (ANEM), the BBC Monitoring Service Summary of World Broadcasts (SWB), Centre for Human Rights and Democratic Studies (CEHURDES), Centre for Journalism in Extreme Situations (CJES), the Committee to Protect Journalists (CPJ), Canadian Journalists for Free Expression (CJFE), Democratic Journalists' League (JuHI), Freedom House, Global Internet Liberty Campaign (GILC),Human Rights Watch (HRW), Inter American Press Association (IAPA), Indymedia, Institute for War & Peace Reporting (IWPR), Instituto de Prensa y Sociedad (IPYS), the United Nations Integrated Regional Information Network (IRIN), the International Federation of Journalists (IFJ/FIP), Journaliste en danger (JED), International Press Institute (IPI), the Media Institute of Southern Africa (MISA), Network for the Defence of Independent Media in Africa (NDIMA), Network for Education and Academic Rights (NEAR), International PEN (PEN), Pacific Islands News Association (PINA), Pacific Media Watch, Periodistas Frente La Corrupcíon (PFC); Press Freedom Foundation (FLIP), Radio Free Europe/Radio Liberty (RFE/ RL), Reporters Sans Frontières (RSF), Southeast Media Organisation (SEEMO), Statewatch, Transitions Online (TOL), World Association of Newspapers (WAN), World Press Freedom Committee (WPFC), and other sources including members of the International Freedom of Expression eXchange (IFEX).

AFGHANISTAN

A new media law that eases some restrictions on journalists, such as bans on criticism of the army and 'unsuitable' photos of women, also tightened bans on perceived 'criticism' of Islam and 'insult' of public officials. Media rights groups felt that its vague definitions left it open to abuse by officials and that it will be used to censor political reporting. Hamed Almi, President Hamed Karzai's deputy press secretary, suggested that journalists unhappy with the statute should bring their appeals to the new parliament, due to be elected in September. (RSF)

Four different journalists' unions in Afghanistan currently compete for members. The oldest is the National Journalists' Union of Afghanistan, formed in 1980 after the Soviet occupation and patterned on communist-era unions. It claims to be completely independent, but faces competition from the Tadaruk Committee, which claims to have 480 applications for membership from Afghan journalists, the allegedly politicised Independent Journalists' Union, and a group that claims to represent female journalists. (IWPR)

An estimated 150 new media outlets have sprung up since the fall of the Taliban in 2001, but local warlords still control parts of the country and limit free expression in their areas. **Fazil Rahman Orya** of the daily newspaper *Mashal Democracy* said: 'I have been threatened several times over articles that we have written against [the warlords].' Sebghatullah Sanger, pub-

lisher of the weekly *Jumhori Ghag* reports that self-censorship is 'visibly high'. (IWPR)

ALGERIA

On 26 May, **Hafnaoui Ghoul**, a correspondent for the daily *El Youm*, was detained and then sentenced to six months' imprisonment with no parole for defamation. Arrested in Djelfa, Ghoul, a historian who runs the Algerian League of Human Rights, was found guilty for articles complaining of the repression of journalists and the corruption of government and police officials. (RSF)

Kamel Gaci, a reporter with the daily *Le Soir d'Algérie*, was charged on 2 June with 'failure to report a fugitive', following the publication of his interview with an escaped convict in the newspaper. The fugitive, a former police officer, contacted Gaci through the newspaper two weeks after his escape from El Khemis prison, saying he wanted to tell his story. The journalist notified the authorities of his interview with the fugitive but did not say where it was to take place. The court granted the journalist a conditional release, placing him under judicial surveillance pending the verdict. (RSF)

G Lofti, a Djelfa-based correspondent for the daily *Liberté*, was given a three-month suspended sentence at the start of June and ordered to pay 200,000 dinars in damages to the Djelfa police chief. The police chief had complained against Lofti over an article he had written on 14 April on the suicide of a local businessman. (RSF)

ANGOLA

Felisberto de Graça Campos, editor of the weekly magazine *Semanario Angolense*, was sentenced to 45 days' imprisonment on 30 March and fined for an article that claimed to reveal the personal wealth of prominent government officials. (MISA)

ARGENTINA

On 1 April, journalist **Pablo Badano** of *Indymedia Argentina* and **Horacio Guzmán**, a leader of the Guaraní indigenous community group Estación El Tabacal, were detained by police for a day in Orán in northern Argentina. Badano had been covering a land rights dispute between the local community and the US company Seaboard Corporation, owner of a mill on the territory. (*Periodistas*)

A scheduled promotion of a book by **Javier Romero** and **Romina Manguel** at Buenos Aires International Book Fair on 24 April was cancelled, allegedly under threat of legal action by the subject of the book, an unauthorised biography of media magnate Daniel Hadad. The book, *Vale Todo*, has been withdrawn from bookshops since mid April. Publishers Ediciones B say they might not reprint it despite successful sales to date. (*Periodistas*)

ARMENIA

At least four journalists were attacked on 5 April by unknown assailants as they covered an opposition demonstration. Police failed to intervene but did arrest another journalist for photographing a roadblock. They also failed to intervene as a group of men in civilian clothes targeted the journalists during a demonstration by the Azgayin Miabanutiun Party in Yerevan. (IFEX)

The first non-government-controlled paper in Armenian-controlled Nagorno-Karabakh opened in April 2004. The newspaper *Demo*, short for *Democracy*, was founded by former journalist Gegam Bagdasarian. The president of the enclave, the former journalist Arkady Gukasian, welcomed the move, saying: 'A free press is a sign of the formation of civil society.' (RFE/RL)

Former deputy defence minister and historian **Gegan Arutyunyan**, now an opposition leader, was arrested and charged on 20 April with 'use of bad language'. He was held at an Interior Ministry office, feeding speculation that he had been detained to prevent his participation at an opposition rally on 21 April. (BBC)

AZERBAIJAN

On 22 April, a Baku court rejected an appeal against plans to turn the city's Juma Mosque into a carpet museum. It is seen as a bid to constrain dissident religious activist **Ilgar Ibrahimoglu**, who is based at the mosque and operates independently of the state-sanctioned Azeri Muslim community. 'We will defend our rights peacefully,' Ibrahimoglu says. (Forum 18)

The International Press Institute called on President Ilham Aliyev to halt the harassment of the independent newspaper *Tezadlar* through the courts. The paper has been hit by an estimated 400 civil lawsuits in recent years, almost all filed by state officials. The paper is now shackled by the plaintiffs' court orders sequestering their income. (IPI)

BAHRAIN

Interior Minister Sheik Mohammed bin Khalifa al Khalifa was sacked on 22 March after he ordered police to stop a demonstration against the US occupation of Iraq. It led to a day of clashes between police and protesters and a royal decree from the king confirming 'the right to express anger and protest'. (BBC)

On 21 April, Nada Haffadh, a member of Bahrain's upper house of parliament, was appointed as Bahrain's first woman minister, taking the health portfolio. She is the first woman to head a health ministry in an Arab state. (BBC)

Five members of Bahrain's opposition were arrested on 6 May after circulating a petition calling for increased democratic reforms and more power for Bahrain's elected parliament. The five were charged with trying to change the political system and undermining the security of the kingdom which requires any alteration to the constitution to be approved by the king. (BBC)

BANGLADESH

Syed Abul Maksud, deputy chief news editor of state-owned *Bangladesh Sangbad Sangstha* (*BSS*), resigned on 3 March after the government criticised his article in another paper describing the 27 February stabbing of author and academic Dr **Humayun Azad** as 'a naked display of fascism'. Azad suffered death threats after publishing a novel about religious groups in Bangladesh who collaborated with the Pakistani army during the 1971 war of independence. A *BSS* official said the paper was fully run and controlled by the government and so there was no scope to write against the establishment. (*Daily Star*)

On 13 March, **Golam Mortoza**, chief reporter of the weekly *Saptahik 2000*, received a package containing a burial shroud and a letter threatening to kill him. On the same day, an anonymous phone caller warned him that 'the Angel of Death will visit you within a few days'. Mortoza said the caller specifically mentioned his reports on the attack on **Humayun Azad** and violence against members of the Ahmadiyya sect. (RSF, *Daily Star*)

On 4 April, **Delwar Hossain**, Keraniganj correspondent of the daily newspaper *Jugantor*, was shot in the head and back in the city's Malibagh area. Delwar allegedly came under attack because of his articles exposing extortion, abduction, murder and other criminal activities of cadres of the ruling Bangladesh National Party. (CPJ, RSF, *Daily Star*)

Thirteen militants of the banned Maoist Purbobanglar faction were accused on 8 April of murdering journalist **Manik Saha** (*Index* 2/04) with a home-made bomb on 15 January. Four of the accused are already in custody. Two have confessed,

saying that the journalist was an 'enemy of the proletariat'. (RSF)

Sumi Khan, Chittagong correspondent of *Saptahik 2000*, was stabbed and critically wounded in the street on 27 April. Witnesses heard her attackers yelling about her reports and she has received more death threats since leaving hospital. Khan's reports included investigations into links between local politicians and religious groups in attacks on members of minority communities and land grabbing by some landlords. (AI, RSF)

Freelance journalist **Aurobindo Pal** was arrested and charged with murder in the northern Mymensingh district on 10 May after he refused to hand over pictures of election-related violence the evening before. Police had fired into the crowd, killing two demonstrators and injuring at least 17 others. (RSF)

Recent publication: *Bangladesh: The Ahmadiyya Community – their rights must be protected*, Amnesty International, 23 April 2004, 7pp

BELARUS

The daily newspaper *Narodnaya Volya* could be forced into closure, after a Supreme Court judgement upheld last year's lower court ruling that the publication should pay US$23,000 in damages to a state TV executive for libel. The damages are to be paid to Yahor Rybakov, in connection with an interview published in *Narodnaya Volya* that quoted the former state TV presenter **Eleonora Yazer-**

skaya as saying that he was a 'bad manager'. Yazerskaya has also been ordered to pay damages of US$460. (RSF)

Svetlana Zavadskaya, the wife of journalist **Dimitri Zavadski** who has been missing since July 2000, has been told by the authorities that investigations into her husband's disappearance have been closed. Zavadski, a cameraman for the Russian TV channel ORT, disappeared on 7 July 2000 at Minsk airport. (RSF)

On 8 April, police confiscated 4,800 copies of the Grodno-based weekly *Den* newspaper as it crossed the border from printers in Russia. The seized edition included an article accusing the police of failure to prosecute two men who tried to break into the newspaper's office. On 11 May, security services raided the *Den* offices and impounded four computers, a few days before officials were due to force the eviction of the paper from the building. (RSF, RFE/RL)

Valery Levaneuski, leader of the newspaper vendors strike committee in Grodno, was jailed for 15 days for circulating leaflets advertising an authorised May Day rally that featured a poem allegedly libelling President Aleksandr Lukashenko. Levaneuski's sentence was later extended by three days. (RFE/RL)

BELGIUM

On 19 March, German weekly *Stern*'s Brussels correspondent **Hans-Martin Tillack** was arrested and his home and office searched by police acting on behalf of the European Union's Anti-

Fraud Office (OLAF), apparently in reaction to Tillack's reports on fraud inside the European Parliament. (IFJ)

A new draft law on protection of journalists' sources introduced on 27 March was generally welcomed, but some groups warned that the bill had exceptions that could worry reporters. In recent years, attacks on journalistic confidentiality have occurred more often in Belgium than in any other Western European country. Cases have been taken to the European Court of Human Rights in Strasbourg, the latest being a landmark case, *Ernst and Others v Belgium*, where judges voted to uphold confidentiality of sources. (IFJ)

BENIN

Jean-Baptiste Hounkonnou, publication director of the daily *Le Nouvel Essor*, was sentenced to six months' imprisonment and forced to pay substantial damages and fines after publishing an article that accused a woman of adultery. He was released after six weeks pending an appeal hearing. (CPJ,RSF)

BRAZIL

Radio journalist **Samuel Roman** was killed on 20 April in Coronel Sapucaia, on the border with Paraguay. Roman ran a popular local radio station called Conquista. He presented a phone-in programme called *Voice of the People* that exposed drug trafficking and criminality by local politicians. (RSF, IAPA)

Journalist **José Carlos Arãjo** of Radio Timbaba FM was murdered on 24 April in north-eastern Pernambuco State as he left his recording studio. Arãjo used his radio programme *Josè Carlos Entrevista* to expose murder squads and the alleged involvement of local figures in criminal cases. (RSF)

In May, *New York Times* Brazil correspondent **Larry Rother** had his visa revoked by the Brazilian Ministry of Justice, after writing an article about the drinking habits of Brazilian President Luiz Inácio Lula da Silva. (CPJ, IAPA, BBC)

BURMA

Writers **Kyaw San** (pen name 'Cho Seint') and **Aung Zin** were released by the Burmese government on 1 March – three months after their seven-year sentence had officially ended. San and Zin were two of five prisoners of opinion freed on the eve of the arrival in Burma of the UN Secretary-General's special envoy, Ismail Razali. Thirteen journalists are presently held in Burmese prisons. (RSF)

Sixty-year-old Burmese journalist and poet **Kyi Tin Oo** was released from prison on 26 March. He was jailed in 1994 for writing political articles. (RSF)

Photographer and cameraman **Khin Maung Win**, also known as 'Sunny', was freed on 9 April after seven years in jail. He was arrested on 13 June 1997 with four other members of the opposition National League for Democracy (NLD) after filming an interview with party leader and Nobel laureate Aung San Suu Kyi (*Index* 4–6/94, 4–6/95, 4/96, 5/96, 1/97, 2/97, 1/99, 3/02, 3/03, 4/03, 1/04) and sending the interview abroad. (RSF)

On 12 May, sports journalist **Zaw Thet Htwe** (*Index* 3/04) had his death sentence commuted to three years' imprisonment. Htwe and three others had been found guilty of high treason in 28 November 2003 for allegedly attempting to assassinate the leaders of the Burmese military junta. Colleagues believe the real reason for his jailing was an article criticising junta members for misappropriating foreign funds meant to support Burmese football. (RSF, BMA, RFA)

CAMEROON

Two journalists from Radiotélévision Siantou (RTS) were sued by former junior soccer team trainer Jean-Paul Akono, who brought the charges after **Mesmin Kangelieu** and **Bonny Philippe** broadcast a report alleging irregularities in the selection of teams for international games. (JED)

Director of pharmaceuticals for the Ministry of Public Health Ndo Ndo Jean Rollin Bertrand sued **Richard Max Bosoh Mpandjo** and **Luther Ouandie** of *L'Indépendant* and journalists from several other newspapers on 6 May. The accusations follow stories alleging Bertrand's involvement in the disappearance of a body from a Yaoundé hospital. (JED)

CANADA

On 12 May, author **Stephen Williams** was awarded a

2004 Hellman/Hammett Grant from Human Rights Watch. Williams, by defying a ban on reporting a controversial murder trial, drove Ontario province officials to bring an unprecedented 97 criminal charges against him for his defiance. (CJFE/PEN Canada)

On 23 April, a team of academics from the University of Cambridge, Harvard Law School and the University of Toronto formed the Open Net Initiative and began formally monitoring worldwide Internet censorship and surveillance. Research reports can be found on the openinitative.net website. (ONI)

CENTRAL AFRICAN REPUBLIC

Director **Mathurin Constant Momet** and chief editor **Patrick Bakwa** of the daily *Le Confident* were detained in Bangui for 24 hours on 16 April and charged with criminal defamation. The charges are linked to a report about a businessman's criticism of his former lawyer and the judicial system in the CAR. (CPJ, WAN)

Judes Zossé (*Index* 2/04), director of the daily newspaper *L'Hirondelle*, was freed by presidential pardon on 14 May, halfway through a six-month jail sentence for 'insulting the head of state'. He had republished an article from the website centrafrique-presse.com alleging that President François Bozizé had taken over the collection of tax revenue in the country. (CPJ, RSF)

CHILE

On 27 April, the hard disks of computers used by journalists **Lino Solis de Ovando** and **Jorge Molina Sanhueza** of the online newspaper *El Mostrador* were removed by police and confiscated for a day. The seizure was ordered by a judge investigating the 24 March bombing of the Brazilian consulate in Santiago. (RSF)

CHINA

On 16 March, cyber-dissident **Ouyang Yi** (*Index* 2/03) was sentenced to two years' imprisonment for 'incitement to subversion'. In November 2002, he wrote an open letter to the Chinese Communist Party Congress advocating gradual moves towards democracy. (RSF)

On 19 March, **Cheng Yizhong** (*Index* 2/04), editor of the Guangzhou-based *Nanfang Dushi Bao*, was charged with corruption on the same day deputy editor **Yu Huafeng** was jailed for 12 years for embezzlement of 580,000 yuan (US$70,000). Former editor **Li Minying** was jailed for 11 years for accepting bribes totalling 970,000 yuan (US$117,000). The accused maintain that the funds were legally acquired profits shared with staff. The newspaper is thought to have been targeted by the authorities for its investigative reporting on the Sars epidemic and other politically sensitive issues. (CPJ)

Ma Yalian was sentenced to 18 months in a work re-education camp on 19 March, after publishing web articles criticising government handling of public complaints on chineselawyer.com and dajiyuan.com, a website run by the Falun Gong sect. Ma was sent to a re-education camp in 2001 after complaining at being evicted from her home in Shanghai as a result of an urban redevelopment plan. (RSF)

On 2 May, freelance journalist **Liu Shui** was sentenced without trial to two years in a re-education camp. Charged with soliciting the services of prostitutes, he had posted numerous articles on the Internet concerning the Tiananmen Square massacre. (RSF)

On 13 May, US resident **Yang Jianli** (*Index* 4/03) was sentenced to five years' imprisonment for 'espionage' and 'illegally entering Chinese territory'. The editor of online review *Yibao* (chinaeweekly.com) and exiled after the 1989 Tiananmen Square protest, he had returned to China to investigate industrial unrest in the country's northeast. He was arrested in April 2002. (RSF)

Chinese authorities placed several human rights activists under house arrest to prevent their commemoration of the 15th anniversary of the Tiananmen Square massacre on 4 June. These include **Liu Xiaobo**, a champion of freedom of expression who has described the subversion charges made against dissidents as 'an aberration under Chinese law', **Hu Jia**, who called attention to official neglect of the Aids crisis in China, and **Ding Zilin**, leader of 'The Mothers of Tiananmen', a group of mothers who lost their chil-

WHO INVITED YOU?

REPRESENTATIVES OF THE MAPUCHE PEOPLE

From an open letter from Mapuche organisations to representatives of the member nations of the Asia-Pacific Economic Cooperation (APEC) attending the meeting of APEC Trade Ministers in Pucon and Villarrica, Chile, 4–5 June

These meetings in Pucon and Villarrica are located in ancestral Mapuche territory, which was usurped by the Chilean state. Likewise, we have summoned the President of Chile, Ricardo Lagos Escobar, to stop the folklorisation of our culture and its existence in this meeting, an open provocation given that we already feel as if we are victims of jail, repression and the criminalisation of our legitimate collective demands as a people – all at the hands of the government and influential factional groups. It is essential to note that, today, important Mapuche leaders within our territories are imprisoned – all of this in the name of the same economic model that your economies represent and that you plan to continue consolidating in our territory, increasing the colonialisation and usurpation of our lands, of our natural resources and of our traditional knowledge.

We firmly believe that you may not continue carrying out trade negotiations behind the backs of the people. The economies that you represent as well as your promotion of market liberalisation within the APEC region and standardisation of trade rules among unequal economies with asymmetrical technologies and development cause vast sectors of society, such as indigenous people, and in this case the Mapuche people whose rights your economies neither recognise nor respect, to be vulnerable within an economy overwhelmed by corporate domination, transnational pirateering, and environmental and social disaster. This future which you control is not the mandate of the peoples that have entrusted you to govern; this is not the future that the people want.

The Mapuche people resisted the Spanish invaders for over 300 years between the sixteenth and early nineteenth centuries, but with independence from Spain, the new Argentinians and Chileans launched a brutal and eventually successful war on the Mapuche. On the Chilean side alone, from 1881 until the beginning of the twentieth century, the Mapuche say the Chilean state plundered 95 per cent of the historical territory of the original Mapuche nation, depriving them of 9,500,000 hectares of their territory. A similar process occurred in Argentina. ❏

dren in the 1989 massacre. Their houses have been surrounded by police for several days, their phones cut off during 'sensitive' discussions and Internet access interrupted. (RSF)

On 11 June, cyber-dissident **Du Daobin** was sentenced to four years' house arrest and two years' privation of civil liberties. Du was charged with 'incitement to subversion and the overthrow of the Chinese socialist system' after publishing around 30 online articles calling for freedom of expression, pacifism and democracy in China. His lawyer Mo Shaoping said neither he nor Du were allowed to speak at the trial. (RSF)

Three Hong Kong radio talk-show hosts, **Allen Lee**, **Albert Cheng** and **Raymond Wong**, resigned due to threats made over their criticism of Beijing's policies towards Hong Kong. The resignations have provoked concern over the compromise of Hong Kong's traditionally free media environment. (Freedom House)

COLOMBIA

On 29 March, a man was attacked, after he was apparently mistaken for journalist **Ademir Luna** of the human rights group CREDHOS. Luna reports that his home in Barrancabermeja is also under surveillance, while his wife, Yaneth Montoya Martínez, has received threats. (AI)

On 22 April, the stepdaughter of **Jorge Corredor** of La Voz del Norte radio in the city of Cecuta was killed and Corredor injured by an unknown gunman who broke into his home. Corredor is known for his sharp criticism of local authorities. (CPJ, FLIP)

On 18 May, journalist **Aníbal Teran** and photographer **Oscar Díaz** of El Universal were assaulted by anti-riot police when they refused to hand over photographs taken during demonstrations against Free Trade Agreement negotiations in Cartagena. **Wilfred Arias** of the Barranquilla-based El Heraldo was also injured by police officers. (FLIP)

DEMOCRATIC REPUBLIC OF CONGO

On 20 May, two agents of the Congolese Intelligence Service (DSR) seized a videotape from cameraman **Alexis Mugisha Ruguba** of Congolese Radiotélévision's Goma station. Ruguba had filmed the closing of a civil society empowerment workshop in North Kivu province. (JED)

Jean-Denis Lompoto, publication director of the satirical biweekly Pili-Pili, was released on bail on 27 March after a week's detention in Kinshasa. He had been charged with defamation after Pili-Pili accused mines minister Eugène Diomi Ndongala of embezzlement. The paper's managing director, **Prosper Dawé**, and another journalist face the same charges. (CPJ, RSF, WAN)

On 29 March, Congo's intelligence service, the Agence Nationale de Renseignements, banned Radio Mutshima in Mutshima in West Kasai province. According to director **Patient Kolela**, the broadcaster was accused of operating illegally. (JED)

On 30 March, the BBC's Kinshasa correspondent, **Arnaud Zajtman**, was summoned to the state prosecutor's office and ordered to reveal his sources for a BBC news report about a women's demonstration on 8 March 2004. The journalist refused but the judge warned him that he would be summoned again. (JED)

On 20 April, **Faustin Bella Mako**, editor of the weekly Congo News and correspondent for Journaliste en danger (JED) in Katanga province was detained by officers of the Agence Nationale de Renseignements. An ANR official told JED that the journalist was arrested because he had referred to President Joseph Kabila as a 'Rwandan'. (JED)

Laurent Lukengu of KHRT radio in Tshikapa was detained for eight hours on 10 May and quizzed on his reports on the maltreatment of Congolese expelled from Angola on their return to the CAR. The town's mayor threatened to sue Lukengu unless he named local merchants who had contributed funds for the penniless returnees. (JED)

COSTA RICA

The Inter-American Press Association (IAPA) called on Costa Rica's attorney general, Supreme Court and the police to step up investigations into the murder of journalists **Ivannia Mora Rodríguez**, killed on 23 December 2003 in San José (Index 2/04) and **Parmenio Medina** (Index 4/01), killed in July 2001. (IAPA)

Article 19 and the World Press Freedom Committee called on the Inter-American Court of Human Rights to rule Costa Rica's criminal defamation law incompatible with rights to free expression. Journalist **Mauricio Herrera Ulloa** (*Index* 2/01) of *La Nación* is still fighting his 1995 sentence for republication of foreign media allegations against a Costa Rican diplomat. (A19, *Periodistas*, WPFC)

CÔTE D'IVOIRE

On 25 March, security forces assaulted at least 10 journalists, and arrested and harassed many more to stop coverage of mass opposition protests. Local transmitters relaying BBC, Radio France International and Africa No. 1 Radio broadcasts were disconnected for four days. (CPJ, RSF)

On 31 March, **Gaston Bony** of the weekly *Le Venin* newspaper was jailed for six months for criminal defamation and fined 500,000 CFA francs (US$930) for articles accusing the mayor of Agboville of corruption. Since his imprisonment his health has reportedly deteriorated and he has received death threats. (RSF, WAN, CPJ)

French-Canadian freelance journalist **Guy-André Kieffer** went missing on 16 April in Côte d'Ivoire. Kieffer has investigated corruption in the country's cocoa and coffee sectors and reportedly received death threats before his disappearance. The magistrate heading a separate French inquiry into the case told the state prosecutor in Abidjan on 21 May that his investigations were being blocked. (CPJ, RSF, WAN)

Thibault Gbei, a reporter with newspaper *L'Intelligent d'Abidjan*, was assaulted by a group of police officers on 6 May on a university campus in Abidjan. He was investigating allegations of police brutality against students. (MISA)

Outtara Kader, general manager of *Le Patriote* newspaper, was kidnapped but swiftly set free on 11 May after the kidnappers discovered they had the wrong man. The intended target, said Kader, was **Méité Sindou**, director-general of the Mayama Group, publishers of *Le Patriote*. (MISA)

Côte d'Ivoire's broadcasting regulator suspended the local rebroadcast of Radio France International for 24 hours on 15 May after RFI reported the results of a UN inquiry into the killing of some 120 demonstrators in a 'carefully planned and executed operation' against banned opposition protests in March. (RSF)

CUBA

On 26 April, **Carlos Brizuela Yera** (*Index* 3/02) of the independent Cooperativa de Periodistas Independientes de Camagüey news agency was jailed for three years after a one-day hearing in Ciego de Avila, central Cuba. Journalist **Lester Téllez Castro** (*Index* 3/02, 2/04) and eight rights activists got sentences ranging from three years' house arrest to seven years' imprisonment, for 'public disorder' and 'resistance to authority' at a demonstration in March 2002. (RSF, WIPC, HRW)

On 3 May, Cuban journalist and poet **Raúl Rivero** (*Index* 3/03) was awarded this year's Guillermo Cano World Press Freedom Prize by Unesco. Rivero is serving a 20-year prison sentence and is reportedly suffering from pneumonia. (Unesco, RSF)

Recent publications: *Cuba: One Year Too Many: Prisoners of conscience from the March 2003 crackdown*, Amnesty International, March 2004

DOMINICAN REPUBLIC

Lawyers for *Editora Listín Diario*, a Santo Domingo-based publishing house, are fighting a state takeover. Three of its papers closed after one of its owners was accused of fraud. A fourth, *Listín Diario*, remains open but under the control of a state administrator and editor. The company was taken over after one co-owner was accused of fraud. An appeals court ruled the takeover illegal on 22 April, but the state has filed a counter-appeal in the Supreme Court. (IAPA)

Recent publication: *Dominican Republic: Human rights violations in the context of the economic crisis*, Amnesty International, March 2004

EAST TIMOR

Australian journalist **Julian King** was detained for questioning about alleged subversive activities on 6 May in Dili, held for two days and threatened with expulsion. A week later, he was detained again. He was accused of possessing weapons and subversion. King, who denies all charges, was also accused by

A REVOLUTION BETRAYED
MIGUEL SÁNCHEZ

Raúl Rivero was a teenager when the revolution triumphed in 1959 and opened up a better future for the people of Cuba. He believed in it with the fervour typical of his age, and gave it his energy and literary and journalistic talent. He occupied important posts in the national print media and has been a prize-winning poet – indeed he was honoured by the very government that now wishes to snuff out his passion, his vocation and his voice in a narrow cell.

His crime was that of being truly honest to his own thought. Now, as before, he loved free thought and free expression. Using his mastery of the language, he defended the ideas of social equality and national redemption that were deployed as the revolutionary creed, until it gave way to the excesses of a power corrupted by age, whose acts betray the ideals it claims to uphold.

Raúl, with admirable courage in the context of Cuban repression, broke publicly with his long-standing political commitments; or perhaps it is fairer to say that he simply reaffirmed his commitment to his own thought, and has since been in the front line of objective and free-thinking journalism, which is the only possible route to expressing the greatest aspirations of his people, and their tragic reality.

The charges on which he is today being punished with a long and unjust prison sentence would make even George Orwell's fateful portrait of Big Brother pale. There is really no need to cite these charges.

He and two dozen other independent journalists condemned in Cuba over the past year, along with economists, librarians, human rights activists, doctors and peaceful dissidents, have done no more than use their ideas as possible arms for an essential national change.

Each and every one of them was driven by the hope and the determination to bring about by peaceful means a better and different future for all Cubans. ❏

On 3 May, Cuban journalist and poet Raúl Rivero was awarded this year's Guillermo Cano World Press Freedom Prize by UNESCO. Rivero is serving a 20-year prison sentence in Cuba and is reportedly suffering from pneumonia. This text was taken from a speech given on his behalf by his stepson Miguel Sánchez at the presentation in Belgrade

Prime Minister Mari Alkatiri of participating in an arson attack on his home in December 2002. (Pacific Media Watch, RSF)

ECUADOR

Patricio Orduoez Maico, a gay man who filed a complaint against police officers who assaulted him, survived an attempt to kill him on 12 March, just one week after he detailed the case at an international human rights meeting in Quito. He is a member of the Guayaquil-based Fundación Amigos por la Vida which campaigns for the rights of lesbian, gay, bisexual and transgendered. (AI)

EGYPT

Three Britons and one Palestinian were among 26 defendants found guilty on 25 March of promoting the Islamist Hizb al-Tahir group. The three Britons, **Reza Pankhurst, Ian Nisbet**, and **Majid Nawaz** (*Index* 3/02, 4/02), are members of the group in Britain, where it is legal, but deny having anything to do with the organisation in Egypt, where it is banned. The trial was carried out in an Egyptian state security emergency court, under an emergency law in effect since 1981. The verdict can only be overturned by presidential decree. (*Cairo Times*)

Egyptian workers, trade union leaders and representatives of political and civil society organisations were denied the right to join in the worldwide Labour Day celebrations on 1 May. Security forces denied access to Tahrir Square, Cairo, and forcibly dispersed people. (Catholic Information Service for Africa, *Middle East Times*)

EL SALVADOR

On 2 April, Canadian company Cintec withdrew its criminal defamation suit against **Enrique Altamirano**, director of *El Diario de Hoy* and two editors. Cintec first sued in December 2003, demanding US$6 million in damages over allegations that Cintec directors were involved in illegal activities. (PFC)

EQUATORIAL GUINEA

Agence France-Presse and Radio France Internationale correspondent **Rodriguo Angue Nguema** (*Index* 1/04) was refused entry to a press conference given by President Teodoro Obiang Nguema. The president's press secretary, Cosme Nguema Bibang Eyang, only allowed state radio and television station journalists to attend the conference, giving no reason for this restriction. (JED)

ERITREA

Recent publication: *Eritrea: You Have No Right To Ask – Government resists scrutiny on human rights*, Amnesty International, May 2004.

ETHIOPIA

Merid Estifanos, former chief editor of the weekly newspaper *Satanaw*, was arrested in Addis Ababa on 2 April when he was unable to post bail in a criminal defamation case. He was charged with defaming Prime Minister Meles Zenawi in a 2001 article that alleged that Zenawi secretly supported the government of neighbouring Eritrea. (CPJ, RSF)

In May, the International Press Institute (IPI) put Ethiopia on the IPI Watch List. The organisation criticised the government's failure to open the airwaves to private broadcasters and condemned the repeated arrests of journalists. (IPI)

Ato Kifle Mulat (*Index* 2/01, 3/02), president of the Ethiopian Free Journalists Association (EFJA), received Amnesty International's Special Award for Human Rights Journalism under Threat on 18 May. Mulat, also editor of the newspaper *Lissane Hizb*, was given the award 'in recognition of his bravery in defending the freedom of the press in Ethiopia and in the face of constant official repression'. (allafrica.com)

FIJI

New Zealand TV reporter **Jeff Hampton** was denied entry to Fiji and deported on 23 May after his name was found on a Fiji government prohibited immigrant list. It is thought that Hampton was listed in 2000 when he reported armed indigenous Fijians holding ethnic Indian Fijians in detention camps during the May 2000 nationalist coup. (TV3, Pacific Media Watch, *The Australian*)

FRANCE

On 15 May, riot police attacked three journalists as they covered a protest by film industry workers in Cannes. **Gwenaël Rihet,** a cameraman for France 3 TV, was thrown down, handcuffed and detained for several hours. His head injuries required six stitches. A journalist with Agence France-Presse and a Norwegian reporter were also manhandled by police. (RSF)

A 9 April amendment to a bill to promote confidence in the digital economy removed a statute of limitations that allow plaintiffs to sue websites for defamation years after first publication. The change was designed, said parliamentarians, to prevent archives holding such material from circumventing the defamation laws (*Index* 2/04). (RSF)

Staff at an Islamic school in the Seine-et-Marne département assaulted reporters **Jérôme Florenville**, **Jean-Yves Charpin** and **Hervé Bouchaud** on 11 March while they filmed outside the school as part of a six-month investigation into the activities of the Islamist Tabligh. The school had declined to cooperate. Five staff were arrested. (RSF)

GABON

Alfred Ngamba, a journalist with the bimonthly newspaper *Le Nganga*, is being held in a prison in Libreville on charges of defamation. His arrest follows an article that allegedly libels an unidentified doctor who is also a director of a well-known non-governmental organisation. (JED)

GAMBIA

The Independent biweekly (*Index* 1/04) was violently attacked by six armed men who set fire to the paper's print house. Despite an attempt to lock the staff in the

burning building, all escaped with minor injuries. The police took five hours to turn up at the scene of the crime. Journalists give little credence to a pledge by Interior Minister Sulayman Masannah Ceesay that the incident would be properly investigated; there has been no progress in his investigation into the last arson attack on the paper in October 2003. (CPJ, IRIN, allafrica.com)

The Independent, Foroyaa, The Point, The Nation, News & Report (*Index* 4/03) magazine and Radio One FM suspended publication and broadcasts for a week in protest at the introduction of compulsory registration for all journalists and other draconian provisions. As a result the deadline for registration was extended for three months, infuriating President Yaya Jammeh, who said the journalists must register 'or go to hell'. (IRIN, Allafrica.com, MFWA)

GEORGIA

Security forces in the troubled autonomous republic of Ajaria continued to harass the media. A crew filming the brief detention of Georgian Finance Minister Zurab Nogaideli by Ajari authorities on 13 March was attacked; the same day journalist **Nestan Checkhladze** and his cameraman **Baka Sharahenidze** were arrested in another incident and their tapes confiscated. Security forces also attacked **Jumber Chevardnadze**, a driver for a Channel 9 TV crew, seizing tapes belonging to journalist **Nata Imedashvili** and cameraman **Ramaz Jorbenadze**. (RSF)

On 4 May, cameraman **Alexi Tvaradze** of Rustavi-2 TV was beaten by police while covering an opposition rally in Batumi in Ajaria. His tapes were also seized. Journalists **Eteri Turadze** and **Lela Bumbadze** of the weekly *Batumelebi* and **Natia Zoidze** of *Inter Press* were beaten at the same event. (IFEX, CPJ)

GHANA

Ghana's inspector general of police met with media representatives to discuss coverage of the December election. He urged the media not to provoke violent clashes as election campaigns progress. He was particularly concerned by phone-in programmes, which he believed fostered political attacks. (allafrica.com)

Justice FM radio in the northern city of Tamale was temporarily closed after commentator **Shamuna Gazi** suggested during a panel discussion that traditional Tamale chief Dakpema-Na Alhassan had been snubbed by the Ghanaian president because Alhassan was not identified as a chief. The Dakpema-Na ordered police to arrest Gazi but allowed the station to reopen after its management apologised to him. (allafrica.com)

GREECE

Greek state ET-3 TV banned its own award-winning documentary *The Other Side* on 3 May. The Athens daily *Eleftherotypia* blamed pressure from 'nationally correct' persons; the director-general of ET-3 linked it to the visit of Turkish premier Recep Tayyip Erdogan. Journalist **Fani Toupalgiki**'s film cov-

DON'T SAY I DIDN'T TELL YOU
GRAND AYATOLLAH
SAYYID ALI HUSAINI SISTANI

Letter from Ayatollah Sistani to the UN Security Council

Greetings.

We have been informed of the attempts to include the so-called 'administrative law for the transitional period' in the new UNSC Resolution on Iraq, with a view to making it appear internationally legitimate.

This 'law' that has been drawn up by an unelected council under occupation, and through its direct influence, would restrict the national assembly which is due to be elected early next year to draw up the permanent Iraqi constitution.

This is against the laws and rejected by most Iraqi people. Therefore, any attempt to make this 'law' appear legitimate by including it in the international resolution is considered as contrary to the desire of the Iraqi people and a forewarning of dangerous consequences.

Kindly convey the position of the Religious Marja'iyya in this regard to their Excellencies the honourable members of the Security Council.

Thank you.

Seal of the Office of Ayatollah Sistani in Najaf, 6 June 2004

On 24 March, the head of the US Coalition Provisional Authority (CPA), Paul Bremer, signed an order setting up the Iraqi Communications and Media Commission (ICMC). The ICMC will regulate the Iraqi media and will be independent of a future Iraqi government. The body has been allocated a budget of £3.2 million (US$6 million) and will be based on Western models such as the UK regulator Ofcom and the US Federal Communications Commission. (BBC)

On 5 March, **Selwan Abdel-ghani Medhi al-Niemi**, a freelance translator working for the US government-funded Voice of America (VOA), was shot and killed in Baghdad along with his mother and five-year-old daughter. He had been driving home from a relative's house. (CPJ)

ISRAEL

The widow of **James Miller**, the British TV cameraman killed in the Gaza Strip in 2003, has called for a 'full and transparent' investigation into his death, and criticised Israel for delaying the release of the military police report into the killing. Miller was shot in Rafah, while holding a white flag illuminated by a torch, as he approached an Israeli armoured vehicle. (BBC)

Mel Gibson's controversial film, *The Passion of The Christ,* will finally be shown in Israel. Tel Aviv's Cinematheque, an art-house cinema, agreed to show the film after Israeli distributors turned it down because of the controversy that surrounded it. (BBC)

ITALY

Reporter **Fabrizio Gatti** of the daily *Corriere della Sera* was given a 20-day suspended jail sentence on 5 May for giving a false identity to a policeman. He had posed as an illegal Romanian immigrant named 'Roman Ladu' to investigate conditions at a refugee centre. His reports of rights violations at the centre won him a top journalism prize. (RSF)

JAMAICA

On 9 March, US media rights group Freedom House called on the Inter-American Commission on Human Rights to repudiate the Jamaican state's efforts to force the *Gleaner* newspaper group and its former chief editor **Dudley Stokes** to pay a punitive US$1 million fine for libelling former Minister of Tourism Anthony Abrahams in 1987. (Freedom House)

On 27 April, Amnesty International asked the director of public prosecutions in Kingston to clarify reports that he had threatened to prosecute radio talk-show hosts who discussed ongoing court cases. He has accused Amnesty and other rights groups of undermining his office by 'agitation'. (AI)

JAPAN

On 5 April, Japanese state NHK TV and the National Association of Commercial Broadcasters began blocking duplication of programmes on digital TV. The scheme is designed to protect producers' copyrights and prevent duplication for commercial purposes, but consumers have strongly objected. (GILC)

KAZAKHSTAN

President Nursultan Nazarbaev blocked a bill on 22 April that critics feared would undermine freedom of expression in Kazakhstan, choosing to endorse a Constitutional Council ruling that the proposed system of media regulation and registration would violate the Kazakh constitution. Organization for Security and Co-operation in Europe Secretary-General Jan Kubis welcomed the step, but critics note that an existing election law will allow the state to limit political reporting in the run-up to upcoming parliamentary elections (*Index* 2/04). (OSCE)

Jailed newspaper editor **Vladimir Mikhailov** (*Index* 2/04) was released on 26 April. Mikhailov, of the independent daily *Diapazon*, had served six weeks of a politically motivated 12-month jail sentence, applied for failure to comply with planning laws that required him to move a wall in his print house 70 centimetres. (RSF)

On 9 March, **Irina Petrushov**, editor of Kazakh opposition newspaper *Assandi Times*, was arrested in St Petersburg at the behest of the Kazakh government, but subsequently released by Russian police, who, she was privately told, were unwilling to get involved in politically motivated warrants. (CPJ)

Sports journalist **Maxim Khartashov** was hospitalised after an attack by two men on 11 March. He was not robbed. Khartashov has often exposed corruption in Kazakh sports. **Nesip Zhunusbayev**, the editor-in-chief of the weekly *Sport* and *KS*, was sacked by his publisher, Sports Minister Daulet Turlykhanov, after publishing an article critical of the country's national sports authorities. (RSF)

KYRGYZSTAN

The 21-year-old son of **Zamira Sydykova** (*Index* 1–3/01), former political prisoner and editor-in-chief of the independent newspaper *Respublica*, was attacked by four men on 24 April. The incident was linked to four articles written by Sydykova that criticised the leadership of the Interior Ministry. (RSF)

The independent TV station **Pyramida** came back on the air on 27 April, after being shut down for 40 days following an intervention by media investor George Soros. The station stopped broadcasting during a dispute over use of state-owned transmitters. Pyramida Director Andrei Tsetkov said the aim was to block critical political debate in the run-up to October 2004 local elections. (RSF)

LESOTHO

Nthabeleng Sefako, editor of Radio Lesotho's current affairs programme *Seboping*, was threatened on air by Home Affairs Minister Thomas Thabane on 19 May, after she cut short an interview with him to make way for a commercial break. Thabane said Sefako needed to be 'sorted out' and that he would 'keep a close eye on her'. (MISA)

LIBERIA

Liberia's labour minister, Lavella Supawood, has sued the *National Chronicle*, *Monrovia Guardian*, *Forum* and *Heritage* newspapers. Supawood, from the rebel Liberians United for Reconciliation and Democracy (LURD) faction, now part of the National Transitional Government, was named in several articles about attacks on civilian victims during the country's 14-year civil war. (MISA, MFWA)

NEPAL

Dhaniram Tharu, anchor, producer and director of local-language programmes for Swargadwari FM, was arrested by security forces on 13 March with several co-workers in Nepalgunj, a town near the south-western border. Tharu might have been targeted because of Swargadwari FM's airing of critical stories about the government and security forces, as well as detailed reports on the rebels. (INSEC, CPJ)

On 4 April, authorities in the western Jumla District arrested **Khadga Bahadur Swar**, also known as 'KB Jumli', a correspondent for the daily newspaper *Nepal Samacharpatra*. Jumli was accused of Maoist activities and jailed for 90 days under the Terrorist and Destructive Activities (Control and Punishment) Act (TADA). Jumli's detention has been linked to his critical reports on the local administration and security forces, and the fact that he has maintained contact with Maoist sources. (CPJ)

On 8 April, Human Rights Watch said the UN should be authorised to help the Nepalese government investigate human rights violations in the country through its National Human Rights Commission. This would include help in investigating, monitoring and reporting human rights violations in the country. The call came amid reports of widespread violence against peaceful protesters. (HRW)

Police detained and beat over 20 journalists on 7 May as they covered a student-organised mock-political referendum on the country's constitution in Butwal, south-west of Kathmandu. The mock referendum asked respondents to choose between absolute monarchy, constitutional monarchy and a republican democracy. (CPJ)

Police attacked **Nepal**, a senior journalist working for privately owned Kantipur Television Network, in the capital on 16 May. According to local sources, Nepal was covering a political demonstration organised by student groups as part of ongoing protests against King Gyanendra's executive powers. Sources told CPJ that the police had recognised and targeted the journalist, who is known for his aggressive coverage of attacks on civilians by security forces. (CPJ)

On 18 May, Maoist rebels looted and destroyed an FM-transmitting station belonging to state-owned **Radio Nepal** in the village of Jhalari in Kanchanpur. Sources told CPJ that the attack was organised to prevent locals from having access to pro-government news. (CPJ)

NICARAGUA

William Hurtado García was jailed for 18 years on 19 April for the murder of journalist **Carlos José Guadamuz** (*Index* 2/04). Hurtado's wife and the owner of the murder weapon were acquitted of complicity. The victim's family initially accused FSLN leader Daniel Ortega, Guadamuz's former close friend turned bitter foe, of orchestrating the murder, but Hurtado denied the allegation. (RSF)

NIGERIA

African Independent Television reporter **Joseph Nafoh** was assaulted as he attempted to film electoral fraud at a polling station. The attackers were allegedly acting on the orders of candidate Boniface Kobani, a member of the ruling People's Democratic Party (PDP). His seized video camera was later returned with the cassette missing. (MISA, MFWA)

Protestors at an anti-government demonstration in Lagos were tear-gassed and arrested, among them Nobel laureate **Wole Soyinka**, human rights lawyer **Gani Fawehinmi** and leading human rights activist **Beko Ransome-Kuti**. All were later freed without charge. The police said the marchers did not have a permit for the protest. Organisers said that this requirement breaches the constitutional right of freedom of assembly. (IRIN)

Some newspaper vendors in the city of Aba were arrested in May for selling newspapers carrying stories on Biafra, a region that fought for autonomy from Nigeria in a 1960s civil war. Other vendors went on strike until Commissioner of Police Olusegun Efuntayo called for an end to the harassment. (allafrica.com)

MALAWI

Police closed the community radio station **MIJ 90.3** on 23 May, after interviewing opposition spokeswoman Kholiwe Mkandawire, who accused the ruling United Democratic Front (UDF) of stealing elections three days earlier. Station manager **Evans Masamba** was arrested and held overnight with another staffer. (MISA)

The Malawi Communications Regulatory Authority (MACRA) have threatened to close the Catholic Church broadcaster **Radio Maria**, accusing it of partisan coverage. President Bakili Muluzi told the media authorities to 'deal with religious stations that are brewing trouble' after a sermon aired on Radio Maria condemned 'the tendency to impose leaders on the people'. (MISA)

MALAYSIA

The Malaysian government warned local media on 15 April to cut back on news related to the alleged affair of Malaysian-born model Sarah Marbeck and England football captain David Beckham, saying the Australian model tarnished the country's moral image. (*The Age*)

On 17 April, the Malaysian government banned state-controlled radio and television from airing Malay songs containing 'unacceptable' English phrases. (*South China Morning Post*)

On 15 May, Malaysian Information Minister Datuk Paduka Abdul Kadir Sheikh Fadzir announced that the government would give private television stations one month to voluntarily stop screening foreign advertisements and movies considered 'obscene', after which time laws and regulations would be introduced to enforce the directive. As an example, Abdul Kadir cited a Pepsi advertisement that features female pop singers Beyoncé Knowles, Pink and Britney Spears dressed as Roman gladiators. (*The Star, Straits Times*)

MALDIVES

On 1 March, journalist **Ibrahim Lutfee** (*Index* 2/02, 4/02, 2/03, 4/03) addressed a press conference for the first time since escaping detention in 2003. Now living in exile in Switzerland, Lutfee spoke out against the jailing of colleagues producing the Sandhannu email newsletter in 2002, and torture and repression in his country. (RSF)

MAURITANIA

Four editors reached an out-of-court settlement and agreed to publicly repudiate their reports between January 2002 and July 2003 that alleged then Finance Minister Bodiel Ould Houmiel took kickbacks during the sale of an oil refinery. Editors **Moussa Diop** of *L'Eveil Hebdo*, **Oumar el-Moctar** of *l'Authentique*, **Yedally Fall** of *Le Journal du Jeudi* and **Abdel Vettah** of *All Moujatama* had been brought before the state prosecutor on 31 March and 1 April accused of libel. (MISA)

The government refused to legalise a new pro-Islamic political party formed by supporters of former president Mohammed Khouna Ould Haidalla. The Interior Ministry rejected the application from the Parti de la Convergence out of hand on 11 April, arguing that the proposed party leadership contained Islamic radicals, fugitives and convicted criminals. Haidalla was stripped of his political rights for five years on 20 April. The Supreme Court upheld the verdict in December 2003 that Haidalla was guilty of planning a coup. (IRIN)

MEXICO

Roberto Javier Mora García, editorial director of *El Mañana* newspaper, was assassinated on 19 March, stabbed 26 times outside his house in Nuevo Laredo. He was known for his exposé of drug trafficking and murder in the region. On 28 March, Mario Medina Vázquez, a US citizen, was jailed for the killing, though he claimed his confession had been extracted by torture. On 13 May, Vázquez was himself killed by another prisoner in Tamaulipas state prison. (RSF,PSF)

Addressing broadcast media union members on 7 May, President Vicente Fox Quesada reported that he had ordered his Interior Ministry to close some 100 so-called 'clandestine' radio stations, starting that month. Community radio supporters fear that the crackdown is just a cover for a campaign against local media critical of national strategy in Mexico's poorest rural regions (*Index* 1/04). (AMARC)

On 27 April, Jalisco state Supreme Court jailed Huichol Indians Juan Chivarra de la Cruz and brother-in-law Miguel Hernández de la Cruz for 20 years, for murdering *San Antonio Express-News* correspondent **Philip True** (*Index* 2/99). True was killed in December 1998 while working on a story about the Huichol indigenous community that lives in mountains crossing Jalisco, Nayarit, and Durango states. (CPJ)

MOROCCO

Anas Guennoun, director of the weekly *al-Ahali*, was jailed for 10 months on 2 April for criminal defamation. Guennoun, who still faces other separate defamation charges, was the first journalist to be jailed in Morocco since 7 January and a statement by the government that committed the country to a 'fast track' approach to democratisation. (RSF)

Anas Tadili, editor of the weekly *Akhbar al-Ousbouaa*, was jailed on 15 April, ostensibly for failing to pay a fine for a 1994 conviction for illegally opening a bank account overseas. However, the arrest came a week after Tadili published an article entitled 'Homosexuality and the political class in Morocco', which was seen as targeting Finance Minister Fathallah Oualalou. On 19 April, Tadili was charged with maligning the honour of a government minister. (RSF)

MOZAMBIQUE

Anibal Antonio dos Santos (*Index* 4/00, 3/01, 4/01, 1/03, 2/03), sentenced to 28 years' imprisonment for the

murder of journalist **Carlos Cardoso**, has again escaped from jail. Reporters Sans Frontières reported the widespread view that he could not have escaped twice from a supposed maximum-security prison without help from highly placed accomplices to Cardoso's murder who have avoided prosecution. (RSF)

PAKISTAN

On 2 March, about 20 rioters ransacked the offices of the private **Geo** television station in Quetta. The incident occurred after a suicide attack on a religious procession of Shi'ite Muslims in the city claimed at least 47 lives and triggered widespread riots. On 24 February, Geo had broadcast a talk show featuring comments that offended some Shia and led to a 29 February protest against the station outside the Karachi Press Club. About 15 of the protesters stormed the building and beat up a security guard. (CPJ, PPF, *Dawn*)

From mid to late March the authorities barred foreign and local reporters from entering Wana, regional capital of the western province of south Waziristan, during a bloody 12-day confrontation between government troops and Islamic militants. The Pakistan Federal Union of Journalists protested against the 'undeclared ban' on covering the military operation. Local reporters who tried to circumvent the ban faced harassment and, in several cases, brief detention. (CPJ, PPF, *New York Times*)

An Afghan stringer for *Newsweek* working in Pakistan, **Sami Yousafzai**, was arrested with US freelance journalist **Eliza Griswold** when they tried to enter North Waziristan, the scene of fighting between Pakistani troops and Al-Qaida sympathisers. Griswold was expelled to the US but Yousafzai and a driver were held for interrogation by the security services, said a Pakistani official, who said Yousafzai could be 'charged with facilitating and accompanying a foreigner to an unauthorised area'. (*Newsweek*)

On 27 March, **Khawar Mehdi Rizvi**, a local journalist, was released on bail after several weeks in detention for sedition, conspiracy and 'impersonation'. Rizvi was arrested last December along with two French journalists (*Index* 2/04) and later claimed in interviews that he had been tortured while in custody. (CPJ)

US CNN TV producer **Syed Mohsin Naqvi** was detained at his home in Lahore on 10 May while police investigated a tip that there was a bomb in his house. As a result, Naqvi was prevented from joining the return flight of exiled opposition leader Shahbaz Sharif from Abu Dhabi to Lahore on 11 May. The BBC's **Zaffar Abbas** and cameraman **Ali Faisal Zaidi** did make the flight, only to be detained and have their film seized on arrival in Lahore. Shahbaz Sharif, brother of former premier Nawaz Sharif, deposed by General Pervez Musharraf in 1999, was put on a plane out of the country soon after landing in Lahore. (CPJ, *The News, Gulf News*)

The US magazine *New Republic* reopened the debate on who killed *Wall Street Journal* correspondent **Daniel Pearl** in 2002 (*Index* 2/02, 4/02, 3/03). It accused Arab extremists linked to leading Al-Qaida figure Khalid Shaik Mohammed, instead of Ahmed Omar Saeed Sheikh, the British-born man sentenced to death for leading the crime. According to the article, the authorities now suspect Sheikh only conspired to murder Pearl, that he might not have been present at the time Pearl was kidnapped and that he might not have given the order to kill. (*New Republic*)

PALESTINE

Khalil al-Zaben, a prominent Palestinian journalist and human rights adviser to Yasser Arafat, was killed by unknown gunmen outside his Gaza office on 2 March. He died after being struck by a dozen bullets. (APFW)

PANAMA

Roberto Eisenmann, founder of the newspaper *La Prensa*, was detained for questioning by Panama City prosecutors about charges of criminal defamation brought by Attorney General José Antonio Sossa. Eisenmann had earlier accused Sossa of 'protecting criminals and charging journalists'. Later released, he is now barred from leaving the country. (CPJ)

PERU

Peruvian police are seeking the journalists behind a March report in the Lima

daily *La Razûn* about a supposed tape recording of a meeting between President Alejandro Toledo and the former head of the national intelligence service Vladimiro Montesinos, presently being prosecuted for corruption. Montesinos is alleged to have passed on the information from prison. (IPYS)

The 16 April issue of the Arequipa-based *El Búho* was blocked from sale by an organised team who bought up all the available copies of the weekly. The issue featured an investigation on mismanagement at San Agustín National University, and was critical of Rector Rolando Cornejo Cuervo, who was seeking re-election that month. (IPYS)

Journalist **Alberto Rivera Fernandez** was assassinated in his office in Pucallpa, eastern Peru on 21 April. The host of the programme *Transparencia* on Frecuencia Oriental radio, a former member of parliament and president of the Ucayali Journalists' Federation, he had recently criticised local authorities for profiteering from the sale of land occupied by squatters. (IPYS, CPJ)

On 6 May, businessman Fernando Zevallos Gonzalez, presently facing charges of drug trafficking, sued the Lima daily *El Comercio* and a number of its staff for defamation in the reporting of his case. **Fernando Ampuero Del Bosque**, head of the newspaper's investigation unit and **Miguel Ramirez Puelles**, author of articles on the Zevallos case, were all cited. (IPYS)

POLAND

A court in Szczecin postponed the sentencing of journalist **Andrezej Marek** (*Index* 2/04) on 23 March for six months until after his wife gives birth. The editor-in-chief of the weekly *Wiesci Polickie* faces jail for defamation. Polish journalists protested against his treatment by locking themselves in a cage outside parliament the day before. (RSF, RFE/RL)

Beata Korzeniewska of the daily newspaper *Gazeta Pomorska* was jailed for a month after an appeal court reversed her earlier acquittal on charges that she had libelled Torun city judge Zbigniew Wielkanowski. The article reported claims that Wielkanowski had written a letter revealing corruption among Torun lawyers but also his denial of responsibility. (IPI)

RUSSIA

Deputy security council secretary Valentin Sobolev signposted state attitudes to the media on 26 April when he described the media as 'retranslators of terrorism' at a conference in Moscow. He claimed terrorists sought to use journalists to influence public opinion. Duma security committee deputy chairman Anatolii Kulikov said at the same conference that Russia must learn to control information more effectively. (RFE/RL, *Nezavisimaya Gazeta*)

On 30 April, a Moscow city court sentenced Ivan Goncharov to 18 years', Denis Melikhova to 14 years' and Denis Vorotnikov to 10 years' imprisonment for beating 23-year-old journalist **Vladimir Sumkholin** to death in January 2003. Goncharov and Vorotnikov worked for the Directorate of Internal Affairs (UVD) while Melikhova worked as a private security man at the time of the murder. (gazeta.ru)

Reuters TV cameraman **Adlan Khasanov** died of wounds sustained in the 9 May bomb attack on the Dynamo Stadium in Grozny, Chechnya, that killed pro-Moscow president of the Chechen republic Akhmad Kadyrov. (Reuters, CPJ)

Former Federal Security Service (FSB) officer **Mikhail Trepashkin** was jailed for four years on 19 May for divulging state secrets and illegal possession of ammunition. He is best known for his private investigation into alleged FSB links to the 1999 apartment-block bombings in Moscow and other cities. (polit.ru)

Popular TV anchorman **Leonid Parfenov** was sacked from the country's leading channel NTV on 1 June after he publicly protested that his bosses had prevented the broadcast of an interview with the widow of Chechen separatist leader Zelimkhan Yandarbiev, killed in Qatar. One of Russia's most prominent journalists, he claimed that the order had come under pressure from the federal security services, who believed that Yandarbiev's widow would further complicate the case of two Russian agents, currently on trial in Qatar charged with the murder. Parfenov got a written order to drop the item from NTV, which he then leaked to a Moscow newspaper. In turn, NTV had him dismissed for breaking the network's code of conduct and corporate ethics.

RWANDA

Recent publications: *Marked for Death, rape survivors living with HIV/Aids in Rwanda*, Amnesty International, April 2004, 23pp; *Rwanda: The enduring legacy of the genocide and war*, Amnesty International, April 2004

SAUDI ARABIA

Academic **Said bin Zair** was arrested on 15 April after appearing on Qatar-based al-Jazeera TV to discuss a tape attributed to Al-Qaida leader Osama bin Laden, in which he condoned suicide bombings. On 11 May, his son **Mubarak bin-Zair** was arrested for 'false allegations' after he appeared on Al-Jazeera and denounced his father's detention. The month before, lawyer **Abderrahman al-Lahem** was jailed for appearing on the station to criticise the 17 March arrest of intellectual critics of the state, following pro-reform protests in Riyadh. (BBC, APFW)

A new immigration bill was approved by the Saudi Shura Council that will allow Saudi women to retain Saudi citizenship when they marry foreigners. The law will also allow foreign women who marry Saudi men to apply for Saudi nationality. The rights of non-citizens in the country are limited. (BBC)

On 24 March, the Saudi authorities blocked access to the website **gaymiddleeast. com**, a news site for the Middle East's homosexual community. The United States-based website **365gay.com** has also been censored. Posting news intended for homosexuals in 15 countries, gaymiddleeast.com focuses mainly on issues dealing with the persecution of homosexuals. 365gay.com, with which gaymiddleeast.com is affiliated, also deals with homosexual rights. (RSF)

SERBIA & MONTENEGRO

On 1 May, in Belgrade, two unidentified men smashed the camera of a journalist covering the arrest of a key suspect in the murder of who covered the arrest of Prime Minister Zoran Djindjic. **Mashan Lekic** from B92 TV was attacked outside the house of the suspect, Milorad 'the Legionnaire' Lukovic. (RTV B92, Belgrade)

The editor of the Montenegrin daily *Dan*, **Dusko Jovanovic**, was murdered in a drive-by shooting on 28 May in Podgorica. The attack happened as Jovanovic got into his car in front of the paper's head office. Jovanovic was considered close to the conservative opposition in Montenegro and critical of Prime Minister Milo Djukanovic. (CNN)

SOMALIA

On 18 March, reporters **Hassan Haji** and **Mohammed Sheik Nur** from Idaacadda Qur'anka Kariima (Holy Quran Radio) in Mogadishu were threatened when they attempted to cover the closing ceremony of a seminar at the Police School. Orders to remove the reporters reportedly came from the acting governor of Banadir, Abdullah Hassan Ganey. (SOJON)

Abdishakur Yusuf Ali, chief editor of the independent newspaper *War-Ogaal* in the Puntland self-declared autonomous region, was detained on 21 April after he published an article claiming that Puntland Finance Minister Abdirahman Mohamud Farole had sold off humanitarian aid donated by the international community. (SOJON, CPJ, IFJ)

On 26 April, reporter **Abdirahman Haji Dahir** of the independent Somaliland newspaper daily *Haatuf* was arrested in Berbera after alleging that Somaliland President Dahir Riyale Kahin and his vice-president disagreed over the need for a Cabinet reshuffle. (CPJ)

SOUTH AFRICA

The Anti-Censorship Programme (ACP) of the Freedom of Expression Institute (FXI) noted the state's attempts to ban peaceful demonstrations. A protest by the Anti-Privatisation Forum in Johannesburg was banned and 57 of its supporters were arrested when they tried to defy the ban. Other methods are being used to deter public protest. When state-employed doctors marched to parliament in Cape Town on 6 March, the Department of Health ordered its provincial departments to name doctors who joined the protest. (FXI)

SOUTH KOREA

A 12 March amendment to the electoral law gives the National Election Commission increased powers over the Internet, including the ability to force service providers (ISPs) to reveal the names and addresses of users. On 23 March, a 21-year-old student known as **Kwon** was arrested and charged with 'disseminating false information'. He had posted more than 70 satirical images of prominent politicians on various websites. (RSF)

Following the receipt of death threats by phone, email and post, the staff of Internet radio station **Free North Korea** moved offices on 19 May, acting on advice from the Institute of North Korean Studies, a privatised body linked to the South Korean secret services. The first independent radio station to be operated by North Korean exiles, it has angered Pyongyang since its launch on 20 April with its severe criticism of the Stalinist regime. (RSF)

SRI LANKA

After the rebel Liberation Tigers of Tamil Eelam (LTTE) warned Tamil candidates in April's parliamentary elections not to stand for parties other than the pro-Tiger Tamil National Alliance, on 1 March, LTTE gunmen killed **Sinnathamby Sunderapillai**, a Tamil candidate standing for the incumbent United National Party in the eastern Batticaloa region. Sunderapillai, the first candidate to die during the campaign, had been wounded by a failed assassination attempt just two days earlier. The LTTE was also blamed for the murder of **P Yogeswaran**, a member of the LTTE's rival Tamil Eelam People's Democratic Party. (*TamilNet*, BBC, oneworld.net)

On 2 March, a production crew from **Young Asia Television** (YA★TV), dedicated to fostering peaceful coexistence in the country, was harassed and their tapes were destroyed by supporters of the extremist Buddhist Jathika Hela Urumaya (JHU) Party at an election manifesto rally in Kandy. (CPJ)

Several thousand copies of the newspapers **Thinakkural** and **Virakesari** were seized and destroyed on 9 March by an unidentified group as they were being delivered to the eastern city of Batticaloa, stronghold of a breakaway faction of the LTTE. The two newspapers support the mainstream LTTE and its leader Velupillai Prabhakaran. (CPJ, FMM)

Citing allegations of widespread bias in favour of the United Peoples Freedom Alliance coalition (*Index* 2/04), elections commissioner Dayananda Dissanayake took control of state-owned media four days before the 2 April parliamentary elections. Dissanayake appointed WDL Perera as the 'competent authority' for the duration of the campaign and the immediate days after the election. (*Daily Mirror*)

On 2 April, parliamentary election day, the Colombo-based Centre for Monitoring Election Violence advised that voting in the northern Jaffna Peninsula be annulled

and repolled at a later date because of 'systematic impersonation'. Despite similar reports from other election-monitoring outfits in the area, the elections commissioner allowed the vote in Jaffna to stand. (CMEV, *Daily Mirror*)

Iyathurai 'Nellai' G Nadesan, a local correspondent for the Colombo-based daily Tamil-language newspaper *Virakesari* and IBC Radio, run by the LTTE in London, was shot and killed on 31 May in Batticaloa. His death was linked to his strong criticism of breakaway Eastern LTTE leader Colonel Karuna. (Asian Tribune, CPJ)

Recent publications: *The Sri Lanka Peace Process at Crossroads: Lessons, Opportunities and Ideas for Principled Negotiations and Conflict Transformation*, Tyrol Ferdinands, Kumar Rupesinghe, Paikiasothy Saravanamuttu, Jayadeva Uyangoda, Norbert Ropers, January 2004, 40pp; *The Worm Turns and Elections Where the People Will Not Count* – Information Bulletin No. 35 by UTHR (J), 8 March 2004, 26pp; *Unpunished Crimes of the Presidential Security Division (PSD)* – Investigative Report by RSF, 25 March 2004, 6pp

SUDAN

On 2 March, Sudan's oldest-established daily newspaper *Al-Ayam* (*Index* 4/02) re-appeared on the streets after a three-month suspension. The English-language **Khartoum Monitor** (*Index* 4/03) re-appeared on 21 March. The government announced on 16 March that newspaper suspensions would from now on be limited to 24 hours. (RSF)

Veterinary surgeon **Ali Ahmed Daoud** and MP **Hussain Dossa** were arrested in March for organising a meeting in South Darfur about the attacks against villages in the region. They have reportedly been charged with spying for the Sudanese Liberation Army (SPLA). Both men have allegedly been tortured. (AI)

On 10 April, **Islam Salih**, Al-Jazeera's bureau chief in Sudan, was convicted of spreading false news and sentenced to one month's imprisonment and a fine of 1 million Sudanese pounds (US$3,800). He was charged following al-Jazeera's coverage of fierce fighting between rebels and government troops in Dafur. (RSF)

In April, Reporters Sans Frontières and the International Federation of Journalists called on the Sudanese government to lift censorship of the events in South Darfur. According to Human Rights Watch, the army and government-backed militias have displaced almost 1 million civilians in a scorched-earth campaign against non-Arab communities in the region. (IFJ/RSF/HRW)

Recent publication: *Darfur in Flames: Atrocities in Western Sudan*, Human Rights Watch, April 2004

SYRIA

Aktham Naisse of the Committee for the Defence of Democratic Liberties and Human Rights in Syria, was arrested on 15 April in Latakia after organising a sit-in outside parliament in March to mark the 41st anniversary of the Baathist seizure of power in Syria and the start of a 41-year state of emergency. At least 30 people were arrested at the time of the demonstration. (APFW)

Fahd al-Rimawi, editor of the weekly *al-Majd* newspaper, was arrested on 9 May on his return from the US. The arrest resulted from an editorial entitled 'Cowardice is guideline for policies' that accused the Saudis of being 'lackeys' of the US. The authorities said it harmed Syria–Saudi relations. (BBC)

Human rights lawyer Anwar Bunni said at least 300 Kurds had been arrested following unrest in Syria's north-eastern province where members of the Kurdish minority were demonstrating to mark the anniversary of the 1988 gas attack on the Iraqi town of Halabja. At least three people were shot dead in the town of Aleppo and four in Afrin. (BBC)

On 23 March, Syrian Kurdish writer **Muhammad Ghanem** was arrested by military intelligence as he returned home from work at a primary school. No official announcement has been made about his arrest or reasons for it. (APFW)

On 22 February, **Hassan Salih** and **Marwan Uthman**, members of the unlicensed Kurdish Yakiti Party, were released early after a court reduced their sentences for taking part in a demonstration to demand equal rights for Syria's Kurdish minority. The pair had been given three-year sentences for 'trying to annex parts of Syrian territory to an unspecified foreign country'. They were released after the sentences were reduced to 14 months. (BBC)

Syrian authorities ordered the state telecoms network (STE) to block access to two Kurdish websites, **amude.com** and **qamislo.com**, it was reported on 29 March. The managing director of amude.com, Heci Berko, said they would continue to keep opening new sites as existing ones are blocked. (kurdishmedia.com, *Info-Turk*)

TAJIKISTAN

President Imomali Rahmonov removed sales tax from newspaper sales on 20 March in a bid, he said, 'to develop [print] media further and ensure its independence'. He then qualified this by warning the media that it was required to observe the law and 'ensure the country's information and cultural security'. This, he added, required journalists to have a developed sense of patriotism and the need to protect Tajikistan's 'state and national interests'. (RFE/RL)

TANZANIA

In March, **Jenerali Twaha Ulimwengu** was given back the Tanzanian citizenship stripped from him in 2001 for allegedly failing to prove his parents' nationality. At the time the order was seen as a way of punishing him for repeated criticism of the government in his articles and broadcasts. (MISA)

THAILAND

Reporters from foreign news agencies were barred in May from entering military-controlled areas in southern Thailand after reports of clashes between Muslim militants in Yala, Pattani and Songkhla provinces on 28 April angered Prime Minister Thaksin Shinawatra (p11). A military spokesman also asked local media to 'sympathise with us and report news for the benefit of our country'. (*Bangkok Post*)

TOGO

Radio France International correspondent **Guy Mario Abalo** was threatened with death after reporting allegations of corruption by two former government ministers, Saibou Samarou and Agboli Hope. Local newspaper and press freedom groups are concerned for Abalo's safety following the murder of RFI correspondent **Jean Hélène** in October 2003. (RSF)

Security forces assaulted **Yves Kpéto** of Nana FM and **K Amouzouvi** of weekly newspaper *Le Combat du Peuple* as they attempted to cover violent clashes between students and security forces at the Université de Lomé. Nana FM staff went on strike to protest against the treatment of their colleagues. The university itself was closed. Student leader Alphonse Tsogbe claims that the protestors were attacked with sticks, tear gas, rubber bullets and live ammunition. (MISA, MFWA, IRIN)

TONGA

Democracy activist **Alani Taione** (*Index* 2/04) was released on bail on 4 March, given back his passport and allowed to return to New Zealand, where he has lived since 1987. Taione, who is accused of importing a banned publication into Tonga, is due to appear before the Supreme Court on 24 March. His release was conditional on his returning to Tonga for his trial. (RSF)

TUNISIA

The International Federation of Journalists provisionally expelled the Association des Journalistes Tunisiens (AJT) on 8 March after a decision by the AJT to award its Plume D'Or award for press freedom to President Ben Ali in late 2003. The IFJ stated that the AJT had acted contrary to the goals of the federation, and in a manner likely to damage the IFJ. (IFJ)

On 27 March, a demonstration led by 10 human rights groups and five political parties in support of a free and independent press was dispersed by police before they could hand a letter to the head of the state broadcaster demanding that civil society groups be given access to the airwaves. (RSF)

On 6 April, a Tunis court sentenced eight Internet users from the southern city of Zarzis to up to 26 years' imprisonment, basing charges of promotion of terrorism solely on the pages the defendants allegedly read on the web. **Hamza Mahrouk**, **Amor Farouk Chelandi**, **Amor Rached**, **Abdel-Ghaffar Guiza**, **Aymen Mecharek** and **Ridha Hadj Brahim** were jailed and **Ayoub Sfaxi** and **Tahar Guemir**, who live abroad, sentenced *in absentia*. Guemir,

19, was accused of being the ringleader and sentenced to 26 years. On 16 April, a ninth Internet user, aged 17 at the time of arrest, was given 25 months in prison. (RSF)

On 3 May, the Coordinating Committee of Press Freedom Organisations (CCPFO) called upon the organisers of the 2003 Geneva World Summit on the Information Society, to reconsider holding a follow-up summit in 2005 in Tunisia. The CCPFO felt that Tunisian state repression of Internet users made the country an unsuitable location. This view was echoed by the International Press Institute at its annual general meeting on 17 May in Warsaw, Poland. (WPFC, IFEX)

TURKEY

In March, an appeals court overturned *Atilim* journalist **Asiye Zeybek Guzel's** 12-and-a-half-year sentence for 'membership of an illegal organisation'. Guzel, also the editor-in-chief of *Iscinin Yolu* (*Worker's Path*) newspaper, was sentenced in 2002 along with 16 others. Guzel said she had been raped at the anti-terrorism unit's Istanbul centre and denied the charges against her. She was released in 2002 and fled to Sweden with the aid of PEN, and was resentenced *in absentia*. Guzel wrote about her experiences in detention in her book: *Asiye: A Story of Rape in Torture*. (BIA, *Info-Turk*)

The retrial of four Kurdish ex-members of parliament to 15 years' imprisonment – required by a ruling of the European Court for Human Rights – led all four to be resentenced by Ankara State

Security Court, it was reported on 21 April. **Leyla Zana**, **Hatip Dicle**, **Orhan Dogan** and **Selim Sadak** (*Index* 1/97, 6/98, 1/01, 4/01, 4/02, 3/03, 2/04) are still scheduled for release in March 2005. The former members of parliament for the pro-Kurdish Party for Democracy (DEP), banned in 1994, had been jailed that year for alleged 'support for the Kurdistan Workers' Party (PKK)'. (*Cildekt*)

A Turkish court acquitted **Guler Yildiz**, former head of the Mersin-based newspaper *Cinar,* after a third trial. The journalist faced jail for reviewing the controversial *Mehmed's Book* by Nadire Mater, a collection of interviews with veterans of the Turkish army's war in the south-east of the country. The prosecutor said the journalist should be acquitted in line with the EU reforms Turkey has recently passed. (BIA)

Hakan Albayrak of *Milli Gazete* was sentenced to 15 months' imprisonment on 20 May under a 1951 law that prohibits 'insult' against Kemal Atatürk, the revered founder of the Turkish Republic. He had written a commentary that criticised the offering of prayers at the funeral of atheist writer Mina Urgan, which he compared to Atatürk 's funeral. (RSF, BIA)

The same day, the owner of the daily *Vakit*, **Nuri Aykon**, his editor **Harum Aksoy** and **Mehmet Dogan**, author of an article published on 25 August 2003, were ordered to pay damages to 312 generals in the Turkish army. Writing under a pseudonym, Dogan had disputed the competence of the army's senior ranks without naming them. (RSF, BIA)

Freedom of expression groups say that legislative reforms adopted by Turkey linked to its joining the European Union have not led to any significant improvements in press freedom, it was reported on 26 May. Journalists that criticise government institutions or broach taboo subjects like the role of the army in the country's political life, are censored and subjected to heavy penalties. (RSF, BIA)

On 13 May, Turkey's parliament passed a controversial bill supporting religious schools in the face of opposition from the establishment and the army, which see it as a threat to Turkey's established secular system. The bill opens up university places to graduates from technical and religious secondary schools. Currently, the latter are barred from degree courses other than theology, a rule deliberately designed to limit the options of students who attend religious schools. A degree is needed to join the country's civil service, for example. All the universities have condemned the bill. (*Cildekt*)

Kurdish human rights activist **Ferhat Kaya** was detained again following protests against the seizure of land to build an internationally financed pipeline in Kurdish Turkey to further open up Caspian Sea oil reserves. Kaya was arrested on 5 May as he documented the case of people whose land was being used for the pipeline without compensation. After bringing

the cases of 38 others to the European Court of Human Rights he received death threats and was arrested. (*Corner House*, KHRP)

Recent publications: Kurdish Human rights project – Legal Review (2003) 4 KHRP LR November 2003; *Middle East Report – 'Sexuality, Suppression and the State'*, Spring 2004, Number 230

TURKMENISTAN

Mukhamed Berdiyev, a Moscow-based correspondent for the Radio Free Europe/Radio Liberty (RFE/RL) Turkmen service, was beaten unconscious by three men and left for dead in his home on 30 April. They also destroyed his computer. Media rights groups suspect Turkmen secret police are to blame. An unnamed official at the Turkmen embassy in Moscow said that the report was an attempt, 'once again', to draw attention to a reporter 'constantly addressing the so-called issue of human rights in Turkmenistan'. (RFE/RL)

Reporters Sans Frontierès and the Committee to Protect Journalists cited Turkmenistan as Central Asia's worst country for free expression. In its 2004 Annual Report, issued on 3 May, RSF ranked Turkmenistan as the fourth worst place to work as a journalist, after Iraq, Cuba and Zimbabwe. President Saparmurat Niyazov was said to have 'constructed a cult of personality that would have made Romania's Ceauşescu blush'. All newspapers cite Niyazov as their founder and he personally appoints all editors. (CPJ, RSF, RFE/RL)

UGANDA

Recent publication: *Uganda: Torture Used to Deter Opposition, Human Rights Watch*, April 2004

UKRAINE

On 24 March, a group of international experts arrived in Kiev to study the 'Melnichenko tapes' which are said to link the country's highest authorities with the murder of journalist **Georgy Gongadze**. However, the prosecutor's office refused to allow the experts a supervisory role in the investigation. (RSF)

On 6 April, **Dimitry Pozhydayev**, webmaster of the online Crimean Linia news service, was attacked by four skinheads who then robbed him. Pozhydayev believes that the attack was connected to Crimean Linia's critical coverage of local Communist Party leader Leonid Grach and its exposé of skinhead gangs. (IFEX, RSF)

Journalist **Volodymyr Boyko** was beaten by police after he tried and failed to report the trial of **Mykhaylo Haladzhi** of the Donetsk newspaper *Svoboda* in April. After he refused to leave the open court, he was ejected and assaulted. (RFE/RL)

On 22 April, President Leonid Kuchma vetoed a bid by the country's national council to make use of Ukrainian compulsory on radio and TV. Kuchma said the council's 14 April ruling was unconstitutional and had no legal force. (BBC)

MEET THE NEIGHBOURS

A PERSONAL AND IDIOSYNCRATIC EXCURSION
INTO 'NEW EUROPE' CONDUCTED BY ITS
POETS, NOVELISTS, JOURNALISTS AND
PUBLISHERS, AND INTRODUCED BY UMBERTO
ECO WHO URGES THE ENLARGED UNION TO
'UNITE OR PERISH'

*With the exception of Umberto Eco and Michael Foley,
all articles reproduced courtesy Courrier International*

MAY THE FORCE BE WITH YOU
UMBERTO ECO

UNITE OR DIE. EITHER EUROPE GETS ITS
HOUSE IN ORDER AND FORMS A STRONG THIRD
FORCE IN THE WORLD – OR IT GOES THE WAY
OF ALL SMALL STATES: SEMI-OBLIVION

This is hardly the best time to be making predictions about the prospects of a united Europe. The divergent positions European countries have taken on the question of the Iraq conflict have shown just how divided the Continent is. The Eastern countries' entry brings in a contrast between old democracies that are prepared to cede at least some of their national sovereignty to the Union, and younger democracies determined to reinforce their newly formed national governments – even if it means making alliances outside Europe's boundaries.

The way things are looking, we have on the one hand a European consciousness and identity that really does exist and, on the other, a set of circumstances that directly threaten that very unity.

Let us take some of the fundamental principles of the so-called Western world: the Greek and Judaeo-Christian heritage, the French Revolution's notions of liberty and equality, the foundations of modern science laid down by the likes of Copernicus, Galileo, Kepler, Descartes and Francis Bacon, the capitalist mode of production, the secular state, Roman or Common Law and the idea of justice achieved through class struggle. These are the achievements, the products of Europe, but they no longer belong to Europe alone. They have been introduced, established and confirmed in the USA and Australia, and in many parts – though not all – of Asia and Africa.

Nowadays, we can talk freely about Western civilisation (a concept that is increasingly confused with the globalisation process in its current form) without any sense that we are referring to a specifically European form of civilisation.

At the same time, a specific European identity is emerging ever more clearly within the wider category of Western civilisation. It is not when we visit other countries in Europe that this is most evident – on such occasions we are more inclined to note how different things are, though a Sicilian arriving in Milan or a Venetian in Calabria senses similar differences. It is when we come into contact with a non-European culture – including that of the United States – that our European identity really comes out. There are moments, during a conference or an evening with friends from different countries, or even on holiday, when I suddenly sense a shared feeling that makes the behaviour, opinions and tastes of a Frenchman, a Spaniard or a German somehow more familiar than those of people from further afield.

Last December, the philosopher and French MP Luc Ferry, opening a convention on peace in Paris, noted that a war against Germany is now absolutely inconceivable for a Frenchman (the English could no more imagine going to war on Italy, or the Spaniards attacking Flanders). Ferry was not saying anything new, but the way he put it was dramatic. After all, precisely these kinds of conflicts and enmities were the norm across Europe for 2,000 years. We are in a historically new situation, unthinkable even 50 years ago. This is not always entirely apparent or present in our consciousness but it is there in everything we do, regardless of how educated or politically aware we are: short holidays or shopping trips regularly take us quite nonchalantly over borders that our fathers would only ever have crossed under arms.

There are any number of reasons why a Frenchman might still feel distinct from a German, but each now has behind him a set of experiences that have marked both countries. Our collective memory as Europeans is extremely important and cannot fail to have informed our thoughts and beliefs. We share an idea that well-being is to be reached through working together in unions and not through unshakeable success-driven individualism. We remember the fall of imperialism and the loss of our respective colonies. We remember dictatorship close at hand; we know what it is and can recognise its early symptoms; it might also be true to say – of a large number of us anyway – that we have been immunised against it. We remember war on our own soil and the continuing presence of danger that comes with it. If two aeroplanes had ploughed into Notre Dame or Big Ben, the reaction would certainly have been one of shock, pain and indignation. But it would not, I daresay, have reached the level of stupefaction – or produced the violent swings between severe depression and an instinct for immediate revenge – seen in Americans after 11 September, when they were attacked on their own soil for the first time in history.

So Europeans have a lot in common – joy and pain, pride and shame, traditions to defend and regrets to consider. Also, every European country has its own experience of proximity to African and Asian countries, with which it has kept up relations. By turns, these have been either friendly or hostile relations; what they have never been is transoceanic relations.

Is all this enough to make a truly united Europe? As we see every day, despite the euro and the simple fact that so many countries wish to be part of this community, the answer has to be a definite no. It seems we all wish to be part of a union for which we renounce part of our national autonomy but not all of it. And nations are quite prepared to provoke new disagreements, as their divergent positions on the Iraq war have shown.

But the fact is, the unity that Europe cannot find within itself is now being imposed upon it by world events. During the Cold War, Europe had just emerged from World War II and had to live its newly divided life behind the shield of other powers: the US for the West and the USSR for the East. China might have become a fearsome adversary for the US in the long term, but at the time it was fighting for its own internal stability and was actually less directly antagonistic towards the US than it was towards the Russians. The US could suffer a stalemate in Korea and a defeat in Vietnam; for it was in Europe that things were really being played out, and it was in Europe that the US found victory with the fall of the Soviet Empire. The European countries were caught in the middle of this game and had to shape their respective foreign policies according to which of the two blocs they belonged to: accepting a common military defence policy through either NATO or the Warsaw Pact.

The panorama changed with the fall of the Berlin Wall, yet it is only in the last few years that the old knots have really come undone. A key turning point was reached when the limits of US interest in the Balkan question became apparent. Now that their enemy of 50 years had been defeated, the US had noticed that it had another enemy, whose territory was not clearly defined but which was certainly located in the Muslim world, between the Near and the Far East. It directed its military force against this new threat: against Kabul and Baghdad, and maybe beyond, in a new military adventure that has even led it to move some of its bases. In any case, the US was realising that NATO could no longer be depended on for full support, not least because it emerged that European countries, for historical and geographical reasons, could not avoid having a relationship with the Arab world that was, in part, contrary to US interests.

In the meantime, it has become clear that the next great confrontation foreseen by the US will, indeed, be with China. There is no reason to suppose that this will take the form of a war, but it will certainly be an economic and demographic conflict. You only have to visit a US university to see how Asian students are taking more and more of the scholarships, research positions and student leadership roles (genetic considerations aside, these people are culturally far more prepared than their European peers to work 18 hours a day in order to succeed). America's scientific development will increasingly depend on the importation of brains – not from Europe, but from Asia: from India, China and Japan. This means that the US will turn its gaze away from the Atlantic and towards the Pacific. Already, for years now, major research and production centres have either moved to or emerged on the Californian coast. In the long term, New York will be America's Florence – still a centre for fashion and culture, but the location for fewer and fewer truly important decisions. The US is on its way to becoming a Pacific rather than an Atlantic country. This has clear implications for Europe: where the Wasps of the 1920s worshipped a Parisian ideal, in future the Americans who matter will be living in places that don't even get the *New York Times* (or at least not until the next day and only at specific outlets). They will live in places where people know barely anything about Europe, and when they hear about it they won't understand the point of this exotic continent, much further removed from them than Hawaii or Japan.

With the US turning its attention towards the Middle East and the vast universe of the Pacific, the old continent could find that it no longer matters. In any case, even the most decidedly pro-American among us will have to admit that the US, roots or no roots (and there are plenty of Americans with Asiatic surnames), will not be losing sleep over a continent that is clearly not about to submit to the Nazi Panzers or let Cossack horses drink the holy waters of St Peter's.

It is something along the lines of Hegelian doctrine to say that reality is rational and leads the way and that all things must follow it. Here, Europe, left alone through force of circumstance, must either become European or disintegrate.

The disintegration hypothesis seems unrealistic, but it is worth outlining. Europe could become Balkanised, or go the way of South America. The new world powers (and in future that might mean China instead of the US) will use the small European countries for their own benefit, according to whether it is more convenient for them to have their bases in Poland or Gibraltar – or to launch attacks via the pole from Tallinn or Helsinki. And the more divided Europe is, the less competitive the euro becomes on the international markets, so much the better. You can't blame a superpower for putting its own interests first.

Alternatively, Europe could find the energy to establish itself as a third power between the US and the Far East (whether that means Beijing or, who knows, Tokyo and Singapore).

There is only one way for Europe to become that third pole. Having achieved market unity, freedom of movement and a single currency, it must build a pan-European foreign policy backed up by a European defence force. This force does not need to be very big – a European invasion of China or war with the US does not figure in any rational outlook – but it needs to be enough to allow Europe the defence system and the possibility of swift intervention that NATO can no longer guarantee.

Will European governments be able to reach agreement on such issues? In his article, Habermas suggests that it would be impossible to achieve this in the immediate future with an enlarged Europe that includes Estonia, Turkey and perhaps, even some day, Russia. But the project could involve the nucleus of countries that founded the European Union. If a proposal came out of that nucleus, maybe other countries might gradually fall into line.

This may be a utopian view. But rational analysis reveals that this utopia is now indispensable if the old continent is to survive in the new world order. Europe simply has to establish a common foreign and defence policy. Either that or nothing. Either that or, without wishing to offend anyone, we will become Guatemala.

This is the point of the appeal we, as European citizens, are making to the national governments of the continent where we were born and in which we would like to continue to live and to take pride. ❑

Umberto Eco's *most recent book is* Baudolino *(Secker & Warburg, 2003).*
This essay will be included in an anthology on the future of Europe with contributions by, among others, Ales Debeljak, Jacques Derrida, Slavenka Draculic, Jürgen Hadermas, Irena Maryniak, Richard Rorty and Fernando Savater, to be published in autumn 2004 by Eurozine; available directly from www.eurozine.com

Translated by Gulliver Cragg and publilshed courtesy Eurozine

ALWAYS THE BRIDESMAID
MARTIN PLUHACEK-REINER

BRNO In the heart of old Brno stands the former town hall with its panoramic tower. As do all towers, it resounds with the pattering of pigeon-feet and the confused flapping of their wings.

The first time I went up there, it was with my grandfather. From the great height of the stone tower, we contemplated the city below in silence.

'So that's Brno,' my grandfather eventually commented.

'I know that!' I retorted, somewhat put out, but my grandfather did not reply; he was gazing into the distance again, across this green-grey-red sea, rippling slightly in the haze of sun and wind. My mother hadn't come with us – she was making lunch. She had not failed to remind my grandfather, as we were leaving, that he really ought to have a shave. She said he looked like Bakunin. But, as usual, my grandfather merely grinned a toothy grin, just like Bakunin's.

I was six years old those holidays and unlike my mother I was very pleased that my grandfather had such a long beard. The wind could bend it right up to his shoulder. I knew full well which town it was that lay below me, though I was a little frightened to approach the railing, and looked down on it from behind the columns, my back against the cold wall. Brno was where I'd been born and I'd already had plenty of memorable experiences there. With my own eyes I had watched Giacomo Agostini cut the perilous Farina bend on the motorcycling Grand Prix circuit so you never thought he'd make it; I'd been deathly sick the summer before after eating a banana by Lake Brno; and I'd have drowned at Sokolak if it hadn't been for Yannis Kiriakidis, who lived with my mother and spent every Saturday at the Slavia café, where all Brno's Greeks used to meet.

But compared with my grandfather, nothing had happened to me here yet, for he had been born in Brno under [the Emperor] Franz Josef, as he was always reminding people. That's why I didn't understand how he could now look over the town with such an air of wonder.

'Look,' he said, placing a heavy hand on my puny shoulder. 'Do you see anything down there?' His right arm was indicating a point in the sky. I opened my eyes wide and stared into the bright blue until they hurt, but I couldn't see anything.

'Grandpa, there's nothing there,' I moaned, a little annoyed.

'Brno is interesting above all for what you cannot see,' my grandfather explained. 'It's true, there's nothing here, but there might have been something. Just there, at the bottom of Koblinza Street, they were going to build an actual skyscraper, the first in Europe.' He paused, then continued: 'You know what a skyscraper is?'

'Of course I do! It's a big tower!'

'Back then it was a major event: at the Brno International Fair at the Bata stand, there was a four-metre model with a giant globe on top that was going to house a café. Twenty-four storeys!'

Today, 30 years later, I'm looking down on the city from the top of the same tower, the wind is blowing and, as you will not be surprised to learn, I am alone. Grandpa has been dead for a long time but Brno, changed beyond recognition, is still fundamentally the same. So that's Brno, I say to myself, remembering my grandfather's legendary phrase. Grandpa, I know now the story of our skyscraper, that shining finger with which our city could have touched the stars of Europe, if only once. Back then, dear Bakunin (he lies beneath the cypresses in Centralka, a stone's throw from Leoš Janáček's grave), the 1930s left-wing avant-garde revolted against the capitalist presumptuousness of the shoe manufacturing magnate Bata, who wanted to stamp out Brno's historic centre with one enormous boot. Do you find it strange that the left-wing avant-garde should have wished to preserve a few crumbling old buildings? But of course they didn't! Bohuslav Fuchs himself, who was not only Brno's most successful architect at that time but also one of the editors of *Blok,* a left-wing magazine, had submitted a project for the skyscraper to Bata. And his wasn't the only bid. But when Bata ended up cancelling the competition only to hand the project shortly afterwards directly to his architect, Vladimir Karfik, newly returned from some US university, the Brno avant-garde made such a fuss that even cats on heat fell silent, slack-jawed.

And do you know what saved us in the end? The famous shifting sands of Brno! Yes, the sand. Like an insatiable anaconda, just picking out a victim every now and again, a giant mouth could suddenly open up in Brno's old pavement and swallow up some innocent old lady and her umbrella, sucking her for ever more into the digestive system of the city's underbelly and towards un unknown destination. And, there's no doubt about it, it was because this anaconda would have been equally capable of swallowing up a 20-storey tower in one go that the city of Brno ended up withdrawing

Tomas Bata's planning permission. I am so obsessed with that skyscraper that it obscures my view of all the wonderful things about Brno that I would have liked to mention, just as much as if it had really been built. What is it that makes this city, quite plain on first impression, so exceptional to my eyes? Just this: this kind of suppressed grief. Great lost hopes.

Brno is often dubbed 'the biggest village in the Czech Republic' though it has over 500,000 inhabitants. In our little country, Brno will always play second fiddle, forever envying its big sister, Prague. And Brno knows how to envy – that's for sure! When you do something for a long time and you do it well, people can always tell. Travel to Brno on the motorway from Prague, for example. You will notice that on the first part of your journey, the road surface is as smooth as a mirror, but as soon as you cross the imaginary border between Bohemia and Moravia, as soon as you've got two wheels on Moravian tarmac, the motorway begins to ripple with bumps and crevasses and you jolt and jerk your way along it until the valley opens up to reveal Brno's unprepossessing panorama. Brno knows how to look ugly. Just like that, out of plain sulkiness. As the city gets fatter, its skin grows blotchy, its Sunday best creased from negligence . . . You didn't want me? Well, never mind: now you'll want me even less!

When Prague, too, lived in the shadow of a big sister – imperial Vienna – Brno was known as 'the suburbs of Vienna'. But that sounds too grand. If Brno was ever a suburb to Vienna it was a nasty one, tainted by factory chimneys – tile manufacturers and textile mills – so many masts giving the city the air of a boat forever about to sail away somewhere else. The old town managed to hold on to its character as a grand old Moravian-German seat until 1918, though its fearsome ramparts were long gone. When the Czechoslovak Republic was created, the city's population was two-thirds German and most of its capital was in the hands of German Jews.

It may well have been thanks to this that Brno did have its hour of glory – the only one so far. The young republic had to do something about what was already its second-largest city, and so it created, by decree, 'Greater Brno', which was in fact the simple annexation to the municipality of 23 nearby villages – all full of Czechs, of course. Thanks to this ruse, Brno became a Czech city – a Moravian city, to be precise. The first Czechoslovak president, the legendary Tomás Garrigue Masaryk, was himself a Moravian and had a soft spot for Brno. The city obtained the status of regional capital and a substantial budget to go with it. It soon showed. Vast exhibition halls sprung up just outside the city centre; they remain the city's

Czech republic: Prague café. Credit: all photographs Ania Dabrowska 2002

most important economic asset even today. In the hinterland, a motor-racing circuit was laid out, and the legendary Tazio Nuvolari roared along it, looking like a petrified lemur in his yellow jersey. But the true symbol of the circuit was to be the French racer Louis Chiron. Even today, people in Brno use the expression 'he drives like a Chiron' to describe an imprudent driver. In those days, the city's intelligentsia used to drink from French tankards in the bars and cafés . . . How on earth did the poet Vitezslav Nezval, that great balloon of hot air who never shut up, manage to seduce the Parisian surrealists into taking an interest in Brno? How did he pull that off, with his execrable French? With ease: he did nothing but flatter them, he fainted with pleasure, stroked the hands – as was his wont – of all these young men with their combative senses of humour, and wept for joy . . . and it worked. In April 1935, André Breton arrived in Brno, accompanied by Paul Eluard, and the old waxing of Breton's lecture entitled 'What is surrealism?' still haunts the archives of Radio Brno.

The most important phenomenon of this short but glorious period of the first republic was the emergence of the avant-garde, mainly functionalist architecture. This became one of the young republic's most important calling cards, and helped the Czechs gain recognition. It is true that the most famous functionalist building, Villa Tugendhat at Cerna Pole, was built by a German – Mies van der Rohe – but it was undeniably born of the peculiar urban context to be found here. It was grandiose and beautiful. It was something people wanted to believe in and that seemed possible.

That's when Hitler came to Brno. On 17 March 1939, the Führer arrived in his black limousine to greet his followers and stood outside the town hall so that a chubby little boy could ceremonially thank him for liberating his compatriots from the oppression and the pain that they had undergone up until then. Brno was thus to remain an important town, albeit a German one . . . thanks to its armaments factory.

After the war, it was the communists' turn. With the aid of a few zealous apparatchiks, they created the local tyrants, the worst imaginable – the ones whose survival instinct is so overpowering that they strike pre-emptively. The chins of those intellectuals who had not left the country after the communist takeover in 1948 grew long, straggly beards while their noses sprouted the red weeds of alcohol and all but the most mediocre soon moved to Prague.

I am at the top of the tower of the old town hall, the wind is blowing and maybe that is why there are tears in my eyes. It is spring 2003. As a child, I never believed I would live to see this day – I thought years beginning with '2' would for ever remain the preserve of books by Ray Bradbury and Jules Verne. But I believed in my grandfather's Brno. And today, I'd like to make a wish: O mystical fish of Lake Brno, please stop the French and international author Milan Kundera from visiting his home town in secret, incognito, as he has always done. ❏

Martin Pluhacek-Reiner, poet, short-story writer and publisher, was born in Brno in 1964. He was imprisoned under communism and became a spokesman for the post-communist Czech Ministry of Culture in 1989. He is now a director of Brno publisher Lidová Demokracie-Petrov, and co-founder of the journals Proglas and Neon

Translated by GC

A HOME NAMED TAMMIKU

JAAN KAPLINSKI

There is a word in Estonian, *kodu*, that does not translate easily into some languages, French or Russian for instance, though there are good equivalents in English — home; in German — *Heim*; and the Scandinavian *hem*. Etymologically, *kodu* is linked to the ancient word *koda*, which referred to the house or hut. So, in fact, the Estonian says the same thing as the Frenchman: to be at home (*kodus*) means to be in one's domestic space or house.

Kodu is therefore the place where one feels at home. The word identifies a geographical place — a house, a flat, a room — as a place where one's nearest and dearest — family, husband and wife, parents and children — gather together. The Chinese word *jia* signifies the house, the home, as well as the people who live there — the family. To get married means to create a common home. Thus there cannot be a home without love, without the feeling of making up a unit, of forming a family. When this feeling disappears, that means the end of the home, too: the couple part, going their separate ways to lead their separate lives. Nowadays, the home is also the most precious possession for most people: it is there that they keep what belongs to them and gather what is near and dear to them.

Love for one's nearest and dearest broadens into love for one's home. It is difficult to separate one from the other. Nostalgia for the home is also nostalgia for the family and our loved ones. To be without a home is a great misfortune, sometimes as tragic as to be bereaved of a close relative. Tens of millions of people across the world have undergone this sad experience, including millions of Europeans driven from their homes by war or by terror. Among these millions were myself and my parents. We, too, lost our home during the war; which is why that loss is what the war represents for us above all. War is a period when man and his home are in danger, where one can find oneself without a home, taken far away, even sent to a concentration camp.

In the Soviet Union, deportation was one of the Stalinists' favourite activities. Families, *kulaks*, villages and even entire peoples, such as the Kalmuks and the Chechens, were displaced. This is what happened in Estonia, too: in June 1940, for instance, one week before the war started, 10,000 people were arrested and sent far east, to the north of Russia or

Siberia. The men, regarded as more dangerous, were dispatched to prison camps, where most of them died – among them my father. The women and children were generally sent to villages that they were not permitted to leave and where they had to work in the *kolkhoz* (collective farm). Most managed to survive and later returned to their country. In Estonia, the fatherland is often called *kodumaa*, the home country, where one is at home.

Estonians were sent to concentration camps on other occasions, too – always in entire families, and most of the time to Siberia. After the war, living conditions were easier over there; some deportees managed to settle adequately in their new place of residence and earn a lot of money. However, after Khrushchev's 'thaw', when camp prisoners began to be freed and deportees were permitted to return home, very few chose to remain on foreign soil. Even those whose situation was excellent – and whom the authorities occasionally tried to persuade to stay (among them some very able workers) – returned to Estonia.

As I mentioned, my father died in a prison camp in Russia. But the other members of my family were left alone, although my grandfather (a former bookseller) and my mother (a prisoner's wife) lost their jobs and had to earn their living by taking on various casual work.

My grandfather's huge house on the edge of town was commandeered by the German army, which assigned us a flat in the centre instead. But this was destroyed in a fire, and we took refuge in a flat where four families lived and shared a kitchen and bathroom. Six of us had to live, study and work in two rooms, where it was impossible to be alone. Not surprisingly, I did not feel at home and wanted to leave – and sometimes wanted us to be sent to Siberia as well, because I thought there was more space there.

Fortunately, nothing of the sort happened; and I was able to escape the cramped world of the city during the summer. Since my childhood I have always spent the summer in the country. It wasn't easy to find places to spend the holidays; we had a lot of relatives in the country, but some had been sent to camps, others declared *kulaks* and driven from their homes. My mother and I spent one summer here, one summer there, depending on what was available – until the day when my great-aunt and her daughter agreed to take me in with them, at Pindi. Throughout the 10 years that followed, their farm became my second home and my second school.

This house, which we called 'Tammiku farm', was a modest 'new farmers' lodging of the kind that was built in the 1930s on estates seized from big German landowners: three rooms, a kitchen, a small cowshed, a barn, a shed, and two or three hectares of land, most of which had been assigned to the collective. This house and its inhabitants embodied for me a large part of twentieth-century Estonian history and culture.

It was my aunt who took me to Pindi the first year. We went by taxi from Võru, the nearest town. We were met by my great-aunt Anna, with her daughter Meeta and her grandson Are. His father and two brothers were not there. They had been arrested for taking part in an [anti-Soviet] resistance movement and sent to a labour camp. Some armed partisans had also been hiding in the house. Fate decreed that the last of them would die on the day of our arrival but in another part of Estonia. Meeta, my mother's cousin, was driven to town the following day, where she had to testify that the 'forest brother' [resistance fighter] lying in the morgue was indeed their distant relative Jaan.

This sinister incident marked the end of the resistance movement in Estonia. I was dimly aware of it, but there were three other more essential things to me at Pindi: contact with nature, the forest and the river; my friendship with Are; and books. For the little house (including the shed) was full of old books, magazines, musical scores, albums; most of the publications printed in Estonia in the course of the last half-century could be found there. My great-aunt and her husband were primary school teachers; her husband was, moreover, organist and choirmaster at the church. He was a subscriber to most of the quality magazines and bought most 'serious' books: he had books on education, technical manuals, children's magazines, literary reviews, religious books, books on nature, and many others besides. Thanks to him, there were many musicians in the family: Meeta's husband Ants and their oldest son played the violin, while the younger son, Kalle, later became a highly renowned music teacher. But for the moment, they were still all in a prison camp and could only write brief cards of a few sentences to their family. All the same, I managed to hear music in the house: my great-aunt would sometimes play some Lutheran chorale on the old harmonium, and Are would play easy pieces on the piano.

There had been searches and raids on the farm: the agents of the security forces were looking for the 'forest brothers', but as they didn't find them they took away whole bagfuls of old books. Yet there were still enough left, and it wasn't their appearance that interested me, but their contents. I would rummage about for hours, for whole days, in the stacks of books, reading what fell into my hands in a haphazard way but passionately, forgetting myself, sometimes not hearing when I was called to dinner. One day, I was so absorbed in my reading in the attic that I didn't come down when my aunt called me, and she went to look for me in the forest (which was right next to the house).

When I had had enough of reading, I would go into the shed and make something out of wood, or wander off into the forest or go fishing by the river. In the shed I would sometimes content myself with watching Are make something – he was a few years older than me and was cleverer with his hands as well. Sitting on the ladder, I used to watch him in silence, sometimes for hours. The forest began 20 paces from the house and stretched out over tens of kilometres. Great pines grew on mounds of sand, while the lowest spots were filled with impenetrable copses of fir trees. A few kilometres from the farm there was a lake, which was easy to reach by passing alongside a ditch that connected it to the river. The owner of the estate had had this ditch dug long before to lower the level of the lake and so to dry out the peaty pine forest that ran beside it. But the slope of the ditch was not correct and the project was a failure. The ditch was half filled in by vegetation. Here and there you could see puddles full of dark water mingled with peat. In the peat bog, the pines were small, more spaced out, and in between them Marsh Ledums and other peat bog plants proliferated. The Marsh Ledum (*Ledum palustre*) has a heady, intoxicating scent. Some people complain that the smell makes them dizzy. Compared with an ordinary forest, there is something strange and mysterious about a peat bog, which I sensed too. I remember one day spending longer than usual coming back from the lake. The forest darkened and I was suddenly seized with fear; all around me seemed unfamiliar and plunged into a silence heavy with menace. I hurried home, almost at a run, and felt a tremendous sensation of relief when I saw the big silver birch growing next to the farm come into view through the trees. Fifty years ago, this lake was a peaceful spot where I never met anyone. Stretching out behind it was a beautiful overhanging sandy forest. Carrying on along the lake, you would reach a farm which was almost at the edge of the road; further still was the river with the mill of Paidra on its the bank. This was where my grandmother and her seven sisters and her brother had spent their childhood. The oldest of the sisters, my great-aunt Anna, had stayed there, wanting to live near her childhood home; fate had led others farther away, one of them as far as Manchuria, where she had vanished in the turmoil of World War II. The Paidra mill was still in operation when I used to spend my holidays with my great-aunt, and once or twice we carried a sack of grain there to be ground.

I was still merely a child with insufficient empathy or imagination to weigh up all the terrible absurdity of this situation in an Estonian village. Nor did I understand the significance for Meeta and Anna of the letters sent by father and son from the camps of Siberia; that I only began to understand much later. The first summers I spent in the attic or the barn, and I read and read. I read absolutely everything: poems, educational reviews, women's magazines, religious publications, manuals on bird breeding and beekeeping, the journal of the young Red Cross, historical and literary reviews. Sometimes I went down to the river to go fishing – the rivers of Estonia were still well stocked with fish at the time – and I went swimming with Are and the boys of the village; I learned to ride a bicycle and took part in small jobs on the farm.

When Stalin died, I was in the city. I remember the day the news was announced. I was at the riverside with a classmate: we were pushing the blocks of ice wedged on the bank out into the current with a stick. There seemed something symbolic about it. In the country, Meeta was working at the cowshed on the collective with the other women. When the radio announced that Stalin was dead, they all began jangling their buckets. With this funeral music these simple working women bade farewell to the man whom the newspapers called 'the great leader and teacher of the working people'.

After his death, great changes took place in Estonia, as they did in the rest of the Soviet Union. We began to receive messages from relatives and friends abroad. Even the prisoners in the camps could now start to send long letters, not just brief cards. The workers on the collective were able to make hay for their cows on the communal grassland, and they were decently paid for their efforts. People gradually repaired the ruined roofs and walls. Meeta's cowshed had a new roof made of light-coloured wood that had a pleasant resinous scent. Throughout the summer, a long ladder stayed in position up there that I used to enjoy sitting on: from the rooftop, the view stretched far and wide. One evening, when the sun had already set, I noticed a tall man walking along the road in the direction of the forest with a suitcase in his hand. A while later, I saw him come out of the forest again. He went into our garden, then into the house. It was then that I realised this could only be the family's second boy, Kalle, who had been freed from the camp and was returning home.

The days that followed provided me, like many other people in the village, with detailed knowledge of the gulag. Kalle, the former prisoner,

Estonia: Tallinn striptease, the new face of Estonia's medieval capital

would be seated in the kitchen, and our relatives, friends and a few neighbours would listen to his story in silence. He told of the cross-examinations, the beatings, the bloody brawls between the common prisoners and the political prisoners, the work in the mines and on the building sites, the hunger, the bitter cold, the prisoners' rebellions and their suppression. These accounts of the reality of the camp were an important complement to the knowledge I had gained from my reading in my great-aunt's attic and barn. Kalle had been freed before his older brother and his father: he had only been 16 at the time of his arrest. But he was a good storyteller, and I still remember some of his stories, just as I remember the little kitchen at the farm, the paraffin lamp lit on the table and the grave faces of the silent villagers.

The return of the first prisoners marked for us the beginning of Khrushchev's 'thaw'. Like swallows or larks, they heralded the spring. In the years that followed, many things changed on the farm: electricity was installed, a little sauna was built, the master of the estate repaired the dilapidated walls, and flowers and ornamental trees were planted. We started to hear the strains of the violin and piano once more. I was already going to secondary school, but I still spent summers at my great-aunt's, dividing my time between reading, walking and working on the farm. I developed a passion for literature. I read Estonian poetry, but also translations from Baudelaire, Leconte de Lisle, Shelley and Keats that I discovered in the house in old literary reviews. These also contained articles on the great philosophers of the twentieth century – Bergson, Whitehead, Dilthey – which I also tried to read, in spite of their difficulty. Yet this gave a certain foundation to my conception of philosophy: I now knew that this could be something altogether different from Marxist-Leninist philosophy, the only kind recognised by the establishment and which I would soon have to study at university.

I can therefore look upon this modest little farmhouse as having been my second school. Had it not been for that attic, that barn and that library in the living room, had it not been for the stories of gulag life told by the men returning from the camps, had it not been for the need to help Meeta make hay and take care of the bees, and the chance to potter about in the workroom, my education would have been much the poorer. When I arrived at university to study the humanities, I had already read many things to which young people of my age had been denied access. I was perhaps more cultivated and with a more critical attitude. This was useful to me subsequently but, at the time, caused trouble with the authorities, who did not look kindly on a young man exercising critical thought.

During my student years, I went to Tammiku every summer; I read books, went on long bicycle rides and sometimes Kalle or Ako would take me for long rides on their motorbikes. Once I was married and the father of a family, my visits to Tammiku became more infrequent, especially after the deaths of my great-aunt and Meeta, when the farm was taken over by Meeta's sons and daughters-in-law, then by their children.

Today I never go to Tammiku except for funerals, and I am aware that my ties to that place are steadily weakening. The house is still the property of Meeta's descendants, but it is no longer occupied year on year. There are hardly any books left in the attic, and in the barn, instead of books, there is a honey centrifuge and some old honeycombs. The garden is starting to disappear beneath the weeds. The forest, which once seemed to me so vast, even frightening, has become lower and thinner. Only the old silver birch at its edge is still as handsome and solid as ever, and the oaks round the house are much taller and thicker than before. Beside the lake that was once so peaceful, one can often hear cars and music; apparently there are plans afoot to build some villas there too. Important areas of forest have been cut down and sold; in some places, the forest is today the only source of revenue for country people, and the new life we want to live demands much more money. Money is also needed for the cars, tractors, lawnmowers and other machines that have taken the place of cows and sheep. I know that the Tammiku of my childhood, the forest and the lake, the hay-making and the piles of books, has vanished for ever. None of it exists except in my memories which, as so often, are beautiful and melancholy. Nothing can eclipse that melancholy beauty, even though I am well aware that my first summers at Tammiku coincided with perhaps the darkest period in Estonian history. And yet, at a time when tens of thousands of Estonians lost their homes, I, at least, found my second home, and my second school. ❑

Jaan Kaplinski (b 1941) is one of Estonia's leading poets and essayists. Nature plays an important part in his poetry, much of which is influenced by Eastern philosophies. His poetry has been translated into nearly 20 languages. He won the Max Jacob Prize for foreign writing in 2003 for his first anthology published in French, Le désir de la poussière *(Éditions Riveneuve 2002)*

Translated by Saul Lipitz

CITY OF PHANTOM GENTLEMEN
LÁSZLÓ KRASZNAHORKAI

GYULA A little boy proceeds along a street, measuring out his steps on the concrete slabs of the pavement. Upon closer examination, we may observe that he steps only on every other slab, humming as he goes. A little boy, blond, with big ears, very thin. He is wearing a coat, a blue top and blue trousers. What he likes most about the trousers is a little secret pocket on the inside, near the seam, which contains his most jealously kept treasure. One of his hands holds an empty bag, the other the change for the yeast and vanilla sugar he has been sent to the shop for. Walking and humming, he appears completely absorbed in his progress: leaning forward with his head down, his eyes are fixed on the concrete slabs to ensure that he only steps on every other one, only the evens. If he sees anyone coming in the other direction, he stops and waits for them to pass so as not to make a mistake. He is very thin, blond, with big ears. The concrete slabs of the pavement are still too big for him, and he has to lengthen his stride so as not to miss. For only the even-numbered slabs are permitted.

For, in the beginning, there was Mr Kerekes, the small fat Romanian cobbler and bell-ringer who left his house on Maróthy Square every evening around six, with his rolling gait, head sunk into his shoulders as he hurried past the windows of the parish church and into the Orthodox church, where he climbed the narrow staircase up the tower in the darkness to ring the bells.

For, in the beginning, there was Mr Csiszár, the master repairer of fountain pens who, every morning at eight o'clock, lifted the curtain in his workshop behind the statue of Ferenc Erkel — who composed the national anthem — glanced at the narrow display window by the door to check all was well, that no pen or box of pencils had moved during the night, and went on into the shop, sat down at his desk — on the special chair for his hunched back, duly curved and cushioned at the level of the hump — lit up one of his favourite cigarettes, a Terv, and, by slowly blowing the smoke upwards while putting his match out in two swift shakes, announced to the town that he was open and ready to receive pens in need of repair.

For, in the beginning, there was Lajos Markizay, the young and hand-some schoolmaster, bachelor of mathematics and physics who, every Friday afternoon around three o'clock, took a young high school girl in full bloom, who was keen on chess, up to the sun-kissed observatory atop the municipal water tower, so that, after devoting around three hours to this pastime, they could eventually lean out of the window of the tower and, smiling at each other happily, remark that there was far too much noise down there and that up high in the tower was the only place where it was quiet enough to play chess.

And there was the alcoholic and obese Dr Petróczky who was best known not for his ability to calm even the most feverish child with just a few words, but for his insistence, against the very best and most well-intended advice, on straddling a certain Cespel motorbike every time he went to see his patients; it was hardly surprising that at least once a week he ended up in a ditch on this same Cespel. For attached though the motorbike was to its owner, it could not keep the infallibly drunken man in its saddle when he continually jolted around, leaning and skidding over the execrable paths, constantly veering towards gutters, ruts, ditches – in a word, towards the ground.

And there was Fr Gyula Kovrig, the Catholic priest of Armenian descent who was interested in stamp collecting and nothing else and who had lined the shelves of the church hall, where the books should have been, with endless albums of stamps; and who had correspondents in 63 countries of particular philatelic interest, with whom he occasionally exchanged one of the rare pieces in his unparalleled collection for an even rarer one.

And there was Mr Osy, lord of the cakes and delicacies of the Százéves confectioners, skinny, speedy and always rather agitated, who was never at ease despite the luxuriant treats that surrounded him, and longed only to jump on his shiny Czechoslovakian racing bike in the pink strip he had worn on that distant day when he had won a national amateurs' race. As, indeed, he did every morning before opening and every evening after closing, when he would pedal for hours and hours towards an imaginary finishing line.

And there was Kálmán Nemes, Gyula's only adventurer, who had actu-ally come back here from his adventures, from Brazil in particular, though only after several years, bringing with him the black Nadir, his magnificent Brazilian wife who had the town in a frenzy for months, years even; much to the consternation of the citizens of Gyula, the couple would throw themselves at each other on a weekly basis in a rage of blows and yells in an unidentifiable, Brazilian, language before suddenly falling silent, usually towards the morning, with an abruptness that no one could ever understand. For how could you understand, in Gyula, how could you understand the international character of exotic passion?

And there was Mr Turai, the tiny tailor from Románváros, who drowned his insatiable respect for the ladies in a detailed study of esoteric philosophy that made him the favourite of the town's women. He had learned that playing on their capacity for feeling was enough to earn him plenty of doting and petting; and given that the strange, rapturous sermons into which Mr Turai launched himself as he took their measurements were merely the expression of his sincere and unconditional admiration for these women, the fact that they were quite lost amid the complexity of his discourse, was of absolutely no importance whatsoever. What could a woman from Gyula gain from knowing, for example, whether the deepest philosophical rift was that between Martin Buber and Angelius Silesius or that between Nostradamus and Rozenweig?

And there were other phantom gentlemen. There was Mr Halmai, the hairdresser on Maróthy Square, constantly enveloped in a most pungent cloud of perfume that he never tired of explaining was not by choice but had simply been inflicted on him by the vocation fate had assigned him. Or Mr Fodor, the rat-catcher, of whose ageless mongrel with its sausage-dog legs, dragging its stomach along the ground and constantly trying to attract people's attention with its heavy eyes and shrill yap, everyone, but everyone, was afraid. And Füredi, the tobacconist, with his countless little plastic soldiers and his stern look, designed to silence the noisy children in their rowdy queue outside. And Béla Szabo, master of the Németváros chapel, with his six gorgeous daughters, all blessed with extraordinary musical talent and brought up in a house where time did not exist and whose doors were shut to parents, visitors and friends alike, but whose permanently closed windows discharged an unbroken stream of music on to the main street in Németváros: Corelli, Vivaldi, Lully or Bach, depending on the occasion.

Put simply, they were all phantoms, for they were locked into a strange, intangible, floating existence. And what's more, they were merely the backdrop to one of the most otherworldly and inexplicable things in all Central Europe.

Hungary, Budapest: real people

For, in the beginning, the town's most important, most mysterious figures, the most authentic of all the phantom gentlemen, stood out against this backdrop; and no one knew for sure from what vanished worlds they came. And no one could ever really know who they were, for they had merged with their own legend, with the town of Gyula itself. So, whenever the citizens thought of the director of the music academy András Herbály, or the psychiatrist Mr Soóky, or the teachers Miskolczi, Banner and Panczél; of the poet Imre Simonyi, or of Mr Gyurka Ladics, they were thinking of the very essence of Gyula itself.

To start with, there was Mr Herbály himself, who amazed everyone with his erudition and understanding of his field, who had spent years earning his living as a Scott Joplin-obsessed bar pianist in the neighbouring villages before suddenly finding himself head of the Gyula musical academy – big Professor Herbály with his breathing difficulties and worn-out clothes, who was always giving elegant, improvised and mordantly witty lectures on that unbearable burden he called the structure of life, and on the mortal illness that human mediocrity represented for the aforementioned structure of life.

And then Mr Soóky, the hospital's chief psychiatrist, to whom no one spoke his whole life because he let his hair flop over his face, though you couldn't say which was the more terrifying thing about him: that or the menacing look in his eyes when anyone did try to look into them, for both of these traits were quite terrifying and elevated Soóky to the highest rank, though he'd have been up there anyway because he lived apart from them, from the people of Gyula, in the hospital with his patients, and because he rented a whole floor above a little hat shop to house his collection of paintings, which sat there in silence, worth millions in this totally empty flat, all doors and windows shut for 40 years. And Chief Doctor Soóky only visited them occasionally, no more than twice a year, unplanned and at night when all Gyula lay quiet under the heavy quilts of deep sleep.

And there was Schoolmaster Miskolczi, who had been drawn to the town by an elemental passion for his first cousin, giving up a promising career as a philologist without hesitation in order to marry her, weather the public scandal and father four children. The two healthy ones were brought up by the couple, but the two mental retards were sent to a home so that Miskolczi and his wife could be hired as English teachers at the local secondary school. Mr Miskolczi who, in an era beset by false readings of Petöfi and by nationalist and socialist stagnation, refused to talk to young people – naturally rebellious – about anything other than the crisis of modernity in the twentieth century: exclusively that and without any pre-amble. Mr Miskolczi was the subject of numerous anecdotes in town, such as this particularly memorable one: in a bid to quieten the rowdiest class in the school, he walked into the room, stood before his pupils and stared, for a full minute, at the upper right-hand corner of the room until they shut up, whereupon, with a theatrical flourish, he pulled out of his pocket one of the first London editions of James Joyce's *Ulysses* and began menacingly to read it aloud, translating directly into Hungarian so well that you could hear the musicality of the language, and then stopped in the middle of a sentence, snapped the tome shut, put it back into his pocket and, glaring at the upper right-hand corner of an imaginary classroom, went out into the corridor without a word.

In the beginning, too, there was Imre Simonyi, the last poet, who shocked those young minds of Gyula who wished to specialise in the study of form by declaring, one spring day as he was walking towards the Turkish baths – and he didn't stop as he passed the young thinkers near the Százéves confectioners, but picked a bunch of flowers from the acacia overhanging the pavement and started to roll them between his fingers – that ultimately the only true poet is one who is ready to give up his life at any moment, for a single, magnificent line, for a single, magnificent actress, or simply for his country.

And in the beginning, there were also the two Latin and Greek teachers, Banner and Panczél, who had earned their places in Gyula's pantheon through their habit, indulged from time to time upon emerging from their lessons at break, whenever one or the other of them felt like it, of cheerily addressing each other in Latin. The other would reply in Latin, and they would stroll along, chatting eloquently in Latin in their dusty, 100-year-old suits, in front of the silent lines of children, towards the staffroom.

For this is how it all started: with Mr Gyurka Ladics. With his spectacular house and everything there was in it, he had come from the nineteenth century. This man who, thanks to his vast, incomparable library in German, French and Hungarian, his select furniture, his lamps, his piano and his sound knowledge, coupled with the peculiar illness that prevented him from sleeping under any circumstances unless he had read a few pages of Goethe or Schiller in the original, had become a symbol of the town. For that really is how it started, with Mr Kerekes and Mr Turai in the background, along with the greenish alleys, markets, the palace, the castle and the world's most melancholy station while in the foreground paraded the most legendary of the phantom gentlemen, from Mr Herbály to Mr Gyurka Ladics; that is really how it started, how they existed. Then, something truly, truly astounding happened: one day, everything abruptly disappeared, and all trace of Gyula was lost.

Time and again I've tried to work out what can have happened when, after more than 20 years, I came back here, a grown man. As I got off the train after such a lengthy absence, I immediately realised that the town was not in its right place. Worse: not only was it not in its right place, it no longer existed at all. And I wandered, haunted and lost, around a town that claimed to be Gyula but wasn't, and I wandered through the streets and stopped to ask people questions, but in vain; no one knew anything, no one remembered anything. Or, which was worse, they had only false memories and were trying to describe a past that had lost something, but either didn't know what it was or didn't think it mattered: they had simply occupied the town, destroyed what was there and built another one for themselves.

First they obliterated the old one, then they moved in and, pretending nothing had happened, fashioned something vulgarly, brutally new from the poetry of the old Gyula, and tried to pass it off as the original. At first, they knew they were lying; later, they didn't even know even that any more since the children were taught about both old and new Gyula in the schools. I asked them if they remembered Mr Kerekes or Mr Turai and they replied:

'No, we don't remember.'

So I asked them if they remembered Professor Herbály or Mr Gyurka Ladics. They said:

'No, we don't remember the poem that this town used to be nor the culture at the root of it, nor the decors of the chamber concerts where Schumann, Chopin, Beethoven and Mozart used to be played. No, no,' they said.

But what about the Kovrig stamp collection or even the Soóky private museum, maybe?

'No, you must understand, no,' they said, and they shook their heads and smiled, and I saw that for them, the new inhabitants of the town, none of that mattered, they couldn't see any loss. So I stopped asking, and merely noted that the great hall of the Hotel Komló, where they used to hold the county balls, had been taken over by a hideous discothèque and an equally hideous casino and junk shop. And I noted that the trees of the shady lane near the parish church had been pitilessly chopped down so that not a single stump was left; and that the Mogyoróssy library had been moved to the town hall, the town hall to the county hall, the county hall to another town and so on; I didn't note all this down in detail, I didn't make a list, I merely found myself suddenly alone in the street one night the last time I visited, between Maróthy Square and the old casino – there was complete silence, with nary even a cat left on the pavements, just the wind gently wafting past the fortress, and I stood there frozen still on the corner of Maróthy Square, looking straight ahead down the road that led to the old casino and the little shop that used to be there when, suddenly, I noticed something moving: a dot in the shadowy street, not far beyond the old casino building, a little dot moving forward in a rather odd manner, but I already knew at that moment what it was: a boy proceeding along the concrete slabs of the pavement and following a rule of some kind. Upon closer examination, I observed that he was only stepping on every other slab, the evens only, and that he was humming a tune. A little boy, I thought, a blond child with big ears, very thin, in a coat, blue top and blue trousers . . . He's walking and humming, completely absorbed in his progress. Leaning forward with his head down, his eyes fixed on the concrete slabs . . . And, overcome by an indescribable dizziness, beset by an inexpressible sadness, I saw that there wouldn't even be anyone to talk to about this boy moving along, always on the even slabs, never the odds. So I'm telling you what I realised in my dizziness: that run though I might, I'd never catch up with him to tell him not to go any further. ❏

László Krasznahorkai *was born in Gyula in 1954 and is one of Hungary's finest contemporary novelists. He has published several novels with Magvetö in Budapest.* The Melancholy of Resistance *was published in English in 2000 by New Directions Publishing, New York. Krasznahorkai is also well known for his collaborations with the film director Béla Tarr*

Translated by GC

LOOKING FOR THE LIVS

NORA IKSTENA

Over there, outside, the same old war rages on in the same old world. The most powerful dupe the powerful, the powerful rule over the strongest, the strongest dominate the strong, and the strong trample all over the weak. Thus are the lines of warriors arranged in descending order of rank: countless fighters bludgeoning each other to death. About the battlefield they stumble with their blunted minds and their lost memories – are they waiting to hear their names called? Do they want to return to reality? But surely as long as there are reasons to make war, war must be made! Forget reality! Man has exhausted his intelligence and the world's dreams have drifted away, leaving the universal consciousness in a state of paralysis. Only the weakest desert – those who no longer have any reason to fight for power.

There are three jetties on the edge of the sea: life, love and death, and the deserters are pinned to these as a warning. Even as the war heroes and the war-wounded throw stones at them, God will see why the 'weak' do what they do. They have no cause left to fight for. Reality crashes like waves against the three jetties, which the Liv language calls *Jelami, Armaztoks* and *No'vo.*

My soul instinctively rejects this world order set by wars, terrorist attacks and politico-economic alliances. It is a frightening, formidable system in the throes of which more and more people are losing sight of their whole reason for being. My soul rejects it and wants to find the truth that lies outside this reality. I know how to get there: with my rucksack on my shoulders and my feet on the Baltic coastline. There are four of us women, and we aim to walk all the way round the Baltic before we're through. And as our feet tread the sand or the shingle beach, when infinity is near at hand, when God is on our side, we shall reach the truth.

In the woods around Mazirbe on the Courland peninsula, large wooden boats sit rotting – they've been there for decades. Flowers, grass and even trees are growing through them. Long ago, Liv fishermen gave names to these boats, tarred their hulls and put out to sea. The salty, happy waters would lap round them and they'd return to shore laden with a hefty catch.

After World War II, villagers used these fishing boats to flee Soviet occupation, crossing over to Sweden and onward to safety elsewhere in Europe

Latvia: in Riga's airport, part of another minority – Russian

and the USA. The Soviet leaders gave orders for the boats to be taken up into the woods to stop the would-be refugees from getting to them. And now, half a century later, their carcasses still lie here, bearing witness to all those destinies cut short by injustice.

Over there, outside, the same old war rages on in the same old world but I, tired out by all this walking, drift off to sleep in a rotting boat, and there I dream a dream. A crowd of people are gathered on a vast white beach. They are waiting for the start of something. A minister comes down from a dune, climbs up on to an upside-down boat, opens a book, and bellows out the following list: 'Diku Inne, the widower of Kosrags, and Trine, widow of the late Otu Ansis of Pitrags. Niks, child of the Nitelis hamlet, landowner, and Gerde, third daughter of Indrikis, the innkeeper of Kolka. Janis, the farmhand of Delnieku Peteris, a foreigner who became the man of the household, and Babe, servant of Kalnu Didrikis, a girl from Saunags. Janis of Pitrags, old landlord of the Randas lands, father of Randu Krisjanis, widower, and Lize, sister of Reinu Niks and widow of the late Adams, of Mazirbe.' Upon the minister's signal, the couples join hands and each go off to create their own lines of truth, while the sea breeze whistles: '*Izandod etabod virpoli, izandod etabod virpoli* (The lords decide our fate).'

Once upon a time, my dream was a reality. This is where the Liv villages were, this is where the Livs lived, loved and died. So what am I doing here? What am I looking for? A feeling of fear of the future, a feeling that nothing is everlasting: a unique feeling that can't be bought at any price. The feeling that there, along the coast, as it meets the past, the present and the future along its way, mine is not just another soul living out the time that has been granted it, but an initiate.

Seen from the coast near Jurkalne, the snowy sea is so indescribably beautiful that it reminds me of a story about [the Soviet film-maker] Andrei Tarkovsky. He and his crew had been waiting for two weeks for a misty day on the island of Gotland. When the mist finally rolled in off the sea early one morning, and the crew, exhausted by all their sleepless nights waiting up for it, were ready to shoot, Tarkovsky cried: 'Don't shoot! It's too beautiful!' Following in his footsteps on a snowy beach untouched by anyone's feet today is like walking into eternity, joining words beyond time.

The orchard at Uzhava is also covered in the soft, light snow that has just fallen in abundance. Passing under the apple trees, their branches do not appear to bend under its weight – this burden is not heavy, but kind and attentive. The snow takes over the naked, wet ground like a splendidly beautiful idea. Like some kind of conviction, but one that couldn't even exist in a rational mind.

At the bottom of the snowy garden, a happy, faithful black dog leaps into the laps of an ancient couple, their faces well weathered by the cold. As its old mistress tells of how the dog was found abandoned on the Ventspils road, its old master confirms the story with his eyes. What can people be thinking when they throw a live dog out into the road? This old couple are of a different stock. They don't understand that kind of behaviour. They keep blue cows at Uzhava. They're on the losing side. In Latvia now, to keep blue cows is to speak a language that only a handful of other people still speak. Blue bulls are even rarer than blue cows – such are the glory and the misery of matriarchy. But Olina is full. Her silvery sides are fat and warm, her udder swollen, and her blue-grey muzzle turns to give any newcomers a good looking-over. Her large and intelligent eyes are like two hemispheres of a single soul. Stroking Olina's bulging belly, the old man's hand feels today the vibrations of a bygone era: the ability of a minority to survive in the majority's world: to create blue miracles inside these people's perfect, rational edifice, and to be governed by a will to change through preservation rather than destruction.

No obstacles block the wintry road. All of a sudden, the mixture of woodland air and cigarette smoke gives me a glimpse of the truth: that nothing happens by chance, that there is always a deeper meaning to the meetings of men and of thoughts, one that can be known only long after the moment of meeting.

The sea around Sarnate is as unruly as wild horses. Nobody in the world could tame it. I stand on the edge of the cliff and stare at the waves below with my arms stretched out like wings. Perhaps this was once a tear of joy from the eye of a God still floating on water. Perhaps it was once a bead of sweat from the universal Mother in labour. Tear or bead of sweat, it floated around the sky for aeons until it was named sea and fell to earth.

The body of the sea is the maternal sphere. Through it, life came to the world through blood, sweat and tears. The soul of the sea is the ever-changing surface of the water, through which life travels until it disappears over the horizon. The language of the sea is a primary language – all Babel understands it. TS Eliot spoke of it as 'the sound of the sea-bell's perpetual angelus'. Before him, simpler bards believed that the language of the sea was born amid the waves, where 'a joyful soul bobs on the water'.

The sea is man as man is the sea. Flesh is salty like the sea, as the sea is salty like flesh. The soul is as transparent as the sea, and the sea is as transparent as a soul. The tide that smashes into the jetties is as the numbered hours of a worried wife, waiting for her sweetheart to come back ashore. And the endless moment when his life is thrown against the rocks is the moment that time stands still the night he doesn't come home. The past and the future. A man's conversation with himself as he stands on the edge of the sea is a prayer. The man's voice, the sea's echo; the man's voice, the sea's echo.

What do the heavens have in store? You must love and you must hate; you must be disappointed, overjoyed, saddened; you must lie, tell the truth, win, lose; you must aggrieve, flatter, betray, forgive, hope, feel, foretell, blame; you must want, you must wait, receive and lose again. You must live and you must die; you must die and you must live. You must, you must.

A mortal pilgrim on the edge of the undying sea gazes out across the water. He sees the opposite shore but persists in believing this space to be infinite. The pilgrim frees his soul so that it may begin its journey along the surface of the water. The wind lashes the pilgrim's face with the salty words of prayer – like a tear of joy from God, like a bead of sweat from the universal Mother.

As my feet tread the fiftieth mile of beach along the road from Akmenrags to the Lithuanian border village of Nida, I have a blank page in my head. Something I mustered my very last efforts to write and which I now leave behind my back. A pure thought is born in the silence, on the beach road. On one side is the swamp, on the other the sea. Someone is protecting you. Someone you should thank for the birth of this pure thought. The past and the future fill you with strength and you sit down on the Nida jetty and make a V-sign for victory at the sun. ❏

Nora Ikstena (b 1969) is a short-story writer and novelist. In 1998, she won the Latvian Ministry of Culture's literature prize. She has had two novels published by Atena in Riga and some of her work was translated into English in April 2004 by the Canadian literary journal Descant

Translated by GC

'They that can give up essential liberty to obtain a little temporary safety deserve neither liberty nor safety' Benjamin Franklin

NOAM CHOMSKY ON
ROGUE STATES

EDWARD SAID ON
IRAQI SANCTIONS

LYNNE SEGAL ON
PORNOGRAPHY

... all in INDEX

UK and overseas

○ **Yes! I want to subscribe to *Index*.**

❑ 1 year (4 issues)	£32	Save 16%
❑ 2 years (8 issues)	£60	Save 21%
❑ 3 years (12 issues)	£84	**You save 26%**

Name

Address

BOB5

£ _____ enclosed. ❑ Cheque (£) ❑ Visa/MC ❑ Am Ex ❑ Bill me
(*Outside of the UK, add £10 a year for foreign postage*)

Card No.

Expiry   Signature
❑ I do not wish to receive mail from other companies.

INDEX

✉ Freepost: INDEX, 33 Islington High Street, London N1 9BR
☎ (44) 171 278 2313   Fax: (44) 171 278 1878
e tony@indexoncensorship.org

SUBSCRIBE & SAVE

North America

○ **Yes! I want to subscribe to *Index*.**

❑ 1 year (4 issues)	$48	Save 12%
❑ 2 years (8 issues)	$88	Save 19%
❑ 3 years (12 issues)	$120	**You save 26%**

Name

Address

BOB5

$ _____ enclosed. ❑ Cheque ($) ❑ Visa/MC ❑ Am Ex ❑ Bill me

Card No.

Expiry   Signature

❑ I do not wish to receive mail from other companies.

INDEX

✉ Freepost: INDEX, 708 Third Avenue, 8th Floor, New York, NY 10017
☎ (44) 171 278 2313   Fax: (44) 171 278 1878
e tony@indexoncensorship.org

THE HOWLING WOLF

MARIUS IVASKEVICIUS

Matches brought us to Vilnius. My grandmother's brother's family was working in a Nazi-occupied match factory. We still don't know whether the matches were going to the front or being used for civilian purposes. Either way, the front was moving west and the factory was following it. Its German boss had relocated to Vilnius and my family moved in along with the matches. That is why I am here today.

You can't talk about Vilnius without mentioning the inter-war period, when the city was so coveted and so passionately defended. In 1918, several Eastern and Central European nations were granted independence, including Lithuania. The birth of these new countries was a lot less peaceful and harmonious than the transition that took place with the break-up of the Soviet Union in the 1990s. Poland decided to revive its old aristocrats' republic – the *Rzeczpospolita* – that had incorporated the whole of the area that was Lithuania before it was conquered by the Russians. In 1920, war broke out between the two countries. Given the discrepancy in size and military power (Poland was 10 times the size of Lithuania), this was like Britain attacking Belgian Flanders. Poland occupied Vilnius and a large swathe of the land surrounding it without any difficulty. 'No peace without Vilnius' became a slogan of the era. The city became the Lithuanian people's obsession, their holy grail. Whatever negotiations Lithuanian politicians entered into, they always ended up arguing over Vilnius. On the eve of World War II, the city was occupied by the Soviets, who decided to 'give it up' to Lithuania. And so a new, rueful phrase entered the Lithuanians' national mythology: 'We got Vilnius and the Russians got us.'

So Vilnius was the town my match-making family moved into in 1944. The Jews had been exterminated and the Poles were fleeing en masse: the city was half empty. Before moving further west, the German boss had obtained a one-bedroom flat for my family in Vilnius's former Jewish ghetto. Shortly afterwards, a Polish family who were moving back to Poland for good offered them a three-bedroom flat on Foundry Street. 'If you want the flat, take it,' they said. 'Live in it, water the flowers, farm the allotment; there are onions, radishes and a greenhouse too. We'll be happier if we know who's living in our old place.' And with that, *adieu*.

Nothing could have torn my maternal grandparents away from their land – nothing except Soviet coercion. If it hadn't been for the Soviets I would be a farmer somewhere in Belarus and know Vilnius only through hearsay. But, thanks to the communists, my grandparents were robbed of their land and sent away to chop down trees in northern Russia for 20 years. During their exile they had two daughters, one of whom was my mother. When they were finally allowed to come back home, there was no home to come back to: the lands had gone and the house had been demolished. So they went to Vilnius to join my grandmother's brother, the match-maker. They lived for several years in the three-room flat I mentioned, on Foundry Street. It is hard to imagine how two families – 14 people in all – managed to live together in that flat, but they did, until my grandparents found another place in the same area, on Tatar Street. It had an outside toilet and the only tap was in the courtyard but having a home of their own was an incalculable improvement all the same. In return for this privilege, my grandparents had to clean Tatar Street daily for 10 years. Farmers, they had first been forced to work as lumberjacks, and then as street-sweepers. I often walk down Tatar Street, on the way to the little National Theatre or just to get back into the old town from Gedimino Boulevard. It isn't long – you can almost see from one end to the other. I always check whether it is clean, to see that the work my grandparents began is being kept up.

I'm 30, but I was not a Vilniuser until I was 18. I grew up in Moletai, a small town 30 miles north of Vilnius. All the kids at my school used to go to visit their grandparents in the countryside at weekends and holidays. For me, the countryside was Vilnius. By then my grandparents had got a bigger flat, with some mod cons: a coal-burning stove, running water and proper plumbing. It was in Tanner Street. Not many streets in Vilnius held on to their names during Soviet times. The Gedimino Boulevard, for example, was called Lenin Boulevard, and St Stephen's Street, which crosses Tanner Street, was renamed Soviets Street. But the names of Foundry Street and Tanner Street don't seem to have bothered the Soviet leaders, since they contained a piece of history: many centuries before, these streets were where the metalworkers and tanners were to be found, two trades that did not contravene communist ideology, since artisans were the bedrock of the proletariat.

Tanner Street was – still is – near the station. Back then, like most of the old town, it was neither the nicest nor the safest street in town, but the kids paid little attention to that. I used to go with my grandfather to watch the trains as they went by, and with my grandmother I used to go to the Gate of Dawn chapel – surely the most famous in Vilnius – that is set into the city wall's east gate. The mother of God at the Gate of Dawn attracts hordes of Christian pilgrims. They often climb the high, steep staircase inside it on their knees, to pray to Mary of the Gate of Dawn for healing and comfort. If you want to talk to God directly, the Gate of Dawn chapel must be the best place in Lithuania for it.

Yet the improvement in my grandparents' living conditions did not stop at Tanner Street. At the end of the 1970s they were given a well-appointed modern flat in a new area of Vilnius, Seskines. This part of town is now universally known as a dormitory suburb, as are all the other areas like it. These dormitory estates are usually referred to by the name of whoever was First Secretary of the Communist Party in the USSR when they were built. So Antakalnis and Zirmunai are Khrushkes, while Lazdynai, Justiniskes and Seskines are Brezhnevkes. My grandparents are now to be found in yet another new development on the outskirts of town, the Karveliskes cemetery.

In the meantime, Seskines has become one of the most frequently visited areas of Vilnius. Up on the Ozas hill, whose lower slopes no doubt still hide a few World War II bunkers, and on top of which they started building a football stadium about 20 years ago, there now stands the acropolis. OK, it doesn't look like an acropolis, architecturally speaking. Even from afar it bears little resemblance to its Greek antecedent. But it attracts almost as many visitors. Lithuania's acropolis is a leisure centre and shopping mall, the biggest in all Central Europe according to some, and for others unmatched even in the West. Whatever the truth of such claims, people from the provinces, and even some foreigners, flock to the mall on specially organised excursions. Not that there's anything particularly out of the ordinary there, just a big supermarket, two indoor arcades lined with boutiques selling clothes, shoes and other things, a huge bookshop, cafés and restaurants to cater for all tastes, an ice rink and a multiplex cinema. When they built it, I thought this thing is way too big for a city of 600,000 inhabitants. But in fact it's too small. They're talking about expanding it and building another one just the same in Riga, the capital of Latvia. They might even build one in Kiev – the Ukrainian president, Leonid Kuchma, visited the mall, went bowling and declared: 'I want one of these.'

My Vilnius life began in 1991, when I went to university. The languages faculty, where I was based, is in one of the old university buildings in the city centre. The legendary Polish writer Adam Mickiewicz studied there,

Lithuania: Vilnius talking

along with a host of other major players in Vilnius's cultural life over the
years. Like all provincial students, I lived in the Sunrise halls of residence.
We never used to get back to our 16-storey building until night-time since
we did our living in the old town, at the faculty and in the cafés nearby.
Generations of students had come to love Pilies (Castle) Street, or Gorky
Street as it was known in Soviet times. It is the most important thoroughfare
in the old town, and the languages faculty is right on it. Vaiva, La Glacière,
Narutis . . . You couldn't imagine student life without those cafés. We used
to go to the Café des Artistes, right by the Artists' Palace on University

Street. It was from here that Lithuania was once ruled by governors appointed by the Russian Tsar. We used to sit on its red velvet benches drinking coffee all day and vodka all evening. Once inebriated, we would burst into song, and then gather around the piano in the corner. You weren't allowed to play the piano in that café. The waitress always used to come and tell us off first, then the owner and then the police. Only men in uniform could tear us away from that instrument, and we soon developed a rapport with the coppers. We knew that once we'd started playing, we had about half an hour before going through the expulsion ritual once again.

Today, the doors of the old Café des Artistes are bricked up and the Artists' Palace is now the president's official residence. We moved on to drink in the Writers' Union café, just off Gedimino Boulevard. This café was a bohemian enclave. The drinks were cheap and, frankly, they were bad. But in those days our stomachs were young and could stand anything. The steep stairs to the toilets were more of a hazard – many were the wounds incurred by falling down those steps.

I now live on the other side of town, in Santariskes. I've had to get used to people asking 'Which ward?' when I tell them: Santariskes, for most people, is simply the name of Lithuania's biggest hospital. It is just over the road from my flat. They say it's bad luck to live opposite a church, a cemetery or a hospital. But everything's fine at the moment, touch wood. I get up, I walk the dog, I visit the newspaper stand in the hospital – they know me there now – and queue up alongside my 'neighbours' who are all in their pyjamas. I spend the occasional evening in town – usually at the Irish pub near the university, where I meet my friends at weekends. We sit around and chat, our numbers swell, we bring more tables over. After midnight we might move on to a club – Vilnius has loads. It's hard to choose which. Some are too full of kids, others too dodgy – you risk ending up with a black eye. At the moment, the one our crowd like best is Broadway. We push on through to five in the morning there sometimes.

Vilnius is changing fast. There are building sites everywhere. The mayor has decided that ours is to be the most modern capital in Eastern Europe. There are plans for a state-of-the-art tram system. Some approve of this, others are against it: what's the point of trams? No one ever minded not having them! And glass skyscrapers are springing up all over the place. The archaeologists have really got their work cut out for them: whenever the builders start digging the foundations of a new building, they find huge mass graves. Recently they discovered the remains of around 3,000 of

Napoleon's soldiers in the old Soviet militarised zone. Apparently it's the biggest Napoleonic mass grave ever uncovered. There are nearly 40,000 bodies buried in the Vilnius area.

People in Vilnius tend to love their city very much. They honour it, you might say. Perhaps this is because of the feeling that Vilnius's time has come. Paris, to my mind, lives off memories. Paris is exceptional because of everything its past represents. The present cannot live up to that. But Vilnius's spirit is more like that of Berlin. We are rediscovering the old town that was so grey, dark and dilapidated in Soviet times. And areas like Copenhagen's Cristiania are being created: in the Uzupis neighbourhood, a former favourite of Western film-makers, a group of artists have created a symbolic republic. They have set up a border post on the edge of the area and named a president and even a corps of ambassadors. The government sits in a café whose terrace looks over the River Vilnele. Flats in this area are more coveted by the hour, not just by the day. And to think that this was once the grottiest, greyest part of all Vilnius.

The television tower is a recent construction. In 1991, it was co-opted as a symbol of Lithuania's singing revolution. It was at the bottom of this tower that the crowd stood against the Red Army's tanks, and 13 civilians died. The tower was then occupied, which only reinforced Lithuanians' opposition to the Soviet regime.

Vilnius has always been thought of as a cosmopolitan city. Perhaps that is why it is getting so European-spirited these days, even as the rest of the country retreats into provincialism. Built by Lithuanians, the city was then dominated by Poles and Jews. Russians and Belarusans moved in en masse during the Soviet era, and sometimes it was hard to make oneself understood in Lithuanian. So where have all those Soviet-era Vilniusers gone? Nowhere. They've simply become Lithuanian. My grandparents died before they could learn the language and my mother still speaks it with a slight Slavic accent; but me, I am a Young Lithuanian Writer. So there you have it: the Lithuanianisation of Vilnius in three generations.

I'm sure all cities want to be like Rome and dream that all roads will one day lead to them. The dream of Gediminas, founder of Vilnius, was simply of a wolf howling on top of a hill. A pagan priest interpreted this dream as meaning Gediminas should build a city on that hill, and the whole world would come to hear about it just as the whole world could hear the howl of that wolf. And Oscar Milosz — an intellectual who lived in France, got drunk with Oscar Wilde on numerous occasions and was ultimately named

Lithuanian ambassador to Paris – declared that Vilnius would one day be known as the Athens of the North, world capital of culture.

It didn't happen. Arriving back from abroad at Vilnius's tiny airport, you sense how unlikely it is. It seems all the more unlikely when you look at a map of Europe. Vilnius is now the closest capital city to the eastern border of the European Union. It is less than 19 miles from Belarus. But since we have this vision of a howling wolf city, we should hold on to it. It is not too late for Vilnius to become the Athens of the North. We've got the acropolis – all we need now is Socrates. Perhaps the whole world really will hear our distant howl some day. ❏

Marius Ivaskevicius (b 1973) is a playwright, novelist and documentary film-maker. His best-known work is The Story of a Cloud, *a novel that takes in 1,000 years of Lithuanian history*

Translated by GC

VANISHING POINT

ANDRZEJ STASIUK

KONIECZNA For some time now, home to me has above all meant the departure point for my journeys. Living on the periphery, a long way from the centre, has many benefits, but proximity to other countries has to be one of the most important. When the weather's so grim in my village on the northern Carpathian slopes that you wouldn't even put a dog out, I can jump in the car and be in Slovakia 20 minutes later, on the other side of the mountains. After two hours, I'd be in Hungary. Two and a half hours, and I could visit Tokaj, amid the ripening grapes of its famous terraced vineyards. Sometimes I venture further afield. Just three more hours' drive away, I can cross the Romanian border into Transylvania. All of which still takes less time than driving to Warsaw, and is certainly a lot more pleasant than a trip to that botched copy of other cities, still clinging to its paranoid dreams of power when really it is no more than a railway junction linking the Berlin and Moscow lines.

There are only 10 houses in my village. In winter, they are often covered in snow, and you can hear wolves howling nearby. You sometimes need chains or even a 4x4 to get to the border post at Konieczna.

One day, I was catching a plane at Warsaw's Okecie airport. At check-in, the customs official started leafing through my passport, examining it from every angle, visibly intrigued. He would hesitantly look up at me, then back down at my passport, as though pondering over an important decision. Just when I was convinced I was going no further, he leaned towards me and said, 'Tell me, sir, where exactly is Konieczna?'

That's how it is. I've been south through the Konieczna border post 53 times, and this guy hadn't even heard of it, though several of his colleagues were stationed there, stamping passports with the exact same funny little spring gadgets. Yet Konieczna is where it all starts. The Slovak side of the border teems with jolly groups of lads, carting five-litre containers back to Poland. Red, yellow, orange and green, they look like the treasures of Ali Baba shining in the sunlight. They also fetch vodka, and beer by the box. The real hardcore take *crvene modranske*, a massive canister of red wine that only costs five zlotys (US$1.20).

The women, meanwhile, can be seen lugging mega-cartons of sugar, rice and flour. The three stands on the other side of the border are heaving – just like the boats full of emigrants 100 years ago, bound for the other side of the ocean, full of the same people, the same faces, almost the same caps even. All this low-budget bounty animates the rolling hills of the Beksides and the promise of an alcoholic bender at half-price lights up the eyes of my home town like the dream of a promised land. Sometimes, Poles will say they're queuing up to get *tmavy smadny mnih*, or a *demanovka*. But actually I believe that the Na Colnicy cash-and-carry is the start of longitude 21° East, a line from here to somewhere in the Ionian sea, by the Peloponnesian coast, with people like these stationed at intervals all along it, like birds on electricity cables. They are there with their bags stuffed full and their ideas for getting ahead in life, and their own cursed customs men and never enough money. That's why they have to keep moving, dreaming up wheezes to trick reality into giving them their share at the end of the day. Košice, Tokaj, Arad, Timişoara and Skopje line up like everlasting pearls on this glittering longitude. I've promised myself that some day I'll travel its whole length in one go, without sleeping, just to prove what I already know.

Nothing could spoil the view over the Kamenec valley that you get from the front of the U Pufieho mart in Slovakia. The guys sip beer there and look south. The light is clearer on this side of the border, so their gaze is even more envious than if they were at home. Košice, Tokaj, Arad, Timişoara, Skopje . . . you could take these very same guys, standing here with their beers, and plant them in front of a shop in Hidasnémeti, where people spend their last forints before leaving Hungary, or in the bazaar in Sucaeva, which is like some great camp, or in Sfîntu Gheorghe, where the Danube finally flows into the Black Sea, or even on Skanderberg Square in Tirana, under a suffocating navy-blue sky, and it wouldn't upset the harmony of the world. No one would think they were foreigners. Not until they opened their mouths, anyway. Yes, it's good, living on the border. Especially on the southern border. That way, you're out of the boring old 'East versus West' loop, that eternal path along which so many armies have tramped back and forth over the centuries. My God, living on the western border would be my worst nightmare. Where would I travel to then? To Germany? Following in the footsteps of politicians, businessmen, *gastarbeiters* and thieves? To Paris, which everyone's already seen or is about to. What about the East? It's probably very interesting, but who knows if that's not just because the Eastern lands are where you can watch the West gradually disappear.

Night-time, February. It's snowing and windy. Snowdrifts are piling up on the Konieczna road. In this weather, there's barely any traffic at the border post. The guards and customs officials are in the main building, playing cards and watching television, be it Polish or Slovakian. Sometimes, getting back to my country in the evening, I have to wait half an hour before anyone comes to raise the barrier. The shops are shut and the whole commotion of border trade seems to have ended. It's dark and empty on both sides, and not a soul in sight. This is my favourite time to cross the

Poland: on a train to somewhere

border, because it casts doubt on whether I actually crossed at all. Seen from afar in the black emptiness, my passing is no more than a mirage. Sometimes I come here just to contemplate this emptiness. My impression is that even at night, the sky is a little clearer than on the other side of the Carpathians. Naturally, this is an illusion, but it is part of the personal mythology that protects me from the melancholy of the vast European plain, the infinite sadness of Poland, and my own *mal de vivre*. Even in the wintry night, images of Transylvania, Dalmatia and Albania can all be seen in this patch of southern sky. It could be that that flipside of the world is in fact the home of pure hallucination. Maybe that's where all these swarming peoples, borders and languages originally come from.

Yes, it is good, living in a country you can leave just as casually as you might leave your house to go shopping. It is good, having your own mental 'checkpoint charlie'. What better way to cheer yourself up than to see your own country end so simply? ❏

***Andrzej Stasiuk** is a writer, poet and literary critic, and runs the Czarne publishing house (www.czarne.com.pl) which specialises in Central European literature. He refused military service as a youth and spent two years in prison, which he recounts in his book* Mury Hebronu (The Walls of Hebron), *excerpts from which were first published in* Index *1/93*

EXCLUSION WITHIN

VALERIU NICOLAE

EUROPE'S ROMA REMAIN HIGHLY SCEPTICAL
ABOUT THE BENEFITS OF EU CITIZENSHIP

'There is nothing to fear, the worst has already happened to us,' says Janos V, a 65-year-old Roma from Hajduhadhaz in Hungary. In 1865, after the end of almost 500 years of forced slavery in Wallachia and Moldova, now Romania, his family moved to Banat. World War II found them once more within Romanian borders. In fear of deportation, they fled to neighbouring Hungary, just in time, he explains, to avoid the fate of 30,000 Romanian Roma who perished at the hands of the Romanian authorities during their deportation to Transnistria (Ukraine).

In 1999, after repeated cases of police brutality against Roma, the Hungarian Ministry of the Interior finally admitted that Hajduhadhaz had the highest level of reported police violence in the country.

Nevertheless, Janos remains somewhat optimistic: if he's lucky, some of Europe's wealth and prosperity will trickle east to his poverty-stricken village where it could help to ease the inter-ethnic tensions among its citizens. Having endured the worst, things can only get better. Or so he thinks.

But Romaphobia is on the rise again in Europe, to the point where it could be one of the few common links that bind the majority 'Europeans'. The media is taking a leading role in playing to anti-Roma sentiment, not only in the new democracies of Central and Eastern Europe, but within the heart of Western Europe.

In January, UK tabloids led a media campaign of racist slurs and innuendos against Roma on the grounds that 'hordes' of Roma from Eastern Europe would 'invade' Great Britain the moment they were EU citizens, to take advantage of the British welfare system. None of the governments in Bucharest, Budapest, Prague, Bratislava or Sofia, where most Roma live, said a word in defence of their citizens. In London, the talk was of measures to stem the 'deluge'; Paris, Berlin, Athens, Madrid maintained a chilling silence. Had this language been used of any other European community, the reaction would have been very different.

Milan and Iveta Gozova from Ceaklov, Slovakia, are two of those Roma accused of preparing to 'flood in' and 'suck dry' British welfare funds.

However, on 1 May, they did not catch the first bus or plane to London but, as they have done every year, put on their best clothes and went out to the small village market to celebrate International Labour Day.

The Gozovas do not expect much from their new citizenship in Europe: unable to find a job in what was once a prosperous Roma village, they want nothing but to regain their dignity by getting off the dole and into work. Ceaklov is in eastern Slovakia, a region with an above-average unemployment rate; the new jobs created on the other side of the country are not accessible to them. 'I am almost an old man and I need help. I worked hard all my life. I did not do anything wrong, but this doesn't matter. For them [the majority Slovaks] I will remain always a Gypsy,' is Milan's disillusioned conclusion.

With enlargement, some 1.6 million more Roma became EU citizens, bringing the total number of European Roma to between 3.5 million and 4.5 million, considerably more than the population of some of the EU's smaller members. When Romania and Bulgaria enter, this number will more than double. But for Roma in the ghettos of Europe, European citizenship does not mean much. They are Europe's most poverty-stricken group, with virtually no political representation and facing powerful discrimination. They are socially isolated and seen as genetically predisposed to thievery and other crimes. Under pressure from European institutions, and international NGOs, the governments of the accession states produced a flood of well-phrased 'action plans', strategies and programmes. Legislation was changed, anti-discrimination laws adopted; bodies to monitor and punish discrimination were set up.

But there is a huge gap between the well-conceived documents and fancy brochures, and the remote villages where many Roma are condemned to live; starvation continues to be part of everyday life, jobs are scarce and, as one of the mayors of Craiova, a Romanian city with a significant Roma population, put it, European funds must first be deployed to solve some of the problems of 'our people' before dealing with those of the 'Gypsies'. It never crossed his mind – nor those of the national politicians – that Roma are 'their people' too.

The situation in the old EU member states is also far from the standards they have imposed on the new countries. International reports by human rights organisations and the UN have regularly highlighted the discrimination and appalling living conditions of Roma in Greece, Italy and Spain; but without effect. In Lyon, two Romani teenagers from Romania were recently burned alive in their hut. The French authorities responsible for this fail to offer adequate accommodation to asylum seekers. The European example offers no cause for rejoicing among its new Roma citizens. And ethnic nationalism is again on the rise in much of 'old' Europe.

After centuries of harsh discrimination there is a strong social stigma associated with the fact of being Roma. Successful Roma professionals tend to hide their ethnicity in order to avoid social isolation in the best case. Politicians 'suspected' of being Roma have to deny any relationship with the Roma community if they want to retain the support of their electorate.

The main fear of new Europeans such as Janos, Iveta and Milan is that the whole of Europe will now treat them as alien 'Gypsies', just as the Slovaks and Hungarians do.

For the younger Roma this could be a disaster. With the Roma population increasing to 8–10 million by 2007, Roma issues will inevitably become more visible on the European agenda. But with no single political representative of the community on the European scene, Roma have little power to influence the course of events. Inclusion doesn't come with the disappearance of customs officials and border controls.

In a taxi in Romania, I hear about the report of the European Commission asking Romania to improve the situation of Roma facing discrimination. The taxi driver articulates the common local view:

'Why don't they [he hints at the EU governments] just take all these fucking Gypsies to their countries to see how easy is to live with them? But they know there is no way to civilise them. Why else would they send them back as soon as they can?' Most EU countries have, in fact, already signed bilateral agreements with Romania for the speedy return of would-be asylum seekers.

The taxi driver looks towards me waiting for automatic agreement. I am wearing a three-piece suit, he picked me up from the Romanian parliament and there is no doubt in his mind that I am anything but what I am: a Roma. ❏

Valeriu Nicolae is deputy director of the Roma Information Office in Brussels. He is a Romanian Roma

HOME OF THE HEAVENLY HAIRDRESSER
DUSAN DUSEK

SASTÍN, ZAHORIA The first signs you're in Zahoria are the pines and the sand. The sea must have been here sometime in the past. It really was, actually. A hundred or so years ago, well-diggers in this region discovered large shells, put them to their ears and listened to the waves. A greenish light is filtered down through the canopy formed by the pine branches, and the forest breathes silence as though it came from the needles. Even the wind is quieter than in deciduous woods. All of a sudden, you feel as though you're in a church – except that instead of incense, there is sap. Nowhere else in Slovakia will you find pines growing in sand. You'll find sand. Pines too, no doubt. But it's only in Zahoria that you'll find them both together.

Shortly afterwards comes the second sign that you're in Zahoria: the humour of the region's inhabitants.

A quick bit of geographical information: this little country within a country is Slovakia's far west. Beyond it lie the Austrian and Czech borders. The capital of Zahoria is Sastín (officially Sastín-Sráze), a small town where my grandmother was born, and my father, and where we still have a little house. Most of the inhabitants of Zahoria would vehemently disagree with what I just said, because all the villages here claim to be the region's capital. But the fact is that the cathedral of Our Lady of the Seven Sorrows, patron saint of Slovakia, stands here in Sastín. We even had a visit from the Pope – if that doesn't prove the town's importance, I don't know what does. None of the other villages and towns can hold a candle to that, and they don't try. But they wish they could, that's for sure.

They say that if you look through the window in the cathedral's clockface, you can see all the way to Vienna. Hard to believe. But then they add: no, it's true, on a clear day after rain, when the sun comes out just after the downpour has washed the air clean. They also say that those who stare long enough have been known to see the peaks of the Alps in their caps of sparkling snow. But those are just rumours. One thing's for sure, though: it's always been a good place to practise gazing into the distance.

Round here, the inhabitants of each village have their own nickname. In one, they apparently eat dogs – so they're known as the 'doggers'. Their nearest neighbours have a tendency to brawl – we call them the 'cripples'. In another village, they're always singing – we just call them the 'singers'. In

DUSAN DUSEK

Slovakia: Bratislava station for trains west to Zahoria

another, they grow peas – the 'pea people', we call them. What we in Sastín like above all is soup, so we're known as the 'soup-slurpers'. When our football team is playing at home, we don't serve them lemonade or any other commonplace drink as a half-time refreshment, but a bowl of soup. You can't serve a meal without soup – lots of it! Ideally, we'd make it in the lake by the cathedral by pouring in a truckload of flour and a truckload of beans and then lighting a fire underneath it. We could mix it up with a gigantic spoon and we'd have enough soup to last the whole year.

Round here, you've got to have lots of everything. Weddings, for example, are judged by the number of dishes served. At a truly successful wedding, even the dog is still feeling bloated the following morning.

Basically, in Zahoria we like to go over the top. Deeds and characters can be blown quite out of proportion by local chatter. They can also be cut short, but always in such a way as to bring out the juiciest point with precision and pertinence. When someone wants to tell their grandmother, with all good intentions, that she has reached an advanced age, they might say something like this: 'Granny, when you got married, the devil was still a little boy.' Someone else might say of themselves: 'I'm as old as the coals.'

A father will tell a greedy son that his appetite would devour everything – like rust. For another example of this subtlety of sentiment, let me tell you about a conversation I once had with our Aunt Tula, a great cat lover. When her cat had kittens, she naturally could not keep them all. She deeply regretted this fact.

'What are you going to do with them?' I asked her. 'Drown them?' She shook her head. 'I could never torture them like that! I just whack them over the back of the head with a spade and then bury them in the garden.' Put so bluntly, it sounds brutal, but her attitude shows all the wisdom and kindness of one who knows that a quick death is much easier and less painful than a long, slow agony.

Also, since I've got on to this unhappy topic, I recall a conversation I once had with the gravedigger in the cemetery, the day after my grandmother's funeral. While she was alive, the old girl had never missed seeing off a single one of her generation when they left for their final journey.

'Considering how many people she buried, there wasn't much of a turnout,' the gravedigger commented, hard at work on digging another grave. Then he stopped for a second to wax philosophical: 'I'm no stickler for life, me. If people die, fair play to them.' He wasn't speaking out of pessimism, but merely forestalling any comments on the sadness of his work: someone has to do it. Shortly afterwards, this was confirmed to me. The gravedigger lit up a cigarette and, seeing his spade leaning against a nearby tomb, suddenly exclaimed, 'There's a happy spade for you: at rest!'

What I have always enjoyed about this directness, this coarseness – but also this *honesty* – is the pleasure of using words and language freely in ordinary conversation. In communist times, this was one of the only freedoms available to all. Humour and wit work like a good defence in football. They are all the fun of the game and of the proper discussions, where we would taunt each other, tussle with each other, and joke around without wishing to do any harm or to hurt anyone's feelings. Or else it would be all about coming up with a caustic response or butting in at the right moment – for everyone had something to say. When you missed the exact point at which your inter-locutor drew breath, you'd missed your chance to reply. Everyday language is the lifeblood of literary language. And humour is a form of happiness.

I've written several books about this region, and have tried surrepti-tiously to slip a few amusing situations, or at the very least a few authentic phrases, from Zahoria into each one – without that they wouldn't be true reflections of life in this part of the world. Lifting them straight from people's mouths, I had to beg permission to use some of these phrases. Others I had to buy, with a bottle of wine for example. Others were given up to me willingly. They're always the phrases I like best. I'm delighted every time I hear around us that ocean of laughter and irony, the magical freedom that enlivens the airy and joyful lightness of being. It must have something to do with the location of this region and its close proximity to three other languages – German, Czech and Hungarian. Zahorians blithely take a word from another language and make it their own. For example, we took the German for aunt, *tante* (in Slovak it's *teta*), and made the Zahorian diminutive *tantinka*. I'm convinced that this free adjustment of the vocabu-lary extends into the construction of phrases and into our ways of thinking, our willingness to chat, to create our own personal languages and pepper them with wit. Exaggerating rather, as any true Zahorian should, but no more than necessary, I would even go so far as to say that humour is the ideal Esperanto – enabling people to communicate the world over. Practi-cally everyone loves to laugh.

The day after the Pope's visit, a well-known joker from Sastín was going on in a local bar about a dream he had had. We were sitting with the village hairdresser, who was known as Goose Feathers, and our raconteur's tale was addressed to him.

In my dream, I was at the Pope's place in Rome. There were hundreds of us there, all together in one big room. After giving us his blessing, the Pope stared at me and pointed his finger. I was petrified: all eyes were on me. I said, 'Me?' The Holy Father nodded and beckoned me towards him. So I started in his direction and the crowd parted as I went by, rolling out a magnificent red carpet right up to his holy throne. I kneeled before the Holy Father and kissed his hand.

'Holy Father, to what do I owe this honour? What do you want from me?' I asked him.

He replied, 'Nothing, my son, I just wanted to know what klutz gave you that haircut?' So I told him it was you!

We burst out laughing. After a brief pause, Goose Feathers started laughing too. And since that day, everyone calls him 'the heavenly hairdresser'.

Thanks to my grandmother, I know that one Sunday afternoon a long time ago, a bugler appeared in the clock-face window, as the village danced to the military band in the adjacent park. From his lofty perch, the bugler launched into a solo that filled the whole sky. The dancing couples froze. That brilliant bugler became the star of the village fête. He was richly applauded and heard all over town. They might even have been able to make him out in Vienna. This sounding of the bugle was no doubt another way of gazing into the distance.

Now, we simply have to stop staring and start moving. That's what our country is about to do. Finally, we have set off towards the rest of the world, hoping also that the world will come and see us. Which is why I would like publicly to draw to your attention the fact that, arriving from the west, Zahoria is the first region of Slovakia you'll come to. All visitors are most welcome.

And in Sastín, we'll serve them soup. Let them become good soup-slurpers, just like us. ❏

Dusan Dusek (b 1946) *is a writer and poet. He teaches screenwriting at the Bratislava Academy of Arts (VSMU). He has scripted a number of films, in particular for the directors Dusan Hanak and Martin Sulík, and has also written several children's books*

Translated by GC

WINDOW ON LJUBLJANA

KATARINA MARINCIC

In the middle of a calm residential area near the Ljubljanica, the river that runs through the Slovenian capital, there is an old house left standing for no good reason, whose fragile, crumbling façade is a constant hazard for passers-by. Every morning when I pass this ruin, I count its broken windows. And every morning, without fail, I lose count when I come to a particular one on the ground floor. Someone has created a mini-jungle with a dozen or so plants in between the inner and outer layers of glazing, still misty though the plants are drying out. Behind the jungle is a yellowing curtain; behind that, an olive-green sewing machine. The sight of the sewing machine disturbs me in the same way as a documentary about the backward regions of Russia might.

I turn my head and immediately see my old aunt, enjoying her first cigarette of the morning at a fifth-floor window in a big modern building. She swapped her old, stucco-ceilinged apartment, which was horribly cold in winter, for this modern, centrally heated studio flat 10 years ago. She lives alone, and in her immaculate hair and make-up and pearl necklace she knows how to chase the devil away. 'I see him in the corner of my bedroom, and I briskly yell at him to get out, and he gets out,' she tells me. The devil defeated behind a plain pastel façade – it's a reassuring thought.

But when I pass my aunt's old building, I doubt whether the people who now live in her big sitting room know how to chase the devil away as she does. The vaulted windows are forlorn and dirty, the venetian blinds peeling and crooked.

The white façade of the Ursuline convent presents a more cheerful sight, with its long rows of windows, all opaque – plus a false one painted in *trompe-l'œil* on the second floor. The sisters, not as numerous nowadays as they once were, rent out part of the building. 'They are merciless,' moans one of their tenants, an architect. 'I've explained my situation to them, but they won't budge an inch when it comes to paying the rent.' It makes me smile to hear this. In my mind's eye I picture one of those magnificent creatures all in white and with great locks of white hair who would come to the hero's aid at the crucial moment in Louis de Funès's comedies. (These are the happy images of a world where the Mother Superior can choose to be

Slovenia: Ljubljana and its windows

obstinate. Images of a free world. It hasn't always been like that in this country.)

In Ljubljana, like anywhere else, there are windows that don't give anything away to passers-by. There's one on the fourteenth floor of a granite tower in the city centre. One day, I happened to discover that it belonged to a notary. In his office, a black-haired young man, tanned in

November, makes me a coffee and for a second I believe I'm in some California soap opera. But no. I look out of the window and see my home town nestling between its two round, green hills, glowing like a child tucked up in a duvet. On the southern hill stands the ochre castle. The bricks of its new roof are all the same red; it doesn't look quite right. It's a picture-postcard castle, a commonplace, but isn't it human nature to love the things we recognise?

In Ljubljana, like anywhere else, there are also windows that seem to have more to tell than they actually do. The Franciscan church is huge, and the windows at the top of its lateral wall are almost out of sight. Their grey opacity tickles my imagination – I like to picture how the light is inside: a pink and silver light like the one that appears on a black-and-white photograph if you open the darkroom door before it is finished. (This year, a few days after Christmas, I went into the church to see the crib. The nave was buzzing with people. Suddenly: silence. A helium-inflated balloon illustrated with Pikachu has slipped out of a little boy's hands and now glides slowly but surely upwards. The shiny object ends up pushing against the indistinct *trompe-l'œil* frescoes on the ceiling. To my amazement, the balloon's former owner does not burst into tears.)

In the heart of the old town, a lovely veranda with coloured panes of glass sometimes makes me think of an era when people lived slower and more sheltered lives than we do now. The charm of the past is not unlike that of childhood; both contain something artificial and deceptive. Childhood suffering only becomes insignificant when it is put into perspective, a purely rational operation that part of us will always resist. (I'm thinking of one night in spring 1895, and a little girl asleep. One of the walls in her house is brought down by an earthquake, but neither the noise nor the cold manage to wake the girl; she sleeps on for hours under the stars.)

Yesterday afternoon, I sat at my desk, overlooking the junction, to write this piece. That very moment, two pigeons started copulating on the balcony. Their passion amazed me, amused me and ultimately moved me to shut the blind. ❏

Katarina Marincic teaches French literature at the University of Ljubljana. She has published three novels. Her most recent, Prikrita Harmonija (Hidden Harmony)*, a tale of Central Europe against the backdrop of World War I, won the Kresnik prize for the best Slovenian novel in 2001*

Translated by GC

WAITING IN THE WINGS

MICHAEL FOLEY

INCLUSION IN THE EU MAY BE THE
ONLY WAY OF RESOLVING CONFLICT
AMONG THE COMPLICATED ETHNIC
MIX OF THE BALKANS

The past is a different country and nowhere is this more evident than in the former communist countries of Eastern and South-Eastern Europe. Take, for instance, Sofia, which expects to be an EU capital in 2007. The degree of change is such that in the early 1990s the *Rough Guide* to Bulgaria was hard pushed to find a decent restaurant outside an overpriced hotel. Sofia, it says, was never the liveliest of Balkan capitals, 'its social life suffering from the endless moralising of a regime which frowned on ostentation and promoted modesty of habits'. Back then it could say things were improving and that state-owned restaurants and cafés were attaining financial independence. In those days, the remnants of communist rule were still in evidence. The Georgi Dimitrov mausoleum that once housed the body of the founder of communist Bulgaria was still in place in central Sofia, even if Mr Dimitrov's body had been removed elsewhere. Today it is gone and until recently a large ad for Tullamore Dew Irish Whiskey stood in its place.

Today Boulevard Vitosha, Sofia's main street, is full of designer shops. All around central Sofia are ultra-cool bars and restaurants. Luxury goods from Western Europe and the US are on sale at Western European and US prices. A large four-wheel drive with tinted windows is a favourite vehicle. But behind the modernity is evidence of another Sofia. Granted, there are still signs of the former regime: the old party headquarters, a magnificent example of Stalinist neo-classical architecture, still straddles a junction looking like a great ship, dominating the centre of the city. But look even closer, and you find that the cracks have not quite been covered over. Criminal gangs are regularly involved in shoot-outs. Journalists tell you that corruption exists at every level and if you are wondering who can shop at all those designer shops, well, hardly anyone actually, as so many are simply money-laundering operations.

But there is another Sofia, where people live on little more than €100 (cUS$75) a month. A 10-minute walk from Boulevard Vitosha and its

*Bulgaria, Sofia: former
Party headquarters.
Credit: Michael Foley*

designer shops is the Ladies' Market, a huge network of stalls and market buildings that sells everything and sells it cheap. Here one can get a glimpse of what Sofia might have been like before the communist takeover of 1947 and the more recent mafia rule. Even some of the buildings have an Ottoman feel. Here, farmers come to sell bags of potatoes, handfuls of herbs and bags of spices, tomatoes and cucumbers fresh from the fields; the smells are not of pizza and McDonald's but of kebabs. Here Sofia becomes the capital of a South-East European country.

Take the metro to the end of the line, to Obelia, one of the communities of crumbling concrete apartment buildings that house Sofia's working class, built during the 1960s and 1970s. Here, green areas are knee-high in weeds. The shops are rusty metal stalls. In some places, residents have tried to brighten the place by sowing some flowers or vegetables but it is just too bleak and desolate to make a difference. In the distance, across a large scrubby green space are more crumbling buildings.

Back in the centre and behind the façades of Western shops and fast-food plastic shopfronts the plasterwork is falling off in chunks, windows are covered in plastic sheeting, pipes are rusty and the walls are discoloured by water stains. The roads, including the main roads, are pock-marked with holes; even the main road from the airport to the centre of the city is pot-holed to excess. The pavements of Sofia are more or less a jigsaw of cracked and broken paving that clicks and kicks back as you walk. Street furniture such as traffic lights, traffic signs and bollards are rusted and broken. There are inexplicable lumps of metal sticking out of the pavements that once presumably had some function, but are now waiting to impale passers-by. In another culture this would be compensation heaven.

Bulgaria may have dangerous levels of corruption and organised crime; it may have high levels of poverty; but it has embraced the market economy and is joining the EU by 2007.

So popular is the EU that almost the first thing you see on arriving at Sofia airport is a huge EU flag descending from the ceiling over passport control. Outside, the blue and golden stars of the EU fly alongside the Bulgarian flag over government buildings. Near the Sheraton Hotel, the sellers of cheap souvenirs and postcards sell little Bulgarian flags and, of course, the EU one as well. One visitor suggested that Bulgaria was hoping some EU official would see so many flags he'd assume the country must already have joined without anyone noticing.

It would be a mistake to see Sofia as simply a European capital waiting patiently for its turn to take up its EU membership. It has, no doubt, achieved a remarkable turnabout; it is, after all, only 10 years since inflation was so high the government just had to chop zeros off the value of the currency as it became increasingly worthless. Today, the economy is stable and inflation under control.

Political observers in Bulgaria do not view its EU membership as a favour but a right. It is the culmination of a debate that was taking place since liberation in 1876 right up to the communist victory in 1947: does Bulgaria face Russia or Europe? Does it modernise or, in the words of one political scientist, become a mafiocracy? If it continues on its journey towards the EU, it means much of South-Eastern Europe follows. If the initial impetus to a union within Europe was to stop further conflict after World War II, then stability in today's Balkans must be ensured by offering the region membership without strings.

Bulgaria will be the first of the old communist Balkan countries to take up its right. In Sofia, journalists and academics remind visitors that Bulgaria was a model of stability and peace throughout the 1990s. It was the first country to recognise Macedonia, despite what some might see as unfinished business in terms of its borders. All of this will confer the further right to join European institutions; and, if Bulgaria has that right, so does the rest of the Balkans; and if the Balkans join, so does Turkey.

Bulgaria may have lived under the Ottoman yoke, as they say in this part of the world, for 500 years, but the people of the country have a shared history; one of the two parties in the present coalition is the party of the

Turkish minority. Three years ago, there was the threat of civil war in Macedonia between Slavs and Albanians – Orthodox Christians and Muslims. Realising only too well how easily this part of the world could flare up and pull Albania, Serbia, Bulgaria and possibly Greece and Turkey into a war, the EU got involved and won a significant victory. The same thinking means that once Bulgaria raises the flag of the EU as a member rather than as an aspirant, the rest of the region, including Turkey, cannot be far behind. ❏

Michael Foley *is a journalist and academic who teaches at the Dublin Institute of Technology and is currently working in partnership with the BBC on an EU journalism project in Bulgaria*

CULTURE: LOOT!
EDWARD LUCIE-SMITH

**WITH THE OLYMPIC GAMES
RETURNING HOME TO ATHENS
THIS YEAR, GREECE IS ONCE
MORE DEMANDING THE RETURN
OF THE PARTHENON MARBLES**

*Arch of Titus, Rome (AD c81), built to celebrate the emperor's sack of Jerusalem in AD 70
and depicting the loot from the city, in particular the candelabra and menorah stolen
from the temple. Credit: Bridgeman Art Library*

Perhaps the best known of all the images that show the looting of artistic property is the relief on the Arch of Titus in Rome that depicts soldiers carrying the great menorah from the Second Temple in Jerusalem, seized when the Roman army captured the city and destroyed the building in AD 70. Its precious ornaments were paraded in an imperial Triumph that emphasised the utter subjection of the Jews. Doubtless after that these were melted down as a contribution to the imperial treasury. Just suppose, however, that by some chance the great seven-branched candlestick survived, and was now dug up at some archaeological site in Italy. Who would have the best claim to it? The modern state of Israel, seeing itself as the legitimate successor, even after nearly two millennia, of the nation that Titus destroyed, would doubtless make a claim. But modern Italians might also think that the object was part of the long history of their nation.

The current agitation about the 'restitution' of artistic treasures of all kinds to their original locations is usually presented as overdue justice for faults committed by European colonialism. In fact, this is a serious over-simplification. Conquering armies have always regarded works of art as legitimate spoil. Swedish collections, for instance, are rich in objects from the collection of the Hapsburg Emperor Rudolph II, taken during the Thirty Years War. These, however, were not generally the work of Czech artists but the possessions of an alien court that had based itself for a while in Prague. The modern Czech Republic does not pine for them too much, even when there is proof that they were actually created in Bohemia.

Modern attitudes to the legitimate or illegitimate possession of famous artworks can be traced to the European Enlightenment that blossomed in the late eighteenth century, and in particular to the impact made by Enlightenment ideas on the men of the French Revolution.

It was Enlightenment thinking that gave those in charge of the revolutionary government the idea of creating a great museum, open to all, in the Louvre. This was inaugurated in August 1793, and soon came into possession of masterpieces seized in the Low Countries during the campaigns of 1794, and in Italy in 1796. There was always disagreement about the moral justification for these seizures. In October 1796, for example, a number of eminent French artists, among them Isabey, Gérard, Horace Vernet and the great flower-painter Redouté, signed a petition asserting that the best place for the artistic treasures found in Rome was no longer Italy but France: 'The French Republic, because of its strength, its intellectual superiority and the superiority of its artists, is the only place in the world that can give a real home to these masterpieces.' Others were not so certain. Another petition submitted to the government queried this policy: 'Citizen Directors . . . we beg you to consider maturely this important question: whether it is useful to France, and advantageous to artists and art in general, to displace from Rome the monuments of antiquity and the masterpieces of painting and sculpture which make up the galleries and museums in this capital of the arts.' Why not, they asked, study instead the ruins of Provence, where the Venus of Arles had recently been found?

The seizures nevertheless went ahead, and in July 1798 there was a public festival in Paris when the treasures taken from all over Italy were paraded through Paris mounted on 29 triumphal cars. The horses from the Basilica of San Marco (originally loot from Byzantium, seized by the Venetians during the Crusader sack of the city in 1204) were on view, as were the Dying Gaul, the Apollo Belvedere, Raphael's *Transfiguration* and paintings by Titian and Veronese. Intermingled with the cars bearing the precious works of art were various exotic animals, dromedaries from Africa and bears from Switzerland. When the procession finally halted at the Champ-de-Mars an official speech of welcome was made, thanking the Goddess of Liberty, 'that avenger of the long-humiliated arts, who has broken the chains that hampered the renown of so many of the celebrated dead'.

One of the signatories of the petition protesting against the looting of Italian art treasures by the forces of the new French Republic was Dominique-Vivant Denon (1747–1825). Originally a diplomat who served the *ancien régime* in St Petersburg and later in Naples, Denon became one of the major functionaries of the Napoleonic Empire. His close association with the Emperor began when he accompanied Napoleon's expedition to Egypt in 1798. Later, he was the director of the great and ephemeral Musée Napoléon created in the Louvre, as well as being the Emperor's general director of the arts.

He is a significant figure in all three roles. The French Egyptian campaign was responsible for the first thorough, scholarly exploration of a non-European civilisation by European savants, and the first attempt to assimilate elements of that civilisation into European culture. It is worth contrasting the attitudes of the scholars who accompanied the French army to Egypt with those of the sixteenth-century Spanish conquistadors in Mexico and Peru. The few objects the conquerors saved from the wreck of the Aztec and Inca empires they pulled down were regarded in Europe merely as incomprehensible curiosities, of no artistic value. In 1798 the attitude was quite different. The great *Déscription de l'Egypte* (1809–28), published in 21 huge, superbly illustrated volumes by Denon and his team, was an attempt to explore every aspect of the country, but particularly its Pharaonic antiquities. In the introductory essay, Egypt was presented as the true birthplace of the arts.

One result of Napoleon's expedition was the discovery of the Rosetta Stone. Found by French soldiers in 1799 at the town of Rosetta (Rashid) in the Egyptian Delta, it was seized when the army Napoleon had abandoned in Egypt was forced to surrender to the British, and is now in the British Museum. Carved under the Ptolemies in 196 BC, the slab carries an inscription in two languages, Greek and Egyptian, using three scripts – Greek, Egyptian demotic and Egyptian hieroglyphic. Thanks to the fact that the texts parallel one another, it proved possible to decipher the hieroglyphic pictograms that had hitherto resisted interpretation. This triumph of scholarship took place only after the fall of Napoleon, but was due to a French Egyptologist, Jean-François Champollion (1790–1832). His linguistic discoveries unlocked the whole story of ancient Egypt and immensely enlarged the perspective of human history. The publication of Champollion's results was arguably the decisive step away from a completely Eurocentric view of world events, even more so than the publication of the *Déscription de l'Egypte*. The ancient Egyptians, thanks to a French interpreter, could now speak for themselves.

Today, the Rosetta Stone is being insistently reclaimed by the contemporary Egyptian government. It is nevertheless possible to say, as this brief account shows, that it actually has more significance in terms of recent cultural developments in Europe than in those that have happened in Egypt itself during the past two millennia.

Denon, meanwhile, as director of the Musée Napoléon, completely reversed his attitudes about the looting of artworks from the territories his master had conquered. In a few brief years he built up the most comprehensive collection of masterpieces the world had ever seen. He might even have succeeded in preserving it more or less intact but for Napoleon's escape from Elba. The dismantling of the vast array of masterworks Denon built up was triggered not by Napoleon's original fall, but by the 100 Days, an episode the victorious allies were determined to punish.

While most of the looted works were returned to their original possessors, some were not. One that remained behind in Paris was Veronese's *Marriage Feast at Cana*, taken from the refectory of San Giorgio Maggiore in Venice. The excuse for failing to return it was that the canvas was too vast to travel safely. It had already had to be cut in half in order to bring it to Paris. A painting by the French artist Charles Le Brun was sent to Venice instead.

Another celebrated painting that failed to go back to its original home was Velázquez's *The Water Seller of Seville*. Found rolled up in the abandoned carriage of Joseph Bonaparte after the battle of Vitoria in 1813,

Velázquez's much-looted picture The Water Seller of Seville *never did get home. Credit: AKG Images*

it was given by the restored Bourbons to the British victor, the Duke of Wellington. It now hangs in Apsley House.

Perhaps the most famous – some would say most notorious – act of transference, or looting, during the Napoleonic period was nothing to do with imperial conquests. It was the arrival of the so-called Elgin Marbles in Britain. These were removed from the Parthenon in 1806, under the terms of a firman obtained by Lord Elgin from the Ottoman government. The contemporary Greek claim to the sculptures of the Parthenon is deeply felt, and public opinion seems now to be swinging to the Greek view of the question. However, the matter is a little more complicated than it seems at first.

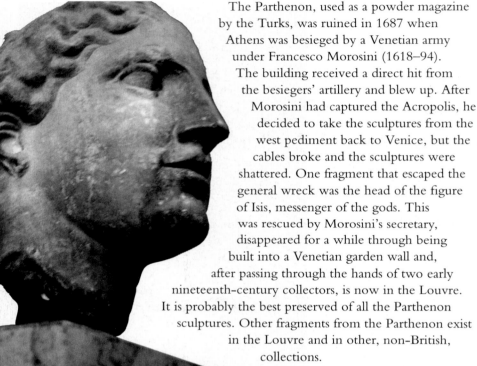

The Parthenon, used as a powder magazine by the Turks, was ruined in 1687 when Athens was besieged by a Venetian army under Francesco Morosini (1618–94). The building received a direct hit from the besiegers' artillery and blew up. After Morosini had captured the Acropolis, he decided to take the sculptures from the west pediment back to Venice, but the cables broke and the sculptures were shattered. One fragment that escaped the general wreck was the head of the figure of Isis, messenger of the gods. This was rescued by Morosini's secretary, disappeared for a while through being built into a Venetian garden wall and, after passing through the hands of two early nineteenth-century collectors, is now in the Louvre. It is probably the best preserved of all the Parthenon sculptures. Other fragments from the Parthenon exist in the Louvre and in other, non-British, collections.

Parthenon pieces: head of Isis now in the Louvre. Credit: Musée du Louvre, Paris

If Morosini had carried off the pediment sculptures, as he intended, they would now almost certainly be housed in the archaeological museum in Venice, which is the one of the oldest public collections of its sort in the world. Athens would have about as much chance of getting them back as Istanbul has of reclaiming the bronze horses from San Marco.

Though both sides in the debate about the Parthenon sculptures attempt to couch their arguments in rational terms, it is clear that reason has little to do with the matter. When Morosini besieged Athens, the Greek nation did not exist. The same situation prevailed when Elgin obtained his firman. Though the Greek authorities sometimes speak of reuniting the marbles with the building they were made for, not simply of reuniting the sculptures themselves, this can never in fact take place, given both the condition of the building itself and the horrible pollution of modern Athens. If the sculptures go back to Greece, they will have to be housed in a new museum, close to the ruins of the Parthenon but not part of them. The Pasok government, led by Costas Simitis, was busy building just such a museum before the recent Greek elections, and it was clear that Pasok thought of the triumphant return of the Marbles as something that might keep his government in power. It failed to get them, lost the contest, and work on the project has been halted, on the grounds that a major archaeological site was being destroyed.

The Parthenon Marbles are, nevertheless, an immensely potent symbol of modern Greek nationhood, intimately part of the national psyche. In particular, they have come to symbolise the determination of the Greeks to reknit their links with the remote classical past – with Greece not only before the Ottoman conquests but even before the Romans. This is, paradoxically, a sentiment with which Lord Elgin himself might well have sympathised. His interest in the sculptures was linked to the conviction, increasingly prevalent in Europe in the opening decades of the nineteenth century, that Greece must be rescued from the Turkish yoke. He was, after all, a contemporary of Byron, who nevertheless made vicious fun of him, mocking his syphilitic nose and adding, for good measure:

Let Aberdeen and Elgin still pursue
The Shade of fame through regions of virtu;
Waste useless thousands on their Phidean freaks;
Misshapen monuments and maim'd antiques;
And make their grand saloons a general mart
For all the mutilated blocks of art.

Yet Byron's words are significant in a sense other than the one he intended. They point, though inadvertently, to the revolution in taste that the marbles' presence in London brought about, accompanied by a revolution in scholarship to a much clearer understanding of the evolution of the classical style. This evolution also owed its impetus to the education based on classical texts that every cultivated person then received.

This broad significance, paradoxically enough, is one of the reasons why the Marbles should go back to Athens without further carping. The legalities cited by both sides are essentially irrelevant. No doubt many of the same points could be made about another set of major Greek sculptures that now resides in a European museum – the reliefs from the Great Altar of Pergamon now in Berlin. Pergamon is now Turkish and the Turks do not regard classical art and its development as an essential part of their history. Greece is right to feel that revived nationhood needs and deserves this symbolic focus, after so many centuries of humiliation.

The debate about the Marbles can still, despite all this, be usefully referred to the Enlightenment ideas I have already cited. The notion of the universal museum, open to all – embracing, eventually, all human cultures – was a British, not a French invention. The key date is the foundation of the British Museum in 1753, which marks the transition from the hugger-mugger accumulations of princely *Wunderkammer* to the idea of a collection of artworks and other objects as an instrument of rational enquiry. When,

Horseman of the Acropolis: will he make it home from the British Museum to Athens?
Credit: AKG Images

for example, we speak of the European interest in 'primitive' or tribal art, we need to remember that the first specimens of this kind to enter European collections were not African but the Maori artefacts and sculptures from Oceania brought back to Europe by Captain Cook. The first exhibition of Maori work was held in 1803, in the British Museum's South Sea Room. Today, 28 of the Maori items in the museum's collection can be traced to Cook's three voyages of exploration between 1768 and 1780. These items are older than almost any Maori items that survive elsewhere, even in New Zealand itself. To think of them as items of loot, unjustly wrenched from the hands of their original possessors, is to do Cook and his contemporaries a serious injustice. Without Cook's intervention, these objects would almost certainly not have survived until the present day.

The depredations committed during a series of nineteenth-century colonial wars are now the chief focus of today's restitutionists, as are the large-scale and often fairly brutal archaeological excavations conducted at non-European sites. Among these were Belzoni's digs in Egypt, Layard's at Nineveh and Schliemann's at Troy (the modern Hissarlik). Schliemann displayed an unscrupulousness that was fairly typical of many of his archaeological confrères at that time. The firman he obtained from the Ottoman authorities in 1871 stated that any treasure found must be divided with the Turkish government. Two years later, Schliemann found the so-called 'Gold of Troy' and promptly smuggled it out of the country. At the end of World War II the Trojan booty was seized in Berlin by the victorious Russian army. It is now in the Pushkin Museum in Moscow. There seems little hope that it will ever return to its place of origin and contemporary Turks do not in any case regard it as part of their own history, any more than they think of the Pergamon sculptures in that context.

Another smuggled object of major importance remains in Berlin – the famous portrait bust of Nefertiti, found in 1912 by a German archaeological expedition working at Tell-el-Amarna. The contract signed with the Egyptian authorities stated clearly that all finds must be equally divided and

Jade Maori Tiki in the British Museum: not 'unjustly wrenched' but given in friendship . . . Credit: Bridgeman Art Library

Karnak, from Denon's Déscription de l'Égypte. *Credit: Bibliothèque Nationale, Paris*

that unique objects must remain in the country. The bust was, nevertheless, sent to Germany, disguised as a box of broken pottery. Here the case for restitution is perfectly clear, and it is surprising that the Egyptian government has not pursued it more vigorously. It is equally surprising that these stories, which are well known and well documented, arouse much less emotion than the conduct of the European powers in Africa.

Where wars are concerned, the attention of modern moralists has been directed largely to the behaviour of the European colonial powers in Africa, for example to the booty taken as a result of the British conquests of Kumasi in 1874 and Benin in 1897.

Until very recently, less attention was paid to the sack, in 1860, of the Summer Palace near Beijing by an Anglo-French expeditionary force. However, in 2000, there was uproar at a Christie's auction held in Hong Kong when two bronze fountainheads representing a monkey and an ox were put up for sale. They brought over US$1 million each and their appearance evoked vigorous protests from the official Chinese Cultural

Relics Bureau. There was also a noisy demonstration at the hotel where the auction took place. A Christie's spokesperson retorted that both items had been seen at auction before – the monkey in New York in 1987, the ox in London in 1989 – and that the auction house was in any case only acting as an agent for the vendors. 'When we undertake to sell property we do so with the understanding that owners have good title under international laws. We always support the claims of rightful owners through due legal process,' she said. This, like legalistic arguments about the Parthenon Marbles, was beside the point. The protest, like the agitation about the Marbles, arose from a sense of cultural humiliation – rage and shame triggered by what happened to the great civilisation of China from the mid-nineteenth century until well past the middle of the twentieth century.

The international laws the spokesperson for Christie's was referring to were largely constructed during the course of the very nineteenth century that perpetrated so many unlawful seizures. Particularly relevant is the Declaration of Brussels on the Customs of War, signed by 15 nations, including Britain, France, Germany, Spain, Belgium and Turkey. Its provisions were further codified in The Hague Conventions on Laws and Customs of War on Land, signed in 1899 and 1907. These specified that the property of religious, charitable and educational institutions, as well as of those dedicated to art and science 'shall be treated as private property' – ie, should be exempt from expropriation by the victor in any conflict. In the colonial period, these provisions, in non-European contexts, were often honoured more in the breach than the observance.

However, recent disputes about the fate and ownership of important cultural artefacts have started to focus on things that the advocates of wholesale restitution find uncomfortable to contemplate. One is that objects regarded as sacred in a particular context – Maori art and Native American artworks come to mind – are often regarded as taboo, not for contemplation or handling by those outside the ethnic group. To restore these to their original context is also an act of deprivation. They are removed from the sphere of general accessibility and therefore from the sphere of universal knowledge.

Another objection to restitution is quite simply that it sometimes seems likely to place irreplaceable works of art in a situation of physical threat. The fate of the national museums in Kabul under the Taliban, and in Baghdad after the US conquest, are sufficient warning.

The conclusion may be that when we talk about the looting of cultural objects we may in fact be working within the wrong framework, both intellectually and emotionally. Disputes about what should live where and what belongs to whom tend to focus, as I have tried to demonstrate here, not on the 'masterpieces' themselves, but on people's feelings about them. We are, for example, almost at the point, technologically, where it would be possible to make perfect facsimiles of the Parthenon sculptures – without even having to make casts. Through the use of lasers, minutely faithful reproduction is possible, without the need for physical contact. Would a set of perfect copies satisfy the Greek government and public? Of course not. Like the rest of us, contemporary Greeks have been imbued with a notion of 'originality' that is a purely Western, post-Renaissance invention. The spread of this idea to cultures other than our own can even be thought of as part of the history of colonialism. It has no real place in the history of Chinese art, for example.

At the same time, there are already an increasing number of situations where the actual originals are not shown. In Vienna, the Albertina has long displayed its incomparable collection of Dürer drawings only in the form of collotype reproductions. The cave at Lascaux is closed to the public, because the palaeolithic paintings were being irreparably damaged by the presence of too many visitors. Go there and all you will see are facsimiles. There is even talk of creating a *faux* version of Giotto's Scrovegni Chapel in Padua, in order to preserve the original.

In other words, all the clamour about physical possession may just be so much self-indulgence. Our real duty may be to the simple physical survival of the masterpiece, even if this means living at arm's length from it. ❏

Edward Lucie-Smith *is a writer and art critic*

Kabul Museum 1995: not protected so much as plundered by warring foreign and Afghan armies. Credit: Steve McCurry / Magnum Photos

Football and Fascism
The National Game under Mussolini

Simon Martin

Published in September by Berg

HB (ISBN 1 85973 700 5) Price £50.00   PB (ISBN 1 85973 698 X) Price £15.99

READER OFFER!

Index readers can buy this book at 20% discount by contacting

the Berg Order Hotline and quoting reference AU18

Tel. (01202) 665432   Fax (01202) 666219   Email: orders@orcabookservices.co.uk

VOICES UNDER OCCUPATION
WENDY PEARLMAN

*Every Palestinian man, woman, and child in the West Bank and Gaza has a story
to tell about how his or her life has been affected by the Israeli occupation in general
and the current violence in particular.* Occupied Voices: Stories of Everyday Life
from the Second Intifada *presents interviews with the few dozen people whom
I was able to meet when I lived and travelled in the Palestinian territories. The
photographs and stories in the book offer one window into the pain, dreams and
resilience of real people enduring a terrible conflict.*

*Some will read the suffering portrayed in these interviews and retort, 'Yes, but
Israelis have suffered, too.' They will be right but they will have missed the point.
I am not trying to argue that Palestinians' miseries trump those of Israelis, only that
Palestinians be given the chance to express themselves in their own terms. Others
may say: 'Yes, but given the suicide bombings, Israel must act to defend itself.' They
too will be right and they too will have missed the point. Many of the hardships
described in this book are difficult to justify on the grounds of security. Moreover, the
volume as a whole paints a portrait of the kind of political and social context that
nourishes extremism. While particular stories will vary, the message remains the
same: a nation's cry for the right to live with freedom and dignity on its own land.*
WP

AZZA, A FILM-MAKER LIVING IN RAMALLAH

The main theme in Palestinian art is usually Palestine,
as if it were illegal to talk about anything else. That is
because it is the main issue, the main priority. But human
lives should never be one-dimensional, so this is very
unhealthy. Maybe when this whole issue is settled we
can start to be self-reflective and think about our own
identities and own culture. We need the space to think
of new things.

I always laugh because liberal Israelis call me and say,
'We're looking for Palestinian films that do not talk about the political
situation, you know, films that talk about day-to-day life.' I laugh because
we don't have anything like that. What are they going on about? We don't
have day-to-day life apart from the political situation. I want to have day-
to-day life.

For example, you should watch Palestinian *Candid Camera*. *Candid Camera* is done all over the world, and they did a Palestinian version on Palestinian TV. They want it to be funny, but it is about Palestinians and Israelis. One of the episodes is about a Palestinian guy who is running from the soldiers and he goes from house to house and says, 'Can you hide me?' And this is supposed to be funny! The point is that *Candid Camera* is supposed to be about day-to-day life, and this is day-to-day life for us.

SUZANNE, JOURNALIST FROM JENIN

I was in the fourth grade when the first intifada started. So you can say that my whole childhood was spent during the intifada. And I suffered as all Palestinians suffered. Because I was a child at the time, most of my experiences revolved around school. I can still remember how it felt to sit in class and hear all the shooting and screaming coming from outside. You just tried to close your eyes and concentrate on the lesson, but it was so hard to do.

There is something else that I will never forget. My school was in an area where there were confrontations, so the Israelis set up barriers to block the road that led to the school. We were able to move the lower barrier but we couldn't move the top one. This made a little open space, sort of like a tunnel.

So every day, we got down on our hands and knees and crawled through the little tunnel. This was the only way to pass through and reach the school. It was so humiliating. Can you imagine? You and your teacher and your classmates – everyone who has to get to school – crouching on their knees. Every day we had to do it. Our hands and knees would get dirty. Our uniforms and socks would get dirty . . . What more do I have to tell you than that?

Because of all of this, I have a hurt inside me, and I don't think it will ever go away. The hurt is called Palestine.

MAHMOUD, OWNER OF A DEMOLISHED HOUSE IN GAZA

I was just taking an afternoon nap when suddenly I woke up to all this noise outside. I looked out of the window and saw a tank and soldiers surrounding my house . . . My wife was eight months pregnant at the time, and I was afraid for her and the baby. So we managed to escape and made it to the house of some relatives not too far away.

We tried to drive back to our house several times, but each time the army and the settlers would come after us and we'd have to flee again. Finally, at 10 o'clock that night a bulldozer came. They bulldozed four houses: my house, my brother's house along with his clinic, and the houses of our two other relatives . . .

We're not asking for a lot. Originally, all of Palestine belonged to us. But we have recognised the State of Israel. We don't say that we want all of Palestine. We don't want to take back Haifa and we don't want the Jews to leave. We don't talk about any of that. We only talk about ending the problems that we have to live with every day . . .

That's my story. One day we had a house and a garden and everything was fine. And then, suddenly, we didn't have a house any more. We didn't have anything besides the clothes on our backs. We had to start over at square one. We had just got married so everything was new. I had all new furniture, including a television, a refrigerator, a bed and dresser, curtains – everything, everything. I had worked for eight years to get married and buy a house, and it was ruined in a single minute. Everything was destroyed. Now it is prohibited for me to return to the land where my house once stood. The Israelis took control over the entire area. But I want to return. I would like to have my house there. I would like to plant a garden again.

Or maybe I'll change my mind and decide to buy another house. The point is that I should decide. There shouldn't always be someone else forcing me to go here or there. It's an issue of rights. I need to take back my rights. But now there are no rights to take.

SANA, NINTH-GRADER FROM HEBRON

We're really scared when we get trapped in the school and there is all this shooting going on outside. The principal will go and try to reach an agreement with the Israelis so they let us go home. She'll ask them to stop

shooting for long enough for us to be able to go out and cross the street. If they don't let us pass, then we end up trapped at school for a long time. If they do agree to let us go, then they won't shoot at us while we're crossing the street. But as soon as we get to the other side, they start shooting again. So then we all just have to run.

MUNA, MOTHER OF A 15-YEAR-OLD KILLED AT A 'CLASH POINT'

He was killed on a Sunday. That Saturday, we worked together in the little garden behind the house. He helped me prune the trees and tend the crops. We worked all morning. I made him the breakfast that he liked, *fatat al-hummus*. I made the food that he loved and I made it as a surprise. When I was preparing it, I said, 'Please God, don't let Mohammed come into the kitchen and see me,' so that it really would be a surprise. I don't know why, I just had this sense. And it was a surprise, because Mohammed was just sitting in front of the TV. So I came in and put the plate in front of him and he was so happy! He said, 'You made the dish that I love, *fatat al-hummus*. It's so delicious!'

His dad left for Kuwait the week before in order to renew his residency visa. He called on Sunday . . . Mohammed asked his dad to bring him new pyjamas, a jacket and clothes for school. And later that day Mohammed was killed. He was killed before his dad got back, before he saw his presents. His dad came back the day after Mohammed was killed and on the third day we buried him . . .

According to our religion, our son is now with God in heaven. He eats, drinks and lives his life. But he has been taken from me! If he had grown up and was a believer and prayed and knew God, then he still would have gone to heaven. They took away life; they took my son's life away. The hardest thing in the world is to lose a child. You want to demand from the whole world that those soldiers be brought to justice, because these children are not dangerous . . .

We are people. We are human beings. We raise our children and we are tired . . . Palestinian women love their children . . . Our children are our land and our lives, we'd do anything to protect them.

KHALED, ACTOR IN BEIT JALA

We have children who come to the theatre to do ballet . . . Palestinians have *debka*, a traditional folk dance. We don't have ballet. But people see

ballet on TV and they see that it is something beautiful. So we brought in a ballet instructor and people loved it. This is culture. It's learning about other people and other ways of life.

So one day, the children were at the theatre practising when they started bombing outside. My co-workers took the girls to take cover in the kitchen during the shelling. Another time, they started bombing when we were in the middle of a drama class. Now children are scared to come to the theatre. We have to think of alternative ways to encourage them to come again.

So you see that Israel is not only bombing buildings and the outside of things. They are destroying our insides, too. They are destroying how we work and the strategies we use to go about our lives.

IMAN, COLLEGE STUDENT IN BIRZEIT

TV is filled with news about funerals and bombings, so I don't watch it any more. I don't even listen to the radio because they just play nationalistic songs and news about those who've been killed . . .

But I also have to live . . . One day a student brought a cake to the university to celebrate his birthday. Those days the news was filled with stories about all the Palestinians who were being killed. The students couldn't believe that he wanted to celebrate at a time like that.

We were all talking about it, but then one of the professors told us to stop. He said that this person was committed to carrying on with life, and we should respect that . . .

Sometimes I feel that it is selfish to be a student when so many people are suffering. At the same time, I need to graduate so I can be of service to my people . . . Each one of us has his own duty . . . It is when we act as one that we can make a statement.

AHMED, PSYCHOLOGIST IN GAZA

The Israelis piled up two mountains of sand on the road. Cars could not cross, but people could go by on foot. They could have stopped people from going altogether, but didn't. Their aim was simply to make things more difficult for people. At first, people were very angry. But after a few days, they adjusted and dealt with the mountains as if they were just another part of ordinary life. People would talk and students would tell jokes as they climbed across. Other people started selling things there, and it became a regular free market zone.

SAMIA, COMMUNITY VOLUNTEER IN EAST JERUSALEM

My children and grandchildren don't know a Jew except as an Israeli military occupier. But I will always cherish the years in which I lived in Palestine before 1948, when all – Palestinians, Jews, Christians and Muslims – lived side by side. I am privileged to have lived during that era.

We had Jewish neighbours when we were living in Safad. I remember that at Easter time my mother would give me a plate of special Easter cookies to take down to our neighbour Hannah. She would in turn send back her daughter with a plate filled with something special that she had baked.

You know something. In the early 1940s, World War II was still raging. We didn't know if Germany or the Allies would turn out to be the winners. Mrs Eisenberg was so scared for her daughter. So she came to my mother and said, 'Linda, if Germany comes into this country, will you consider Batia your daughter?'

My mother used to repeat this story always, and I am telling it to you to show you what kind of relationship we had with each other. Our neighbour had enough trust to let her daughter be in the hands of an Arab family for fear of what she might be exposed to under Germany.

Years after my mother passed away, I was clearing some of her papers. In her address book I found an address with the name Batia and then another last name. I said to myself this must be Batia Eisenberg, who has taken on a new married name. She and her parents had visited my parents once after 1967.

You know, I kept that address on my desk for days and days and months. And, finally, I said I must contact Batia. After all that has

happened, maybe people like us could do something to set things straight and make things make sense. So I finally wrote her a letter. Unfortunately, the letter came back saying 'Address Unknown'.

I didn't say much in my letter. I didn't know if she would be interested in corresponding. Maybe she has lost a son or her husband. You never know. We have all had our share of suffering . . .

But what is important is not to lose hope and not to become bitter. Because if you're bitter, there is no way that you can communicate. And it is important to keep moving forward. That is basically what we try to do – to keep rekindling hope in the hearts of these children here in this school. We do this so that everything we do will have meaning. You're giving them hope in the future. And I hope this succeeds. ❏

Wendy Pearlman *is a PhD student of government at Harvard University, where she studies Middle East politics*

Excerpts from Occupied Voices: Stories of Everyday Life from the Second Intifada *by Wendy Pearlman (Thunder's Mouth Press/Nation Books, 2003) http://www.nationbooks.org*

ALBANIA IN AUGUST

LEDIO CAKAJ & MARIA BURNETT-GAUDIANI

Nestled between Greece, Kosovo and Montenegro, Albania is a forgotten slice of the European continent. The land of the ancient Illyrians borders the European Union in geographical terms, but is many miles away culturally, politically and socially after five centuries of Ottoman occupation and 50 years of tough isolationist communist rule.

While Italy and Greece have been part of the EU since its inception and many Eastern European nations are winding through the legal process for accession, the Albanian government is still attempting to initiate the first phase of negotiations with the EU. An EU report earlier this year criticised the Albanian government for failing to meet the economic and political standards stipulated by EU officials as crucial for negotiations to continue, which means that any prospect for the country's entry in the near future is bleak.

Most Albanians are in favour of joining the EU, attracted mainly by freedom of movement in Europe, which would eradicate illegal immigration, one of Albania's most severe problems for the past 14 years. When Albania might qualify to join the EU as a member state is anyone's guess, but optimists place that date in the 2020s.

But for now, we watch the jagged snow-capped peaks crumble into farmland and the Adriatic stretch out to the horizon line as our plane drops altitude and we skid to a halt in Albania's newly christened Mother Teresa airport. Having arrived there several times over the past few years, we can attest to the fact that there is no airport in the world better suited to a saint's protection.

To our relief, Mother Teresa has undergone a few cosmetic changes. In 2002, Albania announced a US$33 million contract with Lockheed Martin to launch a comprehensive air-traffic management effort, in part to manage the anticipated spike in air travel to Greece for the 2004 Olympic Games. In due course, Lockheed will provide new surveillance radar, navigation and landing aids, communications equipment and a new air-traffic control system. Meanwhile, the floors have been tiled with Italian marble, turning the entire new facility into a skating rink for air passengers. People are slipping in all directions, burdened by luggage spilling with the novelties

Beach in Vlora: where the Adriatic and Ionian seas join, burger bunkers land.
Credit: Maria Burdett-Gaudiani

of the West. A rolling bag clips the heels of its owner and he slips, falling squarely on his tail bone. In the US this would be a lawsuit waiting to happen, Maria tells me.

The newly tiled floors remind me of a story I once heard from the mayor of Tirana, Edi Rama. Sometime during the leadership of Sali Berisha in the mid-1990s, Berisha was given a lion as a gift from a visiting foreign dignitary. The lion was put in a cage in the national zoo in Tirana and several pounds of meat were awarded to him as daily rations. However, times were tough in Albania and the keepers decided that the beef or pork destined for the lion was much better consumed by their own families. To hide the theft, they fed the lion bread and other smaller animals from the zoo, with the exception of the monkey who was too fast for the ailing lion to catch. When the news came out that some government types would be coming to visit the lion, panic spread among the keepers. By this point, the lion was barely alive and very skinny. To make a good impression, they decided to pave the floor with Italian tiles, a luxury for any Albanian homeowner. When the group came to the zoo, they found a worn-out, emaciated lion slipping on to his face with each step as his paws were clearly not built for marble.

We meet my cousin who has come to pick us up, and notice young children trying to help foreigners carry their bags in exchange for a little money. A policeman comes up and screams at one: 'If I catch you, I will kick your ass.' The young one smiles slyly, utterly unintimidated. He offers to buy the policeman a beer later, if he let him make some money. After 50 years of communism, Albania's youngest generation has clearly grasped the basic concepts of capitalism.

Policemen, however, do not have an easy time in the new Albania. Wages are low and rumours of corruption have ruined their reputation. In our experience, the worst that could happen is that one might want a cold beer, especially in the hot summer. Most Albanian drivers are accustomed to that desire and generously try to reward the policemen for standing all day in the heat in the streets guarding the traffic. Last year, when we were travelling to the capital from Gjirokastra, a southern Albanian town, we hitched a ride with a local man. When we were stopped at one of the many police checkpoints, our driver refused to give the policeman any money. The driver logically argued that because his documents were in order, there was nothing expected of him. However, the policeman was not buying that: without an offer of cash, he asked the driver if he could use his mobile phone to make some calls.

My family has gone to the usual great lengths to welcome us home. A huge box of vegetables – tomatoes, courgettes, aubergines – sits in the kitchen. 'Why is it that foreigners like tomatoes so much?' my grandfather once asked. 'Because they are not genetically modified,' I hastily replied. The old man's blank look demanded further information. 'Because they don't have tomatoes like this, not fresh and ripe.'

My grandfather is a part of that generation of Albanians who fought in World War II for a better world, which turned out to be severe isolation for 45 years. He still lives in the same little apartment that 40 years of hard work earned him under communism, uneasy at the fact that many of his offspring are far away from him. As well as me and my brother, who studies in Milan, two of his nephews have emigrated to Greece. Poverty is another burden he has to bear, as well as loneliness. I can only imagine how he feels when at the beginning of every month he stands in a long queue to receive his meagre pension of US$50. 'I can't even have guests at home any more,' he complains. 'I can barely afford bread, let alone meat.'

Meat has always been close to the heart of Albanians and the more honourable the guest the more meat he should receive. In communist times, especially in the late 1980s, food rationing was common. When I was young, I would queue to receive our pound of butter for the month and the three pounds of meat. My mother would cut the meat into small pieces and put it in plastic bags to be refrigerated and used over the whole month. Since we did not have our own refrigerator, we tied our plastic bags with blue thread so they would not get confused with our neighbours' food.

After communism, when there were once again adequate supplies of goods, the desire to consume the luxuries of old was great – even though many people, like my grandfather, can only afford them with the help of their relatives.

Albania's new access to oil and butter has aroused the interest of scientists interested in how 'Westernisation' affects health. In communist Albania, private car ownership was banned and people consumed only what could be produced locally. Today, ageing Mercedes and BMWs tear through the country, and goods from Greece and Italy flood in. Needless to say, smoking has always been a national pastime. Not surprisingly, diabetes, heart disease and obesity are on the rise. In 2002, the Wellcome Trust announced that it would fund a survey to examine diabetes prevalence among the adult population of the capital. The scientists hope to arrive at a better understanding of the impact of rapid mechanisation, transport and changing lifestyles on disease patterns.

Albania's rapid introduction to the West's value system has had devastating impacts on the generation in their twenties, something I am exposed to time and again when I meet my old acquaintances. They usually spend long hours languishing in a local bar. The mixture of people frequenting the place is eclectic, but is mainly pimps and drug dealers, together with 'foot soldiers' who hang out with the pimp and drug-dealer wannabes. And still the bar is pretty normal, even respectable to a certain extent. Maria and I never have any trouble there, of course, because quite a few of these guys used to be my classmates, neighbours or football friends, but we certainly stand out in the crowd. First of all, there aren't many women in this bar and while the men are profoundly courteous to Maria,

Hanging out and keeping in touch in Tirana.
Credit: Maria Burdett-Gaudiani

it's clear they are disconcerted by her growing comprehension of Albanian. But well-placed euphemisms and some Greek keep her baffled all afternoon, and they can still conduct business with the boys.

One afternoon in the oppressive August heat, I am initiated into learning about the business dynamics of Italy. In August, one pimp explains, there is not much work for 'the girls' since most Italians go on holiday that month. Since the end of Enver Hoxha's regime, Albanians can now practise the fine Italian art of the *ferragosto*, a leisurely month of August spent in near-total vacation. That's why all the pimps can enjoy the *ferragosto* themselves: bring the girls back home, deliver some money to their families and enjoy the weather.

They sound just like regular corporate types when referring to their business, profits and currency exchange. When one of them remarks on the benefits the euro has brought to Italy, I naively ask whether it has anything to do with inflation or interest rates. The pimp looks baffled. No, he explains, it is easier to carry bigger sums in euros than in lira, which were worth so little. Clearly, I must have been 'anglicised' far too long not to have thought of such basic practical issues. 'He studies in England,' says my cousin, trying to excuse my ignorance.

On the way home from the bar, we pass the tiny metal kiosks selling newspapers. Though there is a variety to choose from, the public doesn't have great faith in the content. Subtle forms of government interference constrain journalists from speaking out about corruption and poor performance by politicians. When Fatos Nano was appointed prime minister in July 2002 he took a tough stance, instructing ministers to order their staffs to stop speaking to the press. According to Human Rights Watch, civil and criminal defamation suits and political meddling with the allocation of advertising to media outlets are the key tools used to harass and intimidate writers. Surveying six cases against journalists in 2002, HRW found violations of their right to a fair trial and their right to withhold the identity of their sources.

But sometimes the intimidation of journalists is not so subtle. On 14 October 2003, journalist Ilir Babaramo of the Albanian television channel VizionPlus was attacked at a cocktail party by the Albanian Minister for Public Order, Luan Rama, and his bodyguards. Rama apparently punched Babaramo and then dragged him outside and threw him to his bodyguards. Rama was allegedly incensed by a critical statement publicised by Babaramo on the incompetence of the minister in fighting crime. Initially, Rama denied such accusations but others soon came forward attesting to his incompetence and the youth campaign Mjaft began to demand Rama's dismissal. Prime Minister Nano was finally forced to accept his resignation. Rama was the second minister to leave under awkward circumstances during Nano's short tenure and neither was replaced until the end of the year.

To get out of the heat, we decide to go to the beach, 36km south of Fier in Vlora, a city where the Adriatic and Ionian seas meet to create some beautiful beaches, around 100km south of the capital Tirana. We stick to traditional transport, passenger vans that sell individual seats and ferry people around the country on the main thoroughfares. The trick is to get the two seats in the front of the van which are more spacious, allow more airflow and, most important, because they are close to the heavy engine, diminish the sense of being in a blender when flying over frequent gaping holes in the road.

We have learned to stick to the beaches labelled '*Per Familjare*' (For Families). This moniker is found on bars and beaches throughout the country where young women, couples and families might want to hang out without being subjected to the randy young men who might disrupt the mood. Unaccompanied males are simply not allowed in. However, this particular spot hasn't got it quite right. Up the cliffs from our beach there is a large restaurant and bar, which has positioned its tables perfectly for the banned young men to survey the scene at liberty. Needless to say, the women below are perused by sharp eyes.

That particular day, we sat in the middle of three families each speaking different foreign languages. On the left, a mother called to her children in Greek, 'Costas, stop hurting your brother.' Her soft accent gave away her Tirana origin. On the right, parents spoke only Italian to their six-year-old little girl, but Albanian to one another. The family behind us was speaking only Albanian and openly criticising the other 'irresponsible parents' who did not speak Albanian to their children. We started to speak in Albanian in solidarity with the people behind us.

There are around 700,000 Albanians living abroad; according to the Institute of Statistics, most of them are emigrants. There are many reasons for such exodus but 'a perfect world' for an Albanian would probably translate into safety and opportunities. Money is of course a factor but not the most important one. When I asked Ilir Gerdeshi of the Social and Economic Studies Centre about raising wages as a way of keeping people in the country, he replied, 'Even if wages are increased a lot, most would still leave. They want to escape from the Albanian reality.' This Albanian reality is what the mayor of Tirana, Edi Rama, who was just re-elected to a second term in office, refers to as 'a contaminated life' – a result of political corruption, lack of good media and a general sense of apathy. It is only when these problems are dealt with that Albanians can gain optimism and a desire to stay and improve their own country. For now, those that can, leave – and visit in August. ❏

Ledio Cakaj is a student at Oxford University and *Maria Burnett-Gaudiani* at Yale Law School

ABSOLUTE SCARCITY OF EVERYTHING

ESTHER MOIR

Harare: nothing in the basket. Credit: Rex Features

Today I was hoping for a peaceful day, lunch with the local Anglican vicar and his wife Pauline. Pauline says we should lay a place for Matthew, their eldest son, 'just in case he turns up'. He is an accountant in Harare, in his late 20s. He and some friends set out for a weekend at a well-known beauty spot and campsite, planned and booked well in advance. But almost as soon as they arrived they were accosted as 'white tourists' by a gang of youths brandishing axes and other primitive weapons. These are probably some of the young men who are taken away to 'youth camps' where they undergo a week of indoctrination into hatred of all whites. It had not been a good week either for his younger sister Angela, who had had her car windows smashed and everything stolen only a street or two away from the US Embassy. It is hardly surprising to find that both of them are thinking of leaving, part of the huge exodus, both black and white, which has already taken over 2 million to South Africa, half a million to the UK and many elsewhere. To go or to stay? The question runs like an undercurrent through much of the thinking of white families I meet and plays its part in the overwhelming sense of uncertainty underlying everything here. Pressure comes from those who are now in Britain persistently asking their relatives: 'How do you survive?' Among many Christians the answer is quite simply, 'By the grace of God,' and I cannot fail to be impressed by the strong quality of their faith.

I have just spent the weekend in a most beautiful place quite near to Harare which is available for Christian groups to use. I am with a group of mainly white Franciscans and we are the only whites there. I witness first-hand the proliferation of these small indigenous breakaway churches, many I suspect owing much to US funding. Certainly this is true of my immediate neighbours, about 50 children from one of the high-density areas in the city with their Sunday school superintendents. They would like me to attend one of their sessions to hear them teaching the children about HIV/Aids and child abuse. Sadly, I have to refuse; but when Mother Grace gives me the address of her church I see its US connection, which explains why the children insist that I do not come from London but, 'New York, America, New York.'

I have my own Zim dollars! Peter sent them in a large packet (you need such a huge quantity that they become quite bulky). I liked his message: 'Psst . . . Tell no one, wear red, meet me behind the third bougainvillea on the left.' Now I have the chance to visit the art market where local artists and craftsmen have small shops and stalls. This country produces such ingenuity, fantasy, humour. Sadly, there is virtually no one to enjoy it. I buy two paintings, one that shows a woman standing outside a school saying 'closed down'; the other showing a group of women with babies on their backs in front of a road sign, entitled *Which Way Now?*. I wonder why, when most political protest is driven underground, these vivid statements about rural life should have escaped?

On the way home, excited by my new wealth, I stop at our local supermarket to get some wine. 'This is to celebrate being here,' I tell the young man at the checkout, 'I'm from England.' He looks at me quizzically and says, 'In a few days you'll be crying.'

At this time of the year there are clear skies, brilliant flowering trees, glorious colour and birdsong. But living here is totally exhausting for everyone. I cannot fail to be aware of the hazards of trying to move around. Most of the road signs in the city have now been stolen: made of aluminium, they are used for coffin handles, for which there is a huge demand.

There is an exhibition I am keen to see so I am grateful for Donald's offer to go into the city with him when he goes to the weekly gathering of the Zimbabwe Climbers' Club. At the gallery we talk with its owner about Athos, William Dalrymple and St Catherine's in Sinai. This is followed by a visit to the newly built Buddhist centre, with its splendid meditation hall full of people doing yoga, a scene that might be found anywhere in the world. Here are reassuring oases of normality, almost a time warp, but all this is shattered when I visit the Anglican cathedral.

It is still a beautiful building with some fine African carving. But then I notice the empty spaces on the walls from which all memorials to the country's British past have been excised. They look like scars, an assault on Zimbabwe's historical reality. This has, of course, been done at the orders of pro-Zanu bishop Nolbert Kunonga, a close associate of Robert Mugabe, who recently caused scandal by his seizure of a white farm. The seven-bedroom house and its 2,000 acres of prime agricultural land were given to his son. However, since it is so close to the city, some fear it will be used for property development for the benefit of his family. There are far too many terrible stories to recount, but one that caused me delight shows the power of the choir over the preacher – though in this instance they failed. When the bishop began to preach politics the choir started to sing – and were immediately disbanded. The numbers of good men for whose departure from the diocese Kunonga is directly or indirectly responsible is heartbreaking.

Some people refuse to go shopping on the day on which pensions are paid. They find it too distressing to watch older people peering at the prices, picking up things and then putting them back, perhaps having to make a decision at the checkout between a loaf of bread or a few tomatoes.

One voice speaks for so many like her, an older woman in dire straits, trying to put a brave face on ending her life in a country she loves: 'This can no longer be called a civilised country . . . it is so *sad* . . . this is my home, I have been here for 50 years and I have nowhere else to go.'

Waiting for rain is heavy and I am heavy too, with an aching head and aching shoulders. I think it is more than physical. Surrounded by such suffering, corruption and intimidation, and watching a beautiful country being systematically destroyed must take its toll on anyone.

Mashambanzou is a care trust committed to providing support for poor people affected by HIV/Aids in the high-density areas of Harare. It is also committed to empowering the local communities so they are able to deal with this pandemic with understanding and compassion. The name comes from two Shona words for 'washing' and 'elephant', a reference to the early-morning hours when elephants go down to the river to wash. It carries the sense of 'the dawn of a new day' and it was chosen to offer inspiration to those on the threshold of a new life – people living with Aids. At the moment, the trust is caring for 4,500 children. Many of the children did not join in games and physical activities with others because they had no underwear: even the cheapest cotton underpants cost Zim$1,000 (US 19 cents; or, on the parallel market US$6), beyond the reach of most families. So the trust sets about getting sewing machines and making them. I am numbed by the statistics: 33 per cent of the adult population in the country has HIV; 200,000 deaths; 780,000 orphans – and these are the figures for three years ago.

I am faced with the reality of families trying to care for sick relatives in cramped and unsanitary conditions. With the death of both parents, it is only too common to find quite young children in charge of their brothers and sisters: 'child-headed households' has become an often-heard phrase. Then there are households where young widows, infected by their husbands, have been thrown out of the family home by their in-laws. One of the Irish Roman Catholic sisters tells a story that has stayed in my mind like a vignette, contradicting Mugabe's prediction to the United Nations of a bumper harvest in the interests of making the land reform programme appear to be working when, in truth, more than half the people in the country are searching for food and do not know where to get it. Only the day before, she recounts, a young man of 20 had been brought to the house in a wheelbarrow, now increasingly used as the only available form of transport for the sick. He had not eaten for days and he died that morning with tears in his eyes.

Yet, holding on to their belief that things will ultimately be all right, the sisters continue to think positively and would not dream of leaving.

Last night, friends drove me through the Borrowdale Brook area of the city. Mugabe's young wife Grace is building another palace. It is designed by a Serbian architect at the cost of millions and she is taking a huge personal interest in it, apparently meddling with everything from the gold bathroom taps to the chandeliers. It is, of course, to have a swimming pool, a library, a billiard room, a bar.

But this is something that I have seen, to a lesser degree, everywhere throughout the city. Outside one big municipal office there is a space called 'Platinum Parking', full of top-of-the-range luxury cars. There is a new Mitsubishi model, the Pajero, only introduced into the country a few months ago, assembled in South Africa and here worth the equivalent of Zim$220 million (US$43,059) on the current but rapidly changing 'parallel market'. It is clearly important for the extravagantly rich, of which there appear to be great numbers, to own one.

For I know now that this country is short of absolutely everything, that state hospitals and clinics are collapsing through lack of funds, and there is a scarcity of everything. The short drive into the countryside our small amount of petrol allowed enabled me to see fertile land no longer farmed but turning to bush, few crops sown and practically no cattle – I found that numbers had dwindled from 5,000,000 in 1998 to 250,000 today. This is a society that is being undermined by violence, corruption and indifference to innocent suffering. People live in fear of speaking out and are silenced in a variety of ways. The truth is being manipulated through the propagandist media, and the government continues to send out a totally false picture of what is happening. This is a deeply wounded country and at the moment survival is everything. My short time here has shown me what that asks of ordinary people in their day-to-day existence. There do not seem to be any long-term perspectives, no direction, no vision. When I have been really low I have felt there is fatalism rather than vision.

More bewildered and burdened than when I left London, I cannot possibly end on a positive note, not even a coherent one. And yet against the odds I find that I cannot entirely give up hope. And that is why I am determined to return. For that reason all the names of friends have been changed and I am going to sign these letters with a pseudonym. ❏

Esther Moir *is a writer and lecturer. See also 'Uncle Bob and the burial notes',* Index *2/04*

Support for **INDEX** ON CENSORSHIP

It is the generosity of our friends and supporters which makes *Index on Censorship*'s work possible. *Index* remains the only international publication devoted to the promotion and protection of that basic, yet still abused, human right – freedom of expression.

Your support is needed more than ever now as *Index* and the Writers & Scholars Educational Trust continue to grow and develop new projects. Donations will enable us to expand our website, which will make access to *Index*'s stories and communication between free-speech activists and supporters even easier, and will help directly with our Sponsored Subscriptions Programme which provides free copies of the magazine to activists in the developing world and the former Soviet states.

Please help *Index* speak out.

The Trustees and Directors would like to thank the many individuals and organisations who support *Index on Censorship* and the Writers & Scholars Educational Trust, including:

IF YOU WOULD LIKE MORE INFORMATION ABOUT INDEX ON CENSORSHIP OR WOULD LIKE TO SUPPORT OUR WORK, PLEASE
CONTACT HUGO GRIEVE, DEVELOPMENT MANAGER, ON 020 7278 2313 OR EMAIL HUGO@INDEXONCENSORSHIP.ORG

WWW.INDEXONCENSORSHIP.ORG
CONTACT@INDEXONCENSORSHIP.ORG
TEL: 020 7278 2313 • FAX: 020 7278 1878

SUBSCRIPTIONS (4 ISSUES PER ANNUM)
INDIVIDUALS: BRITAIN £32, US $48, REST OF WORLD £42
INSTITUTIONS: BRITAIN £48, US $80, REST OF WORLD £52
PLEASE PHONE 020 8249 4443
OR EMAIL TONY@INDEXONCENSORSHIP.ORG

Index on Censorship (ISSN 0306-4220) is published four times a year by a non-profit-making company: Writers & Scholars International Ltd, Lancaster House, 33 Islington High Street, London N1 9LH. *Index on Censorship* is associated with Writers & Scholars Educational Trust, registered charity number 325003 **Periodicals postage:** (US subscribers only) paid at Newark, New Jersey. Postmaster: send US address changes to *Index on Censorship* c/o Mercury Airfreight International Ltd Inc., 365 Blair Road, Avenel, NJ 07001, USA